D1014985

MERGER OF THE CENTURY

MERGER
OF THE
CENTURY

WHY CANADA AND AMERICA
SHOULD BECOME ONE COUNTRY

DIANE FRANCIS

HarperCollins*Publishers*Ltd

Powell River Public Library

Merger of the Century
Copyright © 2013 by Huntress Company.
All rights reserved.

Published by HarperCollins Publishers Ltd

First edition

No part of this book may be used or reproduced in any manner whatsoever
without the prior written permission of the publisher, except in the case of
brief quotations embodied in reviews.

The citations for, and the content of, the online sources referred to in this
book were current as of the date of writing.

HarperCollins books may be purchased for educational, business,
or sales promotional use through our Special Markets Department.

HarperCollins Publishers Ltd
2 Bloor Street East, 20th Floor
Toronto, Ontario, Canada
M4W 1A8

www.harpercollins.ca

Library and Archives Canada Cataloguing in Publication
information is available upon request

ISBN CANADA 978-1-55468-875-3
ISBN USA 978-00-6232-501-3

Printed and bound in the United States of America
RRD 9 8 7 6 5 4 3 2 1

Powell River Public Library

To both my countries, Canada and the United States

Contents

Introduction

When I have been in Canada, I have never heard a Canadian refer to an American as a "foreigner." He is just an "American." And, in the same way, in the United States, Canadians are not "foreigners," they are "Canadians." That simple little distinction illustrates to me better than anything else the relationship between our two countries.

—Franklin Delano Roosevelt

C ANADIANS AND AMERICANS ARE SO INDISTINGUISHABLE to outsiders that Canadians who don't want to be mistaken for Americans pin Maple Leaf flags on their lapels or backpacks when they travel. Canadians have been jokingly referred to as "Americans with health care and no guns," in reference to the differing levels of public medical care and gun ownership. One prominent Canadian historian described Canadians as "Americans who clearly don't want to be U.S. citizens."[1]

Another variance is that Canadians are hypervigilant about the United States, while the reverse is far from true. Graydon Carter, the editor of *Vanity Fair*, who is originally from Canada, noted, "If you grow up in Canada, you've got your nose up against a window of a much bigger, more fun party happening here, in the United States."[2]

Foreigners typically regard Canadians and Americans as identical twins, when we are more like fraternal twins: we are both multicultural and live in countries based on the same organizing principles of democracy, free enterprise, the rule of law and pluralism, but we have different attitudes and political systems. Perhaps we seem indistinguishable because we get along so well. The last war we fought against each other was two hundred years ago, when 2,500 Americans invaded Canada, then called British North

America, thus causing the War of 1812. The British retaliated and invaded the United States, sacked Washington, D.C., and then lost the Battle of New Orleans. At the war's end, the only land that had changed hands was tiny Carleton Island in the St. Lawrence River, near the mouth of Lake Ontario. The two countries have never fought since—except, perhaps, on skates.

The biggest difference is the survival of a strong French culture in Canada. The French arrived in North America more than four hundred years ago, claimed vast tracts of land and established a few cities, including Detroit, New Orleans and Montreal. In 1763, France lost most of its holdings to the United Kingdom and received a handful of Caribbean islands in return. In 1803, Napoleon sold the rest of the land beyond the Mississippi River to the new United States, stranding the French colonists, who retained their language and culture; today, 8.5 million Canadians are of French heritage, making up roughly 25 percent of Canada's population, and French is an official language of Canada.

The rest of Canada, like Australia or New Zealand, is mostly from the British Isles and is British in its sensibilities, deportment and attitudes. Canada, Australia and New Zealand are Anglo-Saxon nations. The United States is not. I regard the U.S. as a melting pot with a decidedly Germanic sensibility. According to the 2010 U.S. census, some 17.1 percent, or more than 50 million Americans, cite German ancestry—more than those identified as Hispanic, African-American, Irish-American or English-American. Germans have immigrated for hundreds of years to the U.S., often staying below the radar by changing their surnames or calling themselves Pennsylvania Dutch. They have contributed kindergartens, the Christmas tree, beer, frankfurters, hamburgers, metal bashing and manufacturing ability, engineering aptitude, scientific expertise, a strong work ethic, aggressiveness, bluntness and the reason behind America's reluctance to enter the First World War.

Famous Americans with some or all German ancestry include Presidents Hoover, Eisenhower, Nixon, Bush and Obama (his mother's ancestors were from the British Isles and Germany); central banker Paul Volcker, advisor Henry Kissinger, House Speaker John Boehner and defense secretary Donald Rumsfeld; military leaders such as Custer, Nimitz and Schwarzkopf; tycoons Astor, Rockefeller, Gates, Jobs (adoptive father), Zuckerberg, Disney, Baruch, Hilton, Chrysler, Pfizer, Trump, Heinz, Firestone, Hellman, Fruehauf, Merck, Loeb, Maytag, Studebaker, Westinghouse and Weyerhaeuser; scientists such as Einstein, the Manhattan Project's Robert Oppenheimer and Silicon Valley's father, Frederick Terman; brewers Anheuser and Busch, Coors, Hamm and Miller; astronauts Armstrong and Aldrin; native-born celebrities Dillinger, Hoffa, Sousa, Nicklaus, Dr. Seuss, Tom Cruise, Voight, DiCaprio, Presley, Bruce Willis, Rock Hudson, Grace Kelly, Nolte, Depp, Gable, Brando, Astaire, Streep, Mencken, Steinem, Earhart, Dreiser, Plath, Rombauer, Stein, Steinbeck, Letterman, Diller, Lou Gehrig, Casey Stengel and Babe Ruth.

The two countries may have different ethnic mixes, but both have wrestled with social problems involving minorities who have struggled against the psychological damage inflicted by historical injustices, discrimination, violence, inadequate education, poverty, unemployment, substance abuse and crime. The homicide rate of Canada's aboriginals is seven times that of the Canadian population at large, and the African-American homicide rate is six times that of the national average.[3]

A major distinction between the two countries is that the U.S. has been independent since 1776, but Canada has acquired its independence in stages over a long period of time. In 1867, Canada was given Dominion status, but the country's laws had to be approved by Britain. In 1931, Canada was given control over its laws and foreign policy for the first time. In 1947, Canadians attained their own distinct citizenship instead of being simply British subjects. And in 1982, the Queen and British Parliament signed over Canada's constitution.

In part because of its long history as a colony, Canada has remained undeveloped and underpopulated compared to the go-getter republic to the south. More people live in Waco, Texas—some 116,887 in total, according to the 2010 census—than live in the top 39.3 percent of Canada's geographic north. The country's population has rarely exceeded 10 percent of the United States' total, and Canadians live in a narrow band, spanning six time zones, a few hundred miles north of the border. Americans buy nearly three-quarters of Canada's exports and own half of its oil, manufacturing and retail sectors—roughly 10 percent of its economy.[4]

My analysis in 2011 of the Canadian revenues of Canada's fifty biggest foreign-owned companies showed their incomes were $303.178 billion,[5] or 8.5 percent bigger than Quebec's GDP that year, 68 percent bigger than the GDP of the four western provinces combined,[6] and equivalent to 19 percent of the GDP of Canada. And Americans owned more than half of these.

The United States, by contrast, grew rapidly on its own by conquering, buying and colonizing its hinterland throughout the nineteenth century. Lands were violently wrested away from Native American tribes and Mexico, and millions of slaves were imported from Africa. By contrast, slavery barely existed in colonial Canada, and was abolished throughout the British Empire in 1833. In the War of Independence, for instance, those fighting on behalf of the "redcoats," or British side, were mostly Native Americans, German mercenaries, runaway slaves and American colonials who were British Loyalists. Only one-third of these forces were British soldiers.

After the Civil War, the U.S. went on a development tear: it purchased Alaska from the Russians and colonized its West. By 1880, a hundred years after independence from Britain, the United States' population was double Britain's, ten times as large as Canada's, and its economy had overtaken Britain's as the world's biggest economy. The United States then led the Industrial Revolution in North America, while Canada helped provide raw materials, manpower and new markets. Millions of Canadians emigrated south over the next century to work in factories or farms in the U.S., including the forebears of such notable Americans as Hillary Clinton; performers Madonna, Lady Gaga and Angelina Jolie; auto czars such as General Motors founder William Durant, Walter Chrysler and Henry Ford; Thomas Edison; Hollywood moguls Louis B. Mayer, the Warner Brothers and Walt Disney; and author Jack Kerouac.

The Second World War brought the two countries closer than ever as allies, and the two became entwined in every way. Underpinning Canada's economy was American investment, auto manufacturing and resource extraction. America's economy boomed as a result of innovation, cheap labor, technology, entrepreneurship, plentiful resources, financial savvy and marketing.

Lifestyles have gradually become similar. In 2011, according to the World Bank, Americans made $48,442 per capita and Canadians $50,345;[7] Americans had reduced their high levels of consumer debt to about 114.6 percent of personal disposable income, while Canadians were at 152.98 percent (nearly pre-2008 U.S. levels);[8] Americans consumed slightly less energy per capita than Canadians in 2010—a rate of 7,231.80 kilograms of oil equivalent per year compared to Canada's 7,485.54;[9] home ownership levels in 2011 were

64.6 percent for Americans in the seventy-five largest cities, versus 68.9 percent for Canadians in 2006;[10] and, contrary to popular belief, Canadian and American income tax rates, as a percentage of average wages, were similar. In 2011, income taxes on singles averaged 15.5 percent in Canada and 17.3 percent in the U.S., while married couples with two kids paid 9.2 percent in Canada and 4.7 percent in the U.S, according to the OECD.[11] Today, the two sit atop the Western Hemisphere, figuratively and literally. Canada is like Scandinavia, economically smaller and more socially liberal, and the United States is more like Germany on steroids.

Their political systems differ, but it's interesting to note that their mentalities are not that far apart. Voters in the District of Columbia and twenty-odd states—mostly those bordering Canada or linked to those states—are, like Canadians, more liberal-minded and have voted for a Democrat as president since 1992. In 1992 and 1996, thirty-one and thirty-two states, respectively, plus the District of Columbia, voted Democratic; in 2000, twenty states plus D.C. voted Democratic; in 2004, nineteen plus D.C. voted Democratic; in 2008, twenty-seven states and D.C. did; and in 2012, twenty-six states and D.C. did. Interestingly, the 2008 Democratic states represented 72 percent of the United States' GDP and the 2012 Democratic states represented 66 percent of the United States' GDP. So, by this measure, the more prosperous majority of Americans, and those close to the border, think more like Canadians.

As well, one in ten Canadians, or more than three million people, live full or part time in the U.S.; an estimated one million Americans live in Canada (not including their offspring, who are entitled to U.S. citizenship—possibly another million); and the 698,025 First Nations members living in Canada have both U.S. and Canadian citizenship, as stipulated by the 1794 Jay Treaty.

The World Is Becoming More Dangerous

The 9/11 attacks and the financial crisis that started in 2008 damaged the economies of both countries and accelerated the decline of most wealthy democracies. Throughout it all, emerging economies, led by China and India, did not skip a beat. Between 2000 and 2010, they grew by an average of 6 percent per year, while developed nations posted an average of only 3.6 percent, according to *The Economist*'s "Power Shift" report.[12] By 2030, Brazil, Russia, India and China could overtake the U.S., Japan, Germany, Italy, Britain, France and Canada in economic size. And these seven nations, the original G7, cannot catch up because of debt, demographics, resistance to change and an inability to recognize and counteract the strategies of their rivals.

This unprecedented transfer of wealth, from richer to poorer nations, will only escalate because the free-market/free-trade/free-enterprise model does not work as well as controlled and planned economic models such as China's. The methods employed in such countries will beat developed economies to resources and economic growth. In his book *Losing Control: The Emerging Threats to Western Prosperity*, Stephen D. King, the global chief economist of the Hong Kong and Shanghai Bank, said the pursuit of scarce resources such as energy or food may lead to war, hoist prices and impose a "redistribution of wealth and power across the globe [that] will force consumers in the US and Europe to stop living beyond their means."

Nations in distress, and facing uncertainty, must behave like businesses and weigh all options; they must also think laterally and outside the box. The problem for Americans as well as Canadians is that foreign governments, and their vassal corporate entities, have established themselves in Canada and are nibbling away at resource assets or using Canada as a backdoor entry to make direct foreign investments in the United States, sometimes without detection. Their targets include resources, farmland, market access and iconic corporations, assets that they do not allow Canadian or American individuals, corporations or governments to acquire in their own countries. This non-reciprocal and sly strategy is aimed at acquiring assets, undermining competitors and gaining political influence in host countries.

The best option for the U.S. and Canada to survive the new economic reality would be to alter course by devising protective policies and to merge into one gigantic nation. This book, a thought experiment, details the economic benefits of joining forces, the way a deal could be structured in fairness to both nations, the political obstacles littering its path and, lastly, strategies if a merger is impossible. This book is written from my viewpoint, as a dual citizen and business writer, that the interests and values of the two nations are aligned and that a merger makes good business sense.

Many Canadians will be shocked at the notion of being united with America, given how that nation is perceived in the world, its mass murders, gun laws, gangsta rap, movie-star antics, televangelism and political dysfunction. For instance, the U.S. had 9,146 gun deaths in 2007, while Canada, with 10 percent of the population, had proportionally fewer—a mere 173 gun murders instead of 914.[13] Such statistics are worrisome, but Canadians have few choices but to park their prejudices and figure out how to meet the future together with the Americans.

Besides, the United States is not the dangerous, wacky place depicted by Hollywood or by television shows, as the millions of Canadians who study, work, retire, travel or live there can attest. Frankly, the U.S. is as safe as Canada if you live in one of the majority of neighborhoods removed from the drug and gang wars. I would argue that Canadians, like Americans, despite challenges, cannot afford to miss the opportunity to pull off what would become the Merger of the Century.

As for a sheltered and safer Canada, the party is over. It has "snacked off" the United States by tapping into its capital and technology to build companies that produce goods or commodities that, in turn, are mostly exported to the United States. In absolute numbers, most of the two-way trade is made up of transfers between U.S. parent companies and Canadian branch plants, known as intra-trade. But after 9/11, even this trade has slowed and won't grow in the future as the border becomes a problem and Canadian costs escalate.

Canadian demographer David Foot provides another reason a merger might be a good idea. He believes economic success can be forecasted based on whether there are too many young people or too many old people in a country. The United States and Mexico have the right population mixes to sustain future growth, but Canada is aging as rapidly as European nations, even at immigration levels proportionately higher than America's. At the Global Business Forum in Banff, Alberta, in September 2012, he forecast that by 2026, "Canada will have more old than young people, and no amount of immigration can change the figure." This means slow growth, labor shortages and higher pension or health-care costs.

Likewise, the United States needs to recalibrate. The country has prospered, without peer, since the Second World War as the world's largest economy thanks to its resources and little competition. But those days may be over too. Trade deficits have been ruinous and are mostly due to oil imports ($379 billion in 2012,[14] or 78 percent of the total based on the September 2012 average).[15] Forecasts by the International Energy Agency project that the United States may reach energy self-sufficiency by 2035, but only if a new controversial technology called fracking, which taps deep deposits, becomes more successful and if at least 4.5 million barrels a day of oil can be imported from Canada's oil sands, nearly double current amounts. The U.S. also has much to learn from Canada about keeping banks safe and health-care costs reasonable.

If they merged, Canada and the U.S. would become an energy and economic powerhouse, occupying more land than Russia or the continent of South America, and equivalent to 12.25 percent of the world's total landmass. Better yet, Canada is virtually empty, thus providing enormous development opportunities. The two could better tackle environmental challenges together through science and by replacing coal, the biggest culprit worldwide, with shared hydro, conservation and alternative energy sources. Combined, they would have a larger economy than the European Union or than the economies of Japan, China, Germany and France combined. The merged nations would control more oil, water, arable land and resources than any other and would enjoy the protection of America's military. They would be able to eliminate trade and even government budget deficits, and would share a strengthened currency. The merged country's people would have more options, too, in terms of jobs, climates, studies and lifestyles.

The idea of joining countries and erasing borders is not unique, by the way. Many countries around the world are continually debating mergers or forming important regional economies. Networks of people and corporations are replacing the nation-state. In April 2012, a Gallup poll found that 13 percent of the world's adults, or 640 million people, want to leave their country permanently. Another 214 million have already left home, according to the United Nations.

That means roughly one in seven people in the world are dissatisfied with their country.[16] In *End of the Nation State: The Rise of Regional Economies*, Japanese business guru Kenichi Ohmae argues that maps have become "cartographic illusions": "Traditional nation states are unnatural and impossible business units in a global economy. As industry, investment, individuals and information flow relatively unimpeded across national borders, the building-block concepts appropriate to a nineteenth-century, closed-country model of the world no longer hold."

Arguably, the U.S.–Canada border is, in fact, simply the line that the British were able to hold against the expansionist and aggressive Americans. It's interesting to note that most of the borders established by Britain centuries ago are anachronisms. The borders between the U.S. and Canada, or Australia and New Zealand, could disappear while, at the same time, the Québécois and Scottish nationalists in their respective countries could vote to secede and erect new borders. In 2010, New Zealanders and Australians were surveyed about New Zealand becoming a state of Australia. About 48 percent of Australians were in favor, but 52 percent were opposed. Some 41 percent of New Zealanders said the issue should be debated, 29 percent rejected the notion and 37 percent said the country would be better off as part of Australia.[17]

The similarities between New Zealand and Canada are striking. Each is politically, economically and militarily dependent, on Australia and the United States respectively. Australia has dominated with its bigger economy and benefited from a brain drain of New Zealanders. The opening clauses of Australia's constitution still state that New Zealand is part of Australia and can opt to join at any time as a single state. And in 1776, the Articles of Confederation written by the Americans included a provision to the "Canadian" colonies to join the new republic if they chose. Even today's U.S. constitution includes an accession clause that allows entry of territories by Congressional approval. But the issue of a merger between Canada and the United States has never been formally raised.

Past Prime Ministers and Others Have Considered a Merger

The Oregon dispute with Britain, and another in Texas with Mexico, took place during the 1840s. In 1845, the phrase "manifest destiny" caught the public's imagination and became a moral justification for the aggressive expansion of the U.S. to the north, west and south. New York journalist John O'Sullivan coined the phrase, and when repeated, in 1847, it sparked fierce debate and criticism in Britain, the Canadian colonies and New England. O'Sullivan backed off and claimed he was not referring to the conquest of eastern Canada, but the British didn't believe him.

"Away, away with all these cobweb tissues of rights of discovery, exploration, settlement, continuity, etc.," wrote O'Sullivan. "The American claim [Oregon and Texas] is by the right of our manifest destiny to overspread and to possess the whole continent which Providence has given us for the development of the great experiment of liberty and federative self-government entrusted to us."

The British assumed that "manifest destiny" was code for the eventual acquisition of British North America, or Canada. But this never materialized, mostly due to the interruption of the U.S. Civil War and the rapid expansion of its West. But the threat, and the fact that the Union Army was bigger than Canada's total population, propelled Britain to begin granting Canada nationhood. At the time, some thought this was a doomed policy. Goldwin Smith, a British-American academic and abolitionist, wrote in his 1891 book *Canada and the Canada Question* that the British North American project would be untenable, artificial and badly governed, eventually destined to join the United States commercially, then politically. Others have echoed his thesis, that the nation of Canada was doomed, most notably academic George Grant in his *Lament for a Nation: The Defeat of Nationalism*, written in 1965.

Since the beginning, joining the U.S. has always been a taboo subject in Canadian politics, but that didn't stop two prime ministers from privately suggesting mergers long before even free trade became a reality. In 1919, Canadian Prime Minister Robert Borden brought up the subject of a possible three-way merger—between the U.S., Britain and such Commonwealth countries as Canada and Australia, among others—to his British counterpart, David Lloyd George. But Borden's "Anglo-Saxon" merger idea fell on deaf ears, according to Oxford University historian and Canadian Margaret MacMillan (who is also Lloyd George's granddaughter).[18]

"If the League of Nations did not work out, Borden suggested to Lloyd George, they should work for a union between 'the two great English speaking commonwealths who share common ancestry, language and literature, who are inspired by like democratic ideals, who enjoy similar political institutions and whose united force is sufficient to ensure the peace of the world,'" she wrote, citing the Christie Papers, which are minutes taken during these negotiations and part of the National Archives of Canada.

Borden's suggestion was ironic considering that he owed his political career to his fierce opposition to free trade with the United States, which had been proposed by his opponents in the 1911 election. His winning motto had been "No truck nor trade with Yankees."

Then, in 1919, the merger of the U.S. with Britain and its dominions, such as Canada, seemed like a good idea. Even so, Borden dropped the suggestion and went on to other, more urgent initiatives.

The Second World War brought Canada and the United States closer together than ever. And after the war, Prime Minister William Lyon Mackenzie King considered proposing an economic merger with the Americans. The two nations had collaborated well, and the two world wars had "bankrupted" Britain, leaving Canada a geopolitical and economic orphan. King was pro-American because of his background and had even been nicknamed by rivals as "the American." He was born in Ontario, but in 1897 lived and studied at the University of Chicago, worked with Jane Addams at Hull House and went on to earn a master's degree at Harvard University (he also earned a doctorate from Harvard in 1909).

He returned in 1900 and became a civil servant, then politician, then headed back to the U.S. in 1914, a few years after losing a bid for reelection. He was hired by John D. Rockefeller as a senior staff member, researching industrial relations, at the Rockefeller Foundation in New York City. The two became friends and King stayed at the foundation until 1918, also working as an independent labor consultant to some of America's largest corporations.

In 1919, King returned to Canadian politics as leader of the Liberal Party, becoming prime minister in 1921. He lost twice, became prime minister again in 1935 and stayed until he resigned in 1948. In an official telegram to Washington in 1935, the U.S. ambassador to Canada, Norman Armour, wrote that King told him integration was important. "He made it plain that there were two roads open to Canada but that he wanted to choose the American road if we made it possible for him to do so," wrote American historian Gordon Stewart in 1980 of this telegram. "From every point of view it was important that our attachment should be strong and our relations brought closer in every way, political as well as economic."[19]

Stewart said the American ambassador was surprised by King's viewpoint, made during an unannounced visit on Canadian Thanksgiving Day and only a night after King took power. Five years later, in 1940, King quietly signed the Ogdensburg Agreement, which was heavily criticized by Britain's prime minister, Winston Churchill, as well as by opposition parties in Canada. The agreement, later revised, merged the two armed forces and gave the Americans control. The signing was instigated by intelligence reports that revealed Canada would be attacked if Britain were invaded (because of plans to evacuate the King and government to Canada) and would therefore need American military support. While that initiative failed, King continued to search for ways to tether the two countries after the war. "Mackenzie King mentioned the idea of joining with the Americans to a few confidants after the war, but he was a nervous guy politically and didn't think he could pull it off so soon after the war," Donald Macdonald, chairman of the Royal Commission that in 1985 recommended free trade, told me in an interview in 2010.

It would take another forty years for a prominent Canadian like Macdonald—another man with American connections—to resurrect the idea of free trade. Macdonald had also earned a law degree at Harvard University, spent much time in the U.S. on business and had a sister living there. He practiced trade law and became a Liberal cabinet minister in the 1970s.

Critics, including former Liberal colleagues, fiercely attacked Macdonald for his Royal Commission that recommended free trade. Conservative Prime Minister Brian Mulroney and then the Americans followed its recommendations, but fellow Liberal opposition leader

John Turner said he would "tear up" any deal if he became prime minister. He said social programs such as health care and pensions would be threatened because free trade would turn Canada into a de facto "51st state."[20] That was pure hyperbole, but it frightened many Canadians.

"I understood the opposition, but the world had changed," explained Macdonald. "Generally, we grew up as 'Anglo Saxophones' and our spelling and schools were British, our courses were British. We had a narrow view of the world. The Methodists ran English Canada. No newspapers or drinks were allowed on Sundays—you had to go for those to Quebec or the U.S. Essentially I was from the last generation whose mode of life and attitudes were British. The Americans adopted their own mode and, let's face it, Canadian changes in style and living modes have been adopted here from the Americans. And you can find, within every family in Ontario and Canada, relatives who have moved to the U.S. and become Americans."

More than twenty years after the U.S.–Canada free-trade agreement, the world had changed again. The Iron Curtain had disappeared, the Cold War had ended, China was a superpower, dozens of emerging economies had risen out of their slumber, and Canada was getting lost in the shuffle. For instance, if the G8 or even the G7 had been constituted in 2012, Canada would not have made the cut.

So when I asked Macdonald whether a full-fledged merger would be a good idea now, he responded, "Free trade worked fine and they didn't eat our lunch, as some thought would happen. Erasing the border is probably inevitable and would work, but our political institutions are very different and I would worry about the survival of Canada's media and publishing industries."

But media and publishing has changed too. The Internet erased borders and the ability to regulate content. Local and national

newspapers and television networks lost audiences to online information and entertainment rivals around the world. Their business
models imploded as advertisers stopped spending, choosing instead
to chase readers and viewers globally.[21] Technology enabled people
to read, watch or hear whatever they wanted, written by whomever,
whenever and wherever.

This convergence has been most evident in popular culture. In
2010 in the U.S., respondents to a poll named Céline Dion as America's
greatest singer, even though she's Canadian. Conversely, the biggest
television audience in Canada in 2012 watched the Super Bowl, with
an estimated 18 million watching at least part of the game. By contrast, 11 million Canadians watched at least part of their own Super
Bowl, the 2011 Grey Cup.[22]

The Case for a Merger

In 2014, Scots will hold a referendum on independence from the
United Kingdom, and the debate has mostly concerned the economic aspects. One poll showed that 79 percent of Scots would vote
for independence if they reaped an economic benefit of £500 a year
or more per capita, but would not vote for independence if there
was no economic benefit.[23] In the case of a U.S.–Canada merger,
there would be economic gains for both countries. Canadians would
receive compensation in return for their resources, and the new
partnership would yield untold opportunities and benefits for both
populations.

I believe the United States and Canada should and can merge,
but I also recognize why this would be difficult. I believe this is the
most desirable way forward. I also believe a merger is achievable. In

the absence of a merger, or another form of political fusion, energy will be just one of several contentious issues that could cause confrontations and damage to both sides. There are several scenarios that would represent security threats to the United States and lead to conflicts and some form of intervention. For instance, if China, Russia and others succeeded in capturing control over much of Canada's resources and its Arctic region, thus gaining political influence, the relationship between the U.S. and Canada would be disrupted, as would oil shipments. Likewise, if Canada continued to mishandle its First Nations and other aboriginal issues involving land claims and compensation issues, there would be an escalation in the frequency and gravity of incidences involving civil disobedience, border breaches and violence to infrastructure and corporate assets. Finally, if Quebec separatists tried to exit Canada again, economic and political instability would generate undesirable spillover effects on the U.S. economy. There might also be sabotage and violence by environmentalists that Canada would not be in a position to prevent. Any one, or a combination, of these possibilities would, in extreme circumstances, certainly lead to confrontation, violence or even invasion. Such scenarios may appear improbable, but serious incidents have occurred in the past.

The likeliest clash could arise if China's aggressive entry into Canada's economic and political arenas is allowed to continue. In 2012, Beijing was able to pull off its biggest foreign takeover anywhere in the world when Canada's federal government allowed the $15 billion purchase of a large Canadian oil company despite considerable public opposition, warnings by Canadian intelligence agency officials and the recent establishment of precedents against such takeovers. Even more puzzling, Canada agreed to a sweeping trade deal that afforded China special market access for thirty-one years and full legal protection without reciprocal rights to Canadians operating in China. The deal, when signed, cannot be canceled for fifteen years, whereas the North American Free Trade Agreement (NAFTA) can end on six months' notice.

China has targeted Canada for years because of its enormous oil sands, its undeveloped resources, its dominant Arctic position, its backdoor entry into the U.S. market and technology sector, and its vast landmass capable of supporting millions more people. Until 2012, China, like Russia, slowly picked off minority ownership in public companies, often undisclosed, or bought private, small companies. Obviously, gaining more political influence in Canada is in the long-term interests of both nations.

Canadian leaders, convinced the takeover would gain markets and sell oil to Asia, suddenly recognized the China playbook: no sooner had the takeover and trade deal been approved than China rolled out its Arctic scheme. In late 2012, Canada's federal government was asked to approve a gigantic mining plan in Nunavut that involved development of a Chinese-owned-and-operated port, and town, on the Arctic Ocean. This was billed as a one-off transaction, but the Chinese intend to create a string of ports and listening posts to gain control along the Northwest Passage because of its logistical importance to trade in the future.

Such initiatives, and their underlying grand strategy, will eventually place Canada in the middle of a contest among the United States, China and Russia for resources and control of the Arctic. By many measures, Canada is no match for any of these superpowers. By 2011, the four biggest Chinese oil companies—PetroChina, Sinopec, Chinese National Oil Corporation and China National Offshore Oil Corporation (CNOOC)—had combined revenues of $1.1 trillion, equivalent to 78.8 percent of Canada's GDP.[24] Russia's

Gazprom, Lukoil, Rosneft, TNK-BP and Surgutneftegas had combined revenues in 2012 of $406.89 billion, equivalent to 29 percent of Canada's GDP. These companies have political agendas and powerful proprietors—Beijing in China's case and the Kremlin in the case of Russian oligarchs. Neither nation upholds the same values as Canadians or Americans, and they represent Trojan horses that are eager to partition an already weak, fragmented Canada.

At the same time, Canada also faces internal challenges concerning its hundreds of restive First Nations bands, environmental organizations and Quebec separatists. In 1995, during the last Quebec referendum, two First Nations threatened to block the St. Lawrence Seaway and to vandalize power lines serving the industrial U.S. Eastern Seaboard if Quebec attempted to force them to leave Canada. That same year, separatist leaders tried to recruit Canadian military personnel and threatened to seize Canada's fleet of jet fighters, stationed mostly in Quebec, if they won.[25] In 2005, a CBC documentary alleged that Canada's military officials flew jets to a U.S. air base so they could not be seized and used as pawns.[26] In 2012, the separatists regained power in Quebec.

More recently, in 2011, a First Nations chief in British Columbia threatened to harm herself rather than allow construction of an oil pipeline through her band's contested lands. Then, in December 2012, another chief went on a hunger strike to demand sweeping land claims and compensation, and a new youth movement called Idle No More staged protests in Canada and the U.S. The movement was formed out of frustration felt across Canada's over 630 First Nations communities.[27] The elected chief of the Assembly of Nations was pressured to leave office on a medical leave, and thousands staged protests caused work stoppages and blocked highways. Their grievances have remained mostly unaddressed throughout Canada's history.

Against such internal or external incursions, Canada carries no big stick. In 2011, Canada's active military personnel totaled 68,250,[28] or roughly the seating capacity of Candlestick Park in San Francisco. The Canadian coastline, at 151,500 miles, is the world's longest, but its navy, respected worldwide, comprises only 8,500 regular personnel, 5,100 reserve sailors and thirty-three ships,[29] including four submarines, which are not able to spend a significant amount of time under the polar ice because these aging vessels lack the ventilation and other equipment to do so. The second-longest coastline is Indonesia's, at 34,000 miles, guarded by 111 ships and 74,000 personnel. The United States, with the ninth-greatest length of coastline (12,380 miles), has an armada of 287 ships and more than 317,000 active personnel (plus 109,000 reservists) that patrol the world.[30]

Canada's military dependency on the United States is nothing new and is the subtext of the relationship. This dependency, which has existed since Britain faded after 1919 as a superpower, has required Canada, like other smaller nations, to align itself with the grand strategy of its superpower-benefactor or, alternatively, remain pliant. This means that Canada, in other words, cannot bite the hand that guards it.

Occasionally, Canada has crossed the line. Since 9/11, minor disagreements and border irritants have turned into serious bilateral clashes behind closed doors. Few are aware of just how serious the issues are, and that they go way beyond the truck bottlenecks or lengthening lineups at airports and border crossings. The border choke since 9/11 is just one symptom of a deteriorating relationship.

The border clog is harming Canada. Trade has increased in absolute numbers since the peak in 2001 because of the appreciation of commodity prices, but has fallen as a percentage of Canada's GDP as a whole. Two-way trade grew from $409.778 billion in 2000 to $596.235

billion in 2011, but Canadian exports to the U.S. represented 19.1 per-cent of its GDP in 2011, compared to 34.4 percent in 2000. Furthermore, Canada's exports to the U.S. contributed 2.3 percent growth to Canada's economy from 1982 to 2001 and only 0.5 percent afterward.[31]

The U.S. and Canada could have avoided some problems by mov-ing further toward economic integration, as others have in Europe, Africa or the Caribbean. But they have remained at the nascent, or Free-Trade Era stage, in terms of economic integration, since 1989. Others have created customs unions, monetary unions, common markets, economic unions, fiscal unions and even some degree of political union. The U.S. and Canada remained frozen at initial stages, mostly because Mexico was unable to participate. But by 2010, the two had decoupled and begun to negotiate more integration in order to create a security perimeter to address police, immigration and customs issues.

This resulted in the announcement in early 2011, by the two countries, of an initiative called Beyond the Border: A Shared Vision for Perimeter Security and Economic Competitiveness, designed to create stronger perimeter security and accelerate the flow of people, goods and services between the two countries by 2013. The objec-tive was to address bilateral economic and political difficulties, and to open the border to commerce in order to please Canada. But to please Americans, the goal was to block criminals, terrorists, illegal substances and contraband from entering either country through enhanced cooperation between law enforcement and other officials.

Obviously, the announced goals were mutually exclusive. The border is no longer working properly for either nation, and the perimeter deal won't either. The border will continue to close. In fall 2011, the media reported that the U.S. was considering fencing off parts of the U.S.–Canada border, and it has been deploying drones to patrol the border since 2006. The only foolproof way to fix the border—as well as avert conflict—is to eliminate it altogether.

This book makes the case for a merger, and proposes some business and policy approaches to accomplish the goal. The aim is to quantify Canada's value to Americans so they realize just how important Canada is to their future, and to make Canadians realize America's importance to them along with the need for more integration, if not an outright merger. It also outlines the economic and political power Canadians deserve and could wield if the two countries joined forces and how this could remove future logjams in the U.S. political process. I examine world business and political trends, border conflicts, the vanishing options available for America and Canada in their current incarnations, the synergies of a merger, five ways to structure a deal and how to finance a deal, how political resistance and differences could be addressed, and the options available if there is no merger in the near or far future.

Do I believe a merger will happen? I honestly don't know. But it should. Americans and Canadians cannot ignore or refuse to consider such a policy option, no matter how objectionable it may seem and no matter how seemingly impossible or costly. The countries cannot maintain their living standards and are too heavily invested in a free-market model that is being outmaneuvered, and will be destroyed, by nations and regions that purposely divide them or that adhere to their own unique forms of state capitalism.

Politically, their outdated constitutional constructs and democratic institutions are flawed, perhaps impossible to improve or even merge. But an economic union is certainly possible, fully or partially, governed by an improved super-layer of government over existing federal levels. If even that attainable goal is also unlikely, then Canada must transform itself in a way that has historically proved elusive. So must the United States. Each must change, merger or no, because whatever the future, the status quo is not an option. Ideally, this book will help Americans and Canadians realize that they have decisions to make and that the way forward, even if challenging, would be to unite like the Germans, govern like the Swiss and think more like the Chinese.

CHAPTER ONE

International Threats: China and State Capitalism

He took over and said, "If I have to shoot 200,000 students to save China from another 100 years of disorder, so be it."
—LEE KUAN YEW, SINGAPORE STATESMAN, ON DENG XIAOPING'S DECISION TO INITIATE THE 1989 TIANANMEN SQUARE MASSACRE

T HE WORLD WANTS RESOURCES, HIGH LIVING STANDARDS AND power; the race to acquire and hoard them is a zero-sum game. If the Chinese consumed as much as Americans and Canadians do, the world's demand for oil and metals would double. If South Asians also consumed as much as North America's two richest countries, it would triple. And if every one of the world's seven billion people consumed as much as North Americans do now, production would have to increase eleven-fold, as if the world population were to suddenly balloon to 77 billion people. As historian Jared Diamond wrote in 2008 in *The New York Times*, "We often promise developing countries that if they will only adopt good policies—for example, institute honest government and a free-market economy—they, too, will be able to enjoy a first-world lifestyle. This promise is impossible, a cruel hoax: we are having difficulty supporting a first-world lifestyle even now for only one billion people."[1]

The year 2003 marked the beginning of the end of everything. That year, a twenty-year depression in commodity prices ended and a super-cycle of indeterminate duration started. The rise that year of more than a dozen traditional have-not nations, including China, India, Turkey, Indonesia and Brazil, mopped up the surplus inventories of key resources around the world. At the same time, the availability of cheap resources was diminishing rapidly, which led to a demand–supply squeeze that initiated unprecedented price increases and ignited a political transformation.

There is too little acknowledgment of this planetary arithmetic, and of the looming shortage and high price of finite resources. The so-called "peak oil" proponents and some environmental activists are *au courant,* but even among them there is little consensus as to its urgency or remedy. Optimists hope that technology will replace resources before they run out, while pessimists carry on ruthlessly to ensure that when the world hits a wall, they will be safely behind it with plenty of everything. "The Chinese want indoor plumbing and they're going to get it," billionaire geologist and investor Ned Goodman told me in 2006. "It cannot be stopped."

Even so, strangely, it has been business as usual, except that it's not going to be business as usual for long. The first sign of this dire trajectory came in 2003 in the beleaguered mining industry. Suddenly, companies found themselves benefiting from the end of a depression in metal and mineral prices that had lasted two decades. By 2004, those buying energy, metals or minerals began to feel the pinch of higher production costs. Mining company revenues increased, along with profits, and their stocks rose too. When the cost of fuel and foodstuffs began to rise, the public noticed and the politicians paid attention. By April 2008, energy prices were 320 percent higher than they had been in January 2003; metals and minerals were up 296 percent, and food prices were 138 percent higher, according to the World Bank, which described the situation as "the most marked boom in commodity prices in the past century."[2]

A year later, there was a retreat from the highs, and then a pause during the financial catastrophe of 2008 and 2009. But the point of no return had been reached because the emerging economies continued to grow through the crisis. Commodities fell back a bit, but resumed their steady march upward before many of the rich countries were out of recession or out from under their burden of unemployment and debt. Aggravating the predicament was the reality that emerging or developing economies had decoupled from their rich customers and virtually sailed through the collapse, recession and debt crisis. Their rise was tautly quantified in an August 2011 issue of *The Economist,* in which the economic performance of twenty-eight emerging economies was compared with that of the twenty-three original members in 1990 of the Organisation for Economic Co-operation and Development (OECD).

The twenty-three original OECD members

Australia	France	Japan	Spain
Austria	Germany	Luxembourg	Sweden
Belgium	Greece	Netherlands	Switzerland
Canada	Iceland	New Zealand	United Kingdom
Denmark	Ireland	Norway	United States
Finland	Italy	Portugal	

The twenty-eight emerging economies
(including twelve that joined the OECD after 1990)

Brazil	Hong Kong	Morocco	Slovak Republic
Chile	Hungary	Peru	Slovenia
China	India	Philippines	South Africa
Colombia	Indonesia	Poland	South Korea
Czech Republic	Israel	Russia	Taiwan
Estonia	Malaysia	Saudi Arabia	Thailand
Egypt	Mexico	Singapore	Turkey

The Economist's criteria in selecting these emerging economies included national incomes, market infrastructure and size. This analysis demonstrated the extent of the redistribution of wealth. In 1990, the original "rich club" represented 80 percent of the world's GDP; by 2008, the emerging economies generated more than 50 percent of the world's economic output. In 1990, the twenty-three developed nations represented 73 percent of world exports; by 2009, the emerging economies accounted for more than 50 percent. Between 2000 and 2010, the emerging economies managed the financial catastrophe with ease, and at the end of the decade held 81 percent of all government foreign-exchange reserves and only 17 percent of all global government debt. They also held 25 percent of all global financial assets, such as cash, stocks and bonds—double their holdings in 2000.[3] The swing in fortunes led some to dub the first ten years of the twenty-first century the Decade of Emerging Economies. But the converse is also true—it could be labeled the Decade of Decline for Developed Economies.

What this all means is that the world has been developing at three speeds: warp speed for the twenty-eight emerging economies; mediocre growth for the original twenty-three "rich club" members; and zero to negative growth for the other 142 members of the United Nations, euphemistically labeled "developing" or "failed" nations. These countries comprise the billion or so people who subsist on less than $3 a day and live in refugee camps or war zones. Their future is hopeless in this Darwinian race for resources; only nations already featuring booming export economies, and a wealth of capital and resources such as energy and food lands, will win out. This is the era when only the fittest, and fastest, nation-states will survive.

The World Bank estimates that, by 2020, the global economic pie will essentially be divided into two equal parts: the West and the East.

The U.S. economy will grow from $14.8 trillion in 2010 to $22.6 trillion, Germany's from $2.86 trillion to $3.98 trillion, and Russia's from $2.2 trillion to $4.3 trillion. The European Union as a whole is headed for slow or no growth. In the East, China's economy will grow from $9.7 trillion to $28.1 trillion, India's from $3.9 trillion to $10.2 trillion, and Japan's from $4.26 trillion to $6.9 trillion. The International Monetary Fund forecasts that China, India, Japan and the four Asian Tigers—South Korea, Taiwan, Singapore and Hong Kong—will be bigger than the G8 (minus Japan) by 2018.[4]

"The conservative-preferred, free-market fundamentalist, shareholder-only model—so successful in the 20th century—is being thrown onto the trash heap of history in the 21st century," wrote Andy Stern, former president of the Service Employees International Union in 2011.[5] "In an era when countries need to become economic teams, Team USA's results—a jobless decade, 30 years of flat median wages, a trade deficit, a shrinking middle class and phenomenal gains in wealth but only for the top 1 percent—are pathetic." His solution called for long-term planning based on job creation, as is the case in China and elsewhere.

Emerging economies have a superior economic model because they cannot afford to slow down. China must create roughly 300,000 jobs a week, or 15.6 million a year, to keep employment levels steady. India must grow at roughly the same rate. By contrast, America had a workforce of about 154 million in 2011 and Canada's entire workforce totaled slightly more than 18 million. China must build the equivalent of one Chicago a year, in terms of urban infrastructure and buildings, to meet its objective by 2030, which is to triple its middle class by urbanizing a billion of its citizens and relocating them to new cities or to new neighborhoods in old cities. To do that, China must build 50,000 skyscrapers, 170 new mass-transit systems and 200 cities housing more than one million persons each, according to management consultant McKinsey Global Institute.[6]

For rich nations, the redistribution of their wealth to others is well advanced. The 2008 collapse sped up the process, forcing governments to pile on debt to rescue and stimulate their economies, just as their populations were aging and unable to earn, spend or save as much as before. The American version of capitalism, a Wild West of unregulated brokers and bankers, had failed again roughly eighty years after the Great Depression should have taught the country a lesson. Only this time, it nearly took down the world's financial system.

Emerging markets are no less capitalistic or Wild West–like, but they have adapted their versions of free enterprise to fit their cultures. They go by such names as "state capitalism," "planned economies," "command-and-control economies" or "mixed economies." But labels are irrelevant, wrote American historian Joyce Appleby in 2010. "Many believe that capitalism was an inevitable development and that it had deep roots in European intellectual soil. I don't think that either is true . . . capitalism takes different shape in different countries because it is a culture and cultures encompass family mores, religion, politics and personal values."[7]

In 1978, Chinese leader Deng Xiaoping made the same point when describing his new economic development model, one that would change the world. He had also studied the Asian Tigers' successes, and he launched in China what he described as "socialism with Chinese characteristics." It was capitalism mingled with communism and statism, and he sold his concept to skeptical Chinese leaders by citing his favorite Sichuan proverb: "It doesn't matter if a cat is black or white, so long as it catches mice."

What is happening in the world is not about capitalism versus communism, right versus wrong or a battle of ideologies. It's about what works, what doesn't and why. There's no denying that between 2000 and 2010 the emerging economies' black, white or purple "cats" continued to catch lots of mice while others have fallen by the wayside. Going forward, the fat cats must simply realize they need to slim down, learn how to live on fewer mice, and then figure out how to catch enough to survive.

Prey and Predator

The movement of wealth from West to East is old news, and the consumption crisis is so depressing it's mostly ignored. But there is a grand game underway to capture ownership of, or guaranteed access to, the necessities of national life.

In April 2008, when commodity prices peaked worldwide, some 10,000 workers staged street protests against soaring costs in Dhaka, Bangladesh.[8] The protestors caused extensive property damage and injured dozens of police. In Pakistan that same month, the government deployed the army to stop the looting of foodstuffs from farm fields and warehouses. Violence broke out in dozens of countries that spring. Between 2006 and 2008, average world prices for rice rose by 217 percent, wheat by 136 percent, corn by 125 percent and soybeans by 107 percent.[9] The price rises and the unavailability of staples caused severe riots in parts of Asia and Africa, as well as in Haiti. Mexico, Bolivia, Yemen, Uzbekistan, Bangladesh, Pakistan, Sri Lanka and South Africa, among other countries, experienced food riots and social unrest.[10]

On April 8, 2008, an Egyptian boy died from gunshot wounds after police intervened to stop a violent demonstration over the doubling of bread prices in the industrial city of Mahalla.[11] Two days later, the Haitian senate dismissed Prime Minister Jacques-Édouard Alexis after five people were killed during food riots.[12] The price of staples had jumped by 50 percent in one year, and fuel had tripled in price in a matter of months. In February 2008 in Cameroon, large-scale rioting occurred over inflated food and fuel prices, combined with opposition to an attempt by its president, Paul Biya, to extend his twenty-five-year dictatorship. Two dozen were killed, and the violence ended only when the government capitulated by reducing taxes and retail prices on many staples, then announced a two-year emergency program to grow more food.[13] In Mogadishu, thousands of angry Somalis rioted and five protestors died in clashes with government troops and armed shopkeepers over rising food prices and the collapse of the nation's currency.[14]

That same month, Mexican President Felipe Calderón agreed to freeze prices of more than 150 consumer staples, such as coffee, sardines, tuna, oil, soup and tea, until the end of December 2008.[15] The Russian government did the same, pressuring retailers to freeze food prices before key elections. The Brazilian government imposed a temporary ban on the export of rice to protect domestic consumers.[16]

Rich and poor countries alike became ensnarled in this catastrophic rise in prices. Worries about inflation, and share price collapses for food manufacturers and retailers, dominated front pages. Gasoline prices went through the roof. Political careers were threatened in wealthy jurisdictions, and revolutions were imminent in impoverished ones.

Interestingly, the mass protests and insurrections that swept six Arab nations beginning in December 2010 and throughout 2011 may have resulted in part from oppressive food prices and tyrannical regimes that prevented protests back in 2007 and 2008. In a paper for the Carnegie Endowment for International Peace in June 2008,

Ibrahim Saif wrote, "Skyrocketing food prices in 2007 have made basic staples like rice, wheat, and corn unaffordable to lower income groups throughout the world. Arab countries, which import most of their food, found themselves in difficult circumstances with limited options in the short run . . . It is within this context that the riots that erupted in the streets of several Arab countries such as Egypt, Morocco, and Yemen can be understood."[17] In Egypt, a five-fold rise in bread prices led to clashes with the army. Subsidies were put in place, the army was ordered to bake and distribute bread to the poor, and public-sector wages were increased by 30 percent. Yemen, Morocco and Jordan underwent the same upheavals.

In 2010, food inflation contributed to the Arab Spring. Wildfires destroyed most of Russia's wheat harvest, and Moscow halted exports, causing prices to skyrocket. By December, world food prices had reached a new record; although blunted in many of the less-stable countries by various measures, these prices contributed to the explosion of unrest in Tunisia and other North African countries, which were dependent on Russian wheat.[18]

"Assuming a connection among rising prices, hunger, and violent civic unrest seems logical," wrote Evan Fraser and Andrew Rivas in January 2011.[19] It was a replay of the early eighteenth century, when hundreds of food riots in England and France led to the rescinding of an ancient law, called the Assize of Bread, that fixed prices on behalf of farmers. But the urban poor were unable to travel to the farms to get their bread, and merchants took advantage of this by marking up prices extortionately, forcing farmers to bring their commodities to market.

The underlying causes of this mayhem? The usual suspects: the world population explosion and the net daily population increase of 213,810 (367,462 births per day and 153,652 deaths per day according to the 2013 U.S. Census Bureau, World Vital Events); the demand for more meat by Asian middle classes; and a decline in farmland to grow food due to drought, urbanization and other causes. In 1961, there were 1.025 acres of arable land per person globally; by 2010, this had fallen to 0.494 acres, estimated the United Nations' Food and Agriculture Organization.[20]

An internal World Bank report blamed 75 percent of the food price increases on shortages caused by farm subsidies to grow plants for bio-fuels and 25 percent on fuel prices charged to farmers. American biofuel subsidies, part of the U.S. Energy Policy Act of 2005, were designed to reduce dependency on foreign oil imports and included requirements to blend ethanol with gasoline. In 2000, ethanol represented 1 percent of the motor-fuel supply. By 2008, gasoline was being blended with, on average, 5 percent ethanol. Brazil had gone further and become fully self-sufficient in transportation fuels by refining massive tracts of sugar cane into ethanol. By 2011, the U.S. and Brazil produced 90 percent of the world's biofuels. The remaining 10 percent was mostly produced in the European Union, where subsidies have primarily encouraged production of biodiesel from animal fats, oil seeds and a variety of crops such as flax or mustard.[21]

"While many worry about filling their gas tanks," said World Bank president Robert Zoellick in an April 11, 2008, interview with *The Guardian*, "many others around the world are struggling to fill their stomachs. And it's getting more and more difficult every day."[22]

THE ATTEMPTED RAPE OF MADAGASCAR

Soaring food and energy prices forced leaders to prepare long-term food strategies. But few were as efficient or as effective as the four Asian Tigers, which had catapulted rapidly in two or three generations. In Seoul, South Korea's technocrats and leaders were quickest off the mark. The country known as the "Miracle on the Han River" had grown from virtually zero after the Korean War to a $1.4 trillion GDP just fifty years later.

By 2010, South Koreans relied on foreign food imports. The country had become the world's twelfth-largest economy, but during the food price crisis of April 2008 its government responded to the hysterical headlines by rolling out a new national strategy in a press release: Seoul would subsidize Korean corporations to acquire, or lease, farmland overseas in order to guarantee food supplies, at reasonable prices, for South Koreans in the future.[23]

In July 2008, China followed suit by announcing that five of its state-owned farming giants would be deputized to rent or buy foreign farmland for soybean and other production in Central Asia, Russia, Africa, Southeast Asia and South America.[24] Both South Korea and China were simply taking a leaf out of Japan's book. In the 1980s, Tokyo began to lease or buy farmland overseas in order to become self-sufficient in food. By 2010, Japanese private interests controlled an estimated three times as much farmland outside Japan as was being cultivated inside the country.[25]

One of South Korea's business conglomerates, or *chaebols,* was the electronics company Daewoo. In 1997, the Asian crisis destroyed the conglomerate, but it survived as several smaller entities. An offshoot, Daewoo Logistics, decided to take advantage of the government's generous farm subsidy scheme. The company was involved in getting goods to market and building rail, road and ocean transportation facilities. For months, its planners had set up shop in Madagascar, where they had been hired by a major mining consortium to provide logistics and transportation solutions to get its nickel to markets around the world. It was logical that a Korean company with relationships in Madagascar, armed with a mandate and money from its home government, would explore opportunities in the island nation to get control of large tracts of farmland to grow crops to export back to South Korea.

The republic of Madagascar has been an impoverished and unstable former colony of France ever since gaining independence in 1960, and it was badly in need of economic development. The sleepy and dysfunctional island off the southeastern coast of Africa has a population of 20 million and subsists on an economy that generates only $19.5 billion worth of activity a year. The residents are either descendants of Austronesians, who mostly arrived from Borneo twenty centuries ago in outriggers, or East Africans who came to the island to raise cattle.

By the seventeenth century, some 90 percent of Madagascar's rain forests had been cleared for farming. Its small ports had developed into pirate havens, and Arab and European traders bought and sold spices, seafood and slaves there. In 1883, the French invaded the island and made it a colony until 1960, when Madagascar's parliament, modeled on France's, became autonomously but continuously embroiled in battles for political control. There were *coups d'état*, military dictatorships, an assassination and constant conflicts.

Daewoo knew that the Madagascan government was desperate for investment and had millions of unused or underutilized acres of arable land in the charge of subsistence farmers, so the company approached Madagascar's officials and was quickly able to negotiate a sweetheart deal, so favorable that when the deal's details leaked out, political chaos resulted.

On November 20, 2008, Daewoo Logistics announced that Madagascar had granted a ninety-nine-year lease on 3.2 million acres to grow corn and palm oil exclusively for export to South Korea.[26]

The tract of land was the size of Connecticut and represented half of the island nation's farmland. In return, Daewoo said it would invest $6 billion over twenty years to build roads and a port to ship the corn and oil, irrigation systems, power plants, schools and hospitals for farm workers. But there were no job guarantees for locals. And there was no clause in the agreement that would allow Madagascar's government to stop exports to South Korea if there were food shortages at home.

Worse yet, speculation raged that China would become Daewoo's partner and supply all the laborers needed for construction of the infrastructure and for the ongoing plantation operations. One official suggested that workers might also be brought in from poorer African nations. As details dribbled out, the sheer scale of the deal, and the surrender of food security to a foreign nation, shocked many.

The *Financial Times* reported that the Madagascan government had not even had the good sense to negotiate a substantial payment of rent for the land, having agreed to waive the paltry traditional fee of $5 per hectare it charged local farmers for the government-owned lands in return for promises of future investment.[27] In a Bloomberg News interview, an unnamed Daewoo Logistics spokesman contradicted this report, saying there would be a rental fee paid, but that it was "negotiable." "We are in talks with Madagascar officials hopefully to cut it down before finalizing the rental fee," he said.[28]

This was "neo-colonialism," wrote the *Financial Times* in an editorial. "In the name of food or energy security, cash-rich states are seeking to buy up natural resources in poor countries. Foreign capital and technology are desirable, but the terms and scale of the present deal raised serious questions. Any agreement must ultimately be in the interest of the local population. The Madagascan case looks positively neocolonial. If the deal is sealed with the vague promises by

Daewoo Logistics being mooted, the Madagascan people stand to lose half of their arable land."[29]

Madagascar's president, Marc Ravalomanana, an autocratic leader given to dissolving the country's National Assembly whenever it displeased him, came under fire at home and abroad for the deal. Street protests raged throughout the capital city of Antananarivo, and the United Nations' Food and Agriculture Organization publicly raised strong objections, as did the World Bank and others.

The deal, as conceived, would be ruinous for Madagascar. The country was selling its food security for a song, its workers would be held for ransom by the threat of competition from low-cost foreign laborers, its local farmers would be unable to compete or to rent the lands, and the country would be unable to develop its own agribusiness or value-added export industries. Only South Korea, and its corporation, had won, and won big.

Andry Rajoelina, the popular former mayor of Antananarivo and a local media proprietor, led the opposition to the deal, claiming it was unconstitutional to lease sovereign land for ninety-nine years. Protests grew until, in early 2009, soldiers opened fire on demonstrators and killed twenty-eight. In the weeks that followed, violence escalated and a total of 130 people died in uprisings and shootings. By March 2009, the soldiers in the armed forces, and some officers, were siding with protesters, and on March 18 a military *coup d'état* took place, led by the thirty-four-year-old Rajoelina. His first action was to cancel the Daewoo deal and fire all the country's supreme court justices for their decision to allow the land deal that overrode constitutional protection for the country's lands. At the time, he stated, "We are not against the idea of working with investors, but if we want to sell or rent out land we have to change the constitution, [and] you have to consult the people."[30]

Rajoelina promised democratic elections within two years, but many world leaders, guilty of similar practices or also of selling off farmland, condemned him for violently overthrowing a democratically elected president. The African Union, which had a few members leasing off gigantic tracts of land to other Asian governments, demanded reinstatement of the government. Rich nations withdrew foreign aid in protest and imposed economic sanctions. Instead of sympathy, France condemned the coup, as did the United States, Canada, Europe and the rest of the developed world. (In 2013, Rajoelina promised to run for election in 2018.)

But on September 7, 2010, the World Bank fully supported Madagascar's stand and issued a report entitled "The Global Land Rush." The bank documented the extent of farmland "grabs" by South Korea, China, Middle Eastern nations, biofuel companies and others. In the two years following the 2008 food crisis, an estimated 115 million acres of arable land, an area nearly twice the size of the United Kingdom, had been sold or leased to foreign investors. Before the 2008 food crisis, foreign purchases or leases of farmlands had averaged only 9.9 million acres a year.

Tragically, Madagascar's egregious farmland giveaway merely provided a dramatic example of the inability of multilateral institutions to protect greater global interests. The United Nations, encouraged by Japan, decided after the Madagascar controversy to create a code of conduct to regulate overseas investment in farmland. In October 2010, a draft code was completed, including principles advocated by the World Bank such as respect for existing rights, a ban on investments that jeopardized local food security, and consultation with locals. UN members rejected the code, even though its adoption would have been non-binding. "It's terribly disappointing," said Olivier De Schutter, the UN special rapporteur on the right to food. "We are not moving swiftly enough to find an effective answer to the problems posed by land investments."[31]

The result is that business has been brisk for the rich and fleet-footed emerging economies. In 2011, Saudi Arabian business groups were negotiating control over 70 percent of the rice-growing region of Senegal and had already acquired large-scale farms in Egypt, Ethiopia, Tanzania, Syria, Turkey and Ukraine. The Qataris had signed lengthy leases in Kenya, Brazil, Argentina, Australia, Sudan and Ukraine. Argentina and Brazil acquired large tracts of land in Uruguay. In 2010, Nigeria's government offered 175 million acres for lease to Gulf nations. And other South Korean *chaebols,* such as Hyundai Heavy (the country's biggest shipbuilder), were busy signing farmland deals in Russia, Tanzania, Indonesia and the Philippines.

By the end of 2010, the hands-down champion of them all was China. Beijing, along with its state-owned enterprises, had become the single largest owner of farmland throughout Africa, and one of the biggest in Brazil, and was gobbling up target investments in Kazakhstan, Brazil, Canada, Cambodia and Australia, as well as in Malaysia to build palm oil plantations.

Food prices paused or fell in some regions or in some commodities, but have subsequently embarked on a steady increase, as more land in China and India is urbanized and more people are born. Increasingly, the players will turn their attention to the mother lode of farmland: the United States and Canada. Since 2008, dozens of hedge funds and land banks have sprung up, fronting for foreigners, to buy acreage in North America. The opportunity is significant, they promise, to buy low and sell high. American and Canadian farmland is relatively cheap and a way to profit as food prices rise in sync with rising Asian incomes. An added bonus to buying land in the U.S. and Canada is that values will increase more quickly than in Africa or elsewhere because of the sophistication of North America's agribusiness, with its first-rate technologies, logistics and infrastructure.

The potential to acquire lots of land is greatest in the U.S. and Canada too. In 2011, two million farms operated in the U.S., with 907 million acres, nine times the size of California, used to grow crops or as pasture.[32] The United States is the world's largest exporter of agricultural products. Canada is sixth largest in terms of exports, with a quarter of a million farms and 168 million acres in production, 1.6 times the size of California. In addition, the two countries have twice as much land available to grow cash crops or graze livestock as is now in use.[33]

Investors from outside these countries are starting to trickle in. The U.S. Department of Agriculture's Farm Agency tracks foreign ownership, but the figures displayed on its website in 2011 were three years out of date. According to the site, in 2008 there were 22.2 million acres in foreign hands, or 2.4 percent of all privately held agricultural land. While that amount represents a small proportion, it signified an increase of 5.85 percent, or 1.3 million acres, from the year before and twice the level of foreign ownership twenty years before.[34]

Canada's federal and provincial governments don't even track foreign ownership. Alberta, Saskatchewan, Manitoba and Prince Edward Island each restrict foreign farm ownership to between twenty and forty acres. But the National Farmers Union in Canada, a volunteer organization of family farms, believes that neither recent transactions by foreign entities nor growing interest have been carefully monitored. In an essay in 2010 in its newsletter to members, the Farmers Union posited that a big Asian or Middle Eastern country or foreign corporation could easily afford to buy all of Canada's food lands. "Let's use a value of $1,500 per acre which means that one-fifth of all Canadian farmland and buildings could be bought for $44.6 billion, or roughly what Microsoft offered to buy Yahoo! in 2008," said the report. "This single example illustrates the massive capacity of corporate capital to buy farmland. In coming decades, if Canadian (and global) farmland is allocated on the basis of 'ability to pay,' it will not be allocated to local farm families." [35]

North America Is the Next Target

The acquisition of farmland, with a few exceptions, has not been as frenetic as has been the rush to find and buy ore bodies and oil deposits to feed the world's emerging industrial engines. The United States is a prime target, but acquisition strategies by China, Russia and Arab countries such as Saudi Arabia or Dubai have been frustrated by political backlash against their direct ownership of resources or strategic assets. Consequently, these countries have gone elsewhere, invested in easier marks such as Canada, or have gone surreptitiously through Canadian or other intermediaries to buy U.S. assets. The first high-profile opposition to China took place in March 2005, when Congress, taking a stand on control over its resources, chased away the Chinese government–owned China National Offshore Oil Corporation (CNOOC), which had made a hostile bid of between $16 billion and $18 billion to take over California's Unocal Corporation. The House of Representatives referred the purchase to the White House as a "national security" issue, opposition was fierce, and the company withdrew its bid. Months later, Unocal was bought by, and absorbed into, Chevron.

But China has found other ways to gain major footholds in the American economy, using Canada as a back door. In 2012, Canada allowed the same Chinese company, CNOOC, to buy Calgary-based oil giant Nexen for $15.1 billion. This epitomized the long-term nature of China's strategies and illustrated how its players are able to lay the groundwork to gain enormous political influence. Now ensconced in Canada, China's giant corporations may pick off companies one by one, despite the government's assurances that this was the first and last takeover. The Chinese will not take no for an answer; they will bide their time awaiting a change in government, policy or leadership.

China's tactics vary. It may not be allowed to buy American oil giants, but it has become Washington's biggest foreign lender. By January 2011, foreigners held 32 percent of the U.S. government's total debt of $14.1 trillion, and China was a major creditor, with 26 percent of that foreign-held total. The rest was held by Japan, Brazil, Taiwan, Hong Kong and Russia, as well as by intermediaries in Canada, Switzerland, the United Kingdom, nations that export oil, and Caribbean banking centers on behalf of unknown clients. More Chinese, Saudi and Russian investments than show up publicly are likely buried in the U.K., Swiss and Canadian figures, where middlemen act on their behalf.[36]

Foreigners also hold massive investments in American stocks or bonds, as well as in the form of foreign direct investments (FDIs), which are permanent investments in fixed assets and corporations. Their subsidiaries or money managers in Canada, Hong Kong, Singapore and others provide backdoor entries through which China invests in the United States. This is done to camouflage the activities and helps China understate the actual investment figures for political reasons. For instance, China discloses its annual FDI numbers, but does not break down how much goes where. In 2009, the U.S. Bureau of Economic Analysis repeated news reports that China's

FDI in the U.S. totaled $1.2 billion in 2008, but added, "this figure could be larger, as many of the investments made by Hong Kong companies into the U.S. could have sources of capital that originated in mainland China." This was followed by another estimate, by the American Chamber of Commerce in Shanghai, that stated, "In fact, informal estimates place China's 2009 US–bound FDI [foreign direct investment] figures between $3.9 billion to $6.4 billion or a 300 percent increase over 2008 levels. Clearly, the U.S. is increasingly a target of Chinese investment."[37]

This is worrisome to some Americans, and it should be. A 2008 Congressional report on the possible implications of China's stake in U.S. securities outlined the risks. "Some economists contend that attempts by China to unload a large share of its U.S. securities holdings could have a significant negative impact on the U.S. economy (at least in the short run), especially if such a move sparked a sharp depreciation of the dollar in international markets and induced other foreign investors to sell off their U.S. holdings as well."[38]

There is also much to worry about when it comes to China's investments in Canada. Canada is clearly more powerful than Madagascar, but its resources—and pliant governments—have placed a gigantic bull's-eye on its national forehead. This is why, since 2003, the world's resource-starved nations have been flocking north of the border.

Even Canada's most forgotten places, remote and hostile, are targets. On June 22, 2010, I trekked to the town of Inuvik in the Northwest Territories. The journey from Toronto took as long as it would take to reach Moscow, or nine hours of flying time. Inuvik is centered in the resource-rich Mackenzie Delta, about 60 miles from the Arctic Ocean and 120 miles north of the Arctic Circle. Inuvik, with a population of 3,586, is a government administrative center and has a local oil industry. But oil and natural gas exploration in the area mostly shut down in the 1990s, after the federal government eliminated drilling subsidies and after it became obvious that the stuff would never get to market because of political incompetence and squabbling among First Nations bands, levels of government, environmentalists and public agencies. Since the mid-1990s, the town's economy has been moribund, except for government activities, despite the fact that oil companies have found a proven reserve of nine trillion cubic feet of natural gas and an estimated 1.5 billion barrels of oil.

Approval by Ottawa for a gas pipeline to the south had been post-poned for decades because of government delays, public hearings, court cases, a moratorium, hundreds of consultations and dozens of studies. This endless review-and-approval process was frustrating, given the potential in the surrounding area and a consensus within the industry that more exploration and development drilling could find tens of trillions more cubic feet of natural gas and oil in the delta and offshore in the Beaufort Sea. For example, in 1984, Gulf Canada drilled one of the most promising wells in the region, with a flow of up to twenty thousand barrels a day,[39] then abandoned it after Ottawa unraveled its aggressive National Energy Program (NEP), which since 1980 had given millions in grants to Canadian companies to drill in the Arctic and on federal lands. Proponents of the NEP, and industry geologists, speculated that the Northwest Territories and the Beaufort Sea offshore could yield similar hydrocarbon deposits to those found in Alaska and Norway, which contain vast oil and gas fields above the Arctic Circle.

I was there in 2010, along with a dozen others, to speak at the Inuvik Petroleum Show, a small gathering held in the town's biggest building, which housed a recreation center, a civic center, an audi-torium and a school under one roof. The Northwest Territories, the

Town of Inuvik and various oil companies had sponsored the event to once again try to convince the federal government to approve construction of a natural gas pipeline to the south. The usual Canadian proponents of the project attended, along with experts from Alaska and Norway. But so did eight men from South Korea. They had arrived days before the conference and kept to themselves. They were scouting the region, talking with locals and meeting with politicians, and were conducting research on behalf of South Korean gas utilities and various government agencies.

Canada's failure to develop its northern resources proved a magnet to the Koreans. The untapped Mackenzie Delta's gas and oil reserves presented an opportunity. So did low natural gas prices, touted by the pipeline's sponsors as a reason why it would likely never be built. But this did not deter South Korea; just the opposite. The country was, and remains, totally dependent on energy imports, and China and other Asian countries had surpassed them in the race to tie up short-, medium- or long-term supplies from other sources. Korea had become the world's fifth-largest importer of oil and second-largest importer of coal and liquefied natural gas, and securing energy supplies had become vital to its future.

The South Koreans were exploring the possibility of developing a liquefied natural gas plant and seaport. The natural gas would be collected and liquefied in the Arctic, then shipped by icebreaker through the Beaufort Sea, along and down the Alaskan coast, and ultimately to South Korea. Theirs was not a pipe dream—no pun intended. A similar plant, built on a remote Norwegian island in the Arctic by Norway's StatOil, gathered natural gas from as far away as a hundred miles offshore. StatOil liquefied and shipped the fuel to Spain and the United States. And on December 6, 2012, Russia's Gazprom Marketing & Trading, owned by OAO Gazprom, shipped liquefied natural gas from Hammerfest, Norway, to Tobata, Japan, through the Northern Sea Route for the first time in history.[40]

I approached the Korean investors and suggested that gathering, liquefying and shipping natural gas from Canada's Arctic would cost at least six to ten times as much as the going rate of $4 per cubic foot—roughly $25, $30 or more. I wondered how it could ever be economical, given all the new, cheaply produced shale gas being discovered in the U.S. and Canada. "When you don't have natural gas," replied one of the South Koreans, "and may not be able to get any, you will pay anything for it. The word 'uneconomical' is relative. We don't care about North America's prices now or in the future. We are interested in long-term energy security, which is priceless."

That year, the Korea National Oil Corporation and Korea Gas Corporation had followed the same logic and began their move. They committed billions of dollars to produce and liquefy shale gas in remotest British Columbia.[41] Obviously, tying up Arctic supplies was an extension of that strategy. And securing supplies in Canada also made sense from a strategic viewpoint, if only to beat China, India, Japan or the other Asian Tigers to the punch. Perhaps most importantly, natural gas from Canada would reduce, or possibly be able to eliminate, South Korea's dependency on volatile and dangerous Russia for energy in the future.

Naturally, China and others have similar plans afoot. After 2003, as prices began to rise irreversibly, Beijing's national champions had begun to look at resource corporations in Canada and others around the world. The initial foray in Canada was aimed at gaining control of a major resource company with decades of experience around the world, giving China a major foothold in the country and the sector. It would provide relationships and a platform for rapid expansion. So in 2004, Chinese state–controlled China Minmetals began talks with Canada's premier mining company, Noranda. But rumors soon leaked into the Canadian investment community, and columnists, investors and politicians objected. As in the Unocal situation in the U.S., China realized that buying an iconic company was politically difficult and that it needed to develop new approaches.

In 2006, Sinopec Shanghai Engineering Company, a Chinese state-owned enterprise, made a move. Its subsidiary, called SSEC Canada, landed a contract with Canada's largest oil independent, Canadian Natural Resources, to build two tank "farms" involving eleven storage tanks. Their plan to employ cheap Chinese labor undercut all Canadian bidders. The company obtained permission from the Canadian federal government to bring in 132 temporary workers in 2006 and 2007 to build the tanks. The province of Alberta required the employer to pay health benefits, pension entitlements and market wages.

The workers lived in tents, and their wages were withheld pending completion of the job. Supervision and safety controls were non-existent, and workmanship was shoddy. On April 24, 2007, the roof of one of the storage tanks collapsed.[42] Two Chinese workers were crushed to death and five more were injured, two seriously. Routine investigations by Alberta health and safety officials and employment standards personnel took place, and in the spring of 2009 a total of fifty-three charges were laid against the three companies for unsafe working conditions. If convicted, Sinopec, its subsidiary SSEC Canada and Canadian Natural Resources faced millions in fines, and possibly jail sentences. Canada Natural Resources was legally on the hook under Canadian law for any misdeeds committed by subcontractors.

But the prosecution was delayed while Sinopec argued it had no representatives in Canada and therefore could not be served with the court papers and charges.[43] Victims and witnesses had returned to China immediately after the tragedy. A local judge refused to hear the case until Sinopec had been served papers, even after prosecutors explained that they had no jurisdiction to serve them in China.

In addition to alleged workplace infractions, Sinopec and its subsidiary never paid the 132 Chinese workers an estimated $3.17 million in wages for the work they performed in Canada. These employees had been shipped out of Canada immediately after the deaths of their co-workers, presumably because the contract was terminated, but also with the result that none of them could testify about the incident. And none could be contacted, either. Canadian Natural Resources voluntarily placed the unpaid wages in trust, and the Canadian government was asked to try to find the workers in China, or their families, so that they could be paid what they were owed.

Four years after the accident, the court case still had not been heard because of Sinopec's intransigence. Newspapers lost interest in it and so, obviously, did politicians. In 2010, Sinopec International Petroleum Exploration and Production, a sister company, was granted permission by Alberta and Canada to buy, for $4.65 billion, a 9 percent stake in Syncrude, the country's premier and biggest oil sands project. Even more unusual was that governments approved a condition of the deal that gave Sinopec the option to be paid in crude oil. Around this time, Sinopec also became a partner in a proposed $5.5 billion oil pipeline to take oil sands crude to British Columbia for export to Asia. By 2011, various Chinese entities had become partners in several of Alberta's biggest oil sands projects, and there were plans to offer direct flights to Beijing and Shanghai from Calgary.

In 2012, Sinopec took its jurisdictional argument to the Supreme Court of Canada, but the court would not even hear its appeal. Weeks later, likely under pressure from its sister company CNOOC—which was awaiting permission to take control of Nexen—Sinopec's subsidiary, which had not yet contested service, pleaded guilty to three charges of workplace negligence that caused the deaths of two workers and serious injuries to two more. On January 24, 2013, the company received a record fine of $1.5 million.[44]

Horror stories about bad business citizenship abounded, but politicians were mostly indifferent. For instance, Terry Hendrickson, CEO of Hendrickson Construction, and other Manitoba suppliers said they were unable to collect payment for contracts from Chinese-managed CaNickel Mining Limited, whose largest shareholder was King Place Enterprises of China. Hendrickson said the Chinese management accused the Canadians of tricking them or of not doing the work. They also put in place managers without expertise or the ability to speak English and offered below-market wages. In May 2012, the Manitoba Workplace Safety and Health Division issued a stop-work order at the mine over concerns about blasting. The order was lifted in October 2012 after work that was required to ensure safety was completed.

Another mining company, Canadian Dehua International Mines Group in British Columbia, was alleged by B.C. unions of gaming Canada's immigration system to try to bring in 201 temporary Chinese workers for its coal mine, with plans to bring in two thousand more. The company claimed Canadian workers were not available, but it had advertised jobs at below-market wages, then used the lack of response to prove Canadians were unavailable, according to local unions. It also listed Mandarin as a language requirement for its B.C. coal mine. Canadian Dehua is one of several companies owned by a layer of private holding companies out of China. The ultimate owner or owners are not known because disclosure is not required from private businesses.

"These workers will not complain," a British Columbia union official said. "Would you complain if you are going to be sent out on

the next plane? Are there going to be sufficient safety committees? Are workers going to be able to stand up for their own air quality and underground conditions to make sure they're treated properly? Doubt it."

Media attention on this issue, and a looming election in British Columbia, led to reforms. On April 29, 2013, the Dehua controversy led to a change in the federal government's immigration rules governing temporary foreign workers and met union demands by preventing employers from squeezing Canadians out of jobs. "The government addressed that HD Mining [controlling shareholder of Dehua] controversy with a new rule that English and French will now be the only languages that can be used as a job requirement," said a Reuters story about the changes. "The new rules will prevent employers from paying foreign workers less than Canadians, and will ensure that employers who rely on temporary foreign workers have a 'firm plan' in place to transition to a Canadian labor force." But the 201 workers were allowed in by a B.C. court because the rules had not yet been tightened when they entered the country. This decision was appealed by unions in 2013.

In 2008, Chinese state–owned enterprises Jinduicheng Molybdenum Group and Northwest Nonferrous International Investment Company bought the Yukon Zinc Corporation and took the company private. In 2009, a Canadian worker died when his brakes failed underground, and Yukon Zinc and its Canadian-owned subcontractor, Procon Mining and Tunnelling, pleaded guilty to two of eight charges involving unsafe vehicles under the Occupational Health and Safety Act. They were each fined $100,000. In 2010, a second worker died in a cave-in. Yukon Zinc and Procon were charged in connection with the death, and a large portion of the mine was closed for safety reasons. In February 2011, a massive cave-in

occurred, but workers escaped injury. The mine's owners, Yukon Zinc, pleaded guilty to breaches of the Occupational Health and Safety Act in November 2012 in Yukon Territorial Court and accepted the maximum $150,000 fine. Its contractor, Procon, pleaded guilty for the same worker safety violations and also paid a maximum fine of $150,000. "One fatality in a small hard-rock mine in Canada is, these days, real news. Two separate incidents should be seen as shocking," wrote S. Mark Francis, a business consultant and advisor with the Canadian National Stock Exchange.[45]

China's track record in Canada is checkered, and is the same template the country has used in undeveloped nations in Africa, the Caribbean and elsewhere.

Asian Onslaught

In waking a tiger, use a long stick.
—Mao Tse-Tung

The Canadian incidents are an example of China's economic aggression. This poses an enormous danger to living standards in the targeted countries, as a form of neocolonialism, but also to competitors who are not ruthlessly buying and hoarding commodities. For instance, China's clumsy construction mishap in Canada backfired, but the country and its enterprises did not skip a beat; rather, they remained busy buying assets in Canada and negotiating a significant trade deal. This is part of their "resource and periphery strategy," which sees them outmaneuvering most other nations in grabbing economic development contracts and resources. Unable to make great gains in the United States or the European Union, they are investing and penetrating the so-called peripheral countries like Canada, Turkey and eastern European nations.

But their biggest thrust and greatest successes have been in poor and undeveloped countries.

China's biggest target has been Africa, and the impact of its presence on the continent has been brutal. In Kenya, for instance, the Chinese underbid others and loaned money to build five massive roads. A lucrative sideline to this project is elephant poaching. Half of the elephants murdered in that country illegally by poachers have been killed within twenty miles of either side of these road projects. Even more telling, according to an August 2011 story in *Vanity Fair*, such poaching had been virtually eliminated until the Chinese got these contracts.[46] Poachers have been in the process of harvesting, to within a decade of extinction, elephants and rhinoceroses to satiate the egos and sexual demands of millions of Chinese men. All of Africa's elephants are endangered. Of the estimated 650,000 or so remaining, the International Fund for Animal Welfare estimates 100 elephants are being killed each day, or 36,500 per year. In 1979, Chad was home to 15,000 elephants, and by 2011 there were only 400 left. Sierra Leone's have disappeared. The tusks are smuggled all over Asia. In April 2011, police reported the confiscation in Kenya of a ton of ivory on its way to Asia, and 1,300 pounds in Vietnam from Tanzania.[47]

The murder of elephants and rhinos, whose horns are ground down and used as an aphrodisiac, is only part of the rape of Africa. China's real strategy is its "minerals for infrastructure" deals. These involve convincing weak or corrupt regimes to make asymmetrical deals that mostly benefit China. In a typical arrangement, China extends loans to build infrastructure, which are to be repaid in farmland, resources, market access for its cheap products and construction contracts using Chinese labor. What is in it for the countries involved? Good question.

Through these transactions, by 2010 China had become the

biggest buyer of copper in Zambia, the biggest oil buyer in Angola and Sudan, and the largest buyer of African timber, vanadium, tin, tungsten, chromium and manganese. In Latin America and the Caribbean, Beijing had negotiated bilateral deals to buy most of Chile's copper production, most of Brazil's soybean and iron ore production and the lion's share of Cuba's nickel.

In 2006, China also pulled off the biggest "Madagascar" deal, with the president of oil-rich Angola. Beijing agreed to lend the country $14.5 billion to help rebuild roads, bridges and other infrastructure after its devastating civil war. In this case, China would be paid back the $14.5 billion, plus interest, in crude oil. In return, China promised to create economic activity and provide jobs by helping train Angolans to rebuild their country. But four years later, some fifty Chinese state-owned firms and four hundred Chinese private companies employed 60,000 to 70,000 Chinese expatriates in Angola. Angolans were supposed to get at least 30 percent of the jobs for the country's projects, but that promise has not been kept.

"Chinese companies can't employ 30 percent Angolans. It's impossible, it's not realistic," the Chinese ambassador told MediaCorp's Channel NewsAsia in an interview in 2011. "In our contracts here, we have a very short time-frame and a high requirement for quality. The majority of Angolans can't satisfy that demand."[48]

But like the Sinopec fiasco in Canada, the Chinese have performed shoddy and unsafe work. In July 2010, more than 150 patients had to be evacuated from a new Chinese-built hospital in Angola's capital, Luanda, after its walls began cracking and bricks began disintegrating. China Overseas Engineering Group (COVEC) built the hospital for $8 million. COVEC is a subsidiary of China Railway Group, more than 50 percent of which is controlled by the Chinese government. By 2012, this group had become the 112th largest corporation in the world, according to *Fortune*'s Global 500 list. But COVEC was criticized in African media outlets, who claimed that virtually all of the roads, schools, hospitals and other infrastructure completed by the Chinese were substandard or unsafe. In 2012 in Macau, following the controversial closure of a Chinese-built hospital, another China Railway Group subsidiary, China Tiesiju Civil Engineering Group Co., announced it would build a new hospital on the same site as the one that was condemned for construction problems.

Similar deals have been shopped successfully by Beijing to Caribbean countries. On recent trips, Chinese workers were visible everywhere in Antigua laying sewer pipes and building streetlights, and they were in the Bahamas building Chinese-financed hotels. In 2010, Beijing rolled out its periphery strategy in eastern Europe, the Balkans, Greece and Turkey. "What is happening is that the Chinese are expanding in Europe as they did in Africa," said François Godement, a senior policy fellow of the European Council on Foreign Relations. "But in Europe, they're coming in through countries on the periphery, which is extraordinary."

China bought Greek and Spanish government bonds during the euro crisis and made deals in those countries to buy distressed assets. But Beijing has mostly concentrated on building ports, highways and other facilities that link the European Union with eastern Europe or Turkey. Billions in financing loans have been made available for such strategic public works projects, which also use Chinese companies and workers. "Such moves could give China a bigger presence in the European chain of distribution and production, while allowing it to build a track record of investments that it hopes will also encourage Europe to support its position on divisive currency issues and in trade disputes at the World Trade Organization," speculated a *New York Times* piece in November 2010.[49]

Chinese companies are getting inside North America's tent. They are conducting private meetings with cash-starved local governments to finance and build infrastructure projects such as airports, bridges and roads with American or Canadian partners. They will also start buying local and state government bonds to give them leverage in such discussions, and then, once in, will insist on sourcing equipment, manpower and technology from China or Chinese-controlled American companies. This strategy is the thin edge of the wedge, and it has worked in other cash-starved jurisdictions.

In Canada, the Chinese are being bolder. However, its forays may eventually backfire as they did in the European Union. In 2010, COVEC landed a major highway contract in Poland, bidding half what rivals did. But the Europeans were wise to China's techniques, so Polish officials stipulated in the deal that the Chinese could not use Chinese labor and supplies. The Chinese contractor ignored the conditions and brought in some workers on the basis that the Polish workers were not cooperative. They also sourced some supplies from China, saying that they had no choice because local suppliers refused to discount prices to Chinese levels. It was a classic case of low-balling.[50] On June 13, 2011, Poland sued the contractor for $270 million in damages for breach of contract.

In August 2012, China reacted to the lawsuit and bad publicity by removing COVEC's president from his post and sending its state-owned assets regulator, the Assets Supervision and Administration Commission, to investigate the Polish problem. COVEC had joined forces with two other Chinese-owned companies to win the road contract in Poland.

Beijing uses the Toronto office of the China Investment Corporation, a sovereign wealth fund, to mount many forays into the U.S. and Canada. The office has invested in minority positions in resource and manufacturing companies. Investments are often made quietly through Canadian intermediaries. (In 2012, a Chinese entity's attempt to buy a building was thwarted by government officials because one tenant stored high-level security intelligence on site. In Washington, D.C., security sources say that a Chinese entity tried to lease property too close to key government buildings and was discouraged from doing so.)

Another troubling trait is China's designs on its own neighborhood. Taiwan and a number of tiny islands claimed by Japan, and others claimed by the Philippines or Vietnam, are in Beijing's crosshairs. In September 2012, for instance, Japan agreed to pay $26 million to the Kurihara family for tiny uninhabited islands, called the Senkakus in Japan and Diaoyu in China, and China's adverse reaction was threatening. A flotilla of ships was sent to saber-rattle, and government-staged protests led to violence against Japan's embassy and Japanese businesses, forcing Toyota to temporarily close down some factory operations. When Taiwan also made claims and sent ships, China and Japan began to negotiate, but Chinese overreaction underscored regional ambitions, old grievances and a worrisome willingness to use force.

The Sheikhs Target North America

[Dependency on OPEC] is the greatest transfer of wealth from one group to another in the history of mankind.
—T. Boone Pickens

Asia's resource importers are not the only emerging economies buying assets in the West. So are the resource exporters who are interested in acquiring energy or mining assets in countries other than their own. Middle Eastern interests have watched North America's energy markets—Canada's oil sands in particular—like peregrine falcons eyeing their prey. The strategy of the Saudis, Kuwaitis and Emirates has always been, since the advent of OPEC, to fly well below the radar and employ intermediaries or others to do their bidding and buying.

My first brush with the sheikhs, and how they operate worldwide, took place in Calgary in October 2007. I had been approached by a public relations firm to interview Peter Barker-Homek, CEO of the Abu Dhabi National Energy Company, whose Canadian subsidiary is TAQA North (*taqa* is Arabic for energy).[51] Abu Dhabi, with one and a half million very wealthy citizens, is one of the seven emirates that comprise the United Arab Emirates. The company, listed on the Abu Dhabi exchange, had just paid $2.5 billion for two small U.S. oil companies and then, in short order, another $7.5 billion to buy a Canadian oil company and various other petroleum assets.

In 2007, Barker-Homek explained to me TAQA's global strategy, business model and ownership. His intention in Canada, through TAQA North, was to invest another $12.5 billion by 2012 in natural gas or power-generation assets. It was not, he emphasized, to invest "in the oil sands." Another $20 billion would be invested in Europe, in gas storage and liquefied natural gas infrastructure—Abu Dhabi has the world's fifth-largest gas reserves. Another $20 billion would be invested in the Middle East. He said Abu Dhabis owned 75 percent of the Abu Dhabi National Energy Company, and Saudis owned the rest. Canada was a natural target of the Arabs for very specific reasons.

"We chose Canada because it has the rule of law, lots of gas reserves and is easy to get into," he said. "It also does not have the Patriot Act." Falling under the purview of that U.S. law is undesirable because of its worldwide investor disclosure requirements.

TAQA was doing some prudent jurisdiction shopping, and Barker-Homek was a sophisticated global player. But he also had an unusual background. He showed up for the interview meticulously groomed and expensively tailored. Barker-Homek is from New York and has an MBA. He was at one time a U.S. Marine Corps pilot and worked around the world "arming factions," as he put it. He completed a stint at the U.S. Department of State as an economics and political analyst. Eventually, he moved on to Merrill Lynch and British Petroleum.

His interest in granting the interview, in tandem with lobbying in Ottawa, was to fully explain his business model so that the Canadian public—and more importantly the Canadian federal government—would allow TAQA's two takeovers to proceed. Both transactions needed approval from Investment Canada, a federal government agency that reviews and must approve large foreign purchases, according to Canadian law. If a deal was deemed to be in Canada's "national interest," it would be approved. If not, it could be vetoed. I was perceived as a columnist friendly to the Conservative government.

At the time of the interview, the deal was under review. In point of fact, the agency had rubber-stamped virtually every deal that had come before it. Canada had an open-door policy toward all foreign investment because of its huge capital needs. Since commodity prices had begun rising, a succession of important resource corporations had been picked off by British, Brazilian and other foreign-based corporations. The first deal to be rejected by Investment Canada—after Richard Haskayne of Calgary and others, including me, joined the premier of Saskatchewan, Brad Wall, in fighting against it—was the proposed buyout of Potash Corporation in 2010. Investment Canada, under a great deal of public pressure, rejected that proposed buyout as not being in the national interest.

But TAQA got inside the Canadian tent, and Investment Canada approved its two purchases in January 2008. My criticism of that deal focused on the lack of reciprocity: the two Canadian companies, and another $12.5 billion worth, would disappear into the hands of the Abu Dhabi government and its stock market, which forbade Canadians, Americans or any foreigners from investing in its country's resources or in companies listed on its market.

"Abu Dhabi should not be allowed to operate in Canada because it does not offer any reciprocity to Canada or other nations to operate or invest there," I wrote in the *Financial Post* at the time. "It cruises around the world, through state-owned corporations, looking for assets on the cheap with its petro-dollars and denies anyone else the right to drill for oil or to buy companies in their economies."

Intriguingly, TAQA North's planned shopping spree in Canada never materialized beyond the two companies taken over. But something else happened. TAQA enlisted the support of the Canadian federal government in 2008 to land a contract to build a thermal plant in Ghana, presumably using Canadian equipment and know-how. A Canadian government agency signed the deal, on behalf of the Abu Dhabi Company, with the Government of Ghana. Then scandal hit.

Barker-Homek claimed he had been fired by the company in 2009 after he brought attention to alleged "fraudulent and unethical practices" at TAQA. He sued TAQA in Michigan, but the merits of B-H's allegations were never decided.[52]

Arab countries have also demonstrated a willingness to play hardball if Canada does not give them what they want. For instance, the United Arab Emirates' airline applied for landing rights in Toronto and was turned down in 2010. In retaliation, the UAE reneged on a deal to let the Canadian military use its Dubai air base, which had been used to deploy Canada's troops and *matériel* as part of their NATO contribution in Afghanistan. Canada's minister of defense, Peter MacKay, had been due to land in Dubai in October 2010 for refueling on his way back from Afghanistan, but Dubai controllers suddenly denied his plane the right to land.[54] The jet had to make a six-hour detour to land in Rome instead.

Arab nations are not the only ones that have taken advantage of Canada's liberal foreign ownership laws and entitlements without offering reciprocal investment privileges in return. This one-way investment relationship is economic colonization because it allows aggressive emerging economies to buy North American corporations and resources while protecting their own assets from North American ownership.

Non-reciprocal, large-scale foreign ownership hollows out the economy, removes head offices and quality jobs and results in foreigners wielding political influence and power through lobbying, campaign contributions and relationships with leaders. Divided, the U.S. and Canada can be played off against one another, but united they could defend against economic and political incursions at home and abroad. A merger would make them self-sufficient in most resources, a net exporter and a more formidable competitor around the world.

THE RUSSIANS ARE COMING

Russia's greatness lies in its culture.
—VLADIMIR PUTIN

Business leaders in Moscow can be masters at dirty tricks, and they've been lurking around the U.S. since the end of the Cold War, which left many of its spies and KGB operatives, including Vladimir Putin, unemployed. Many commercialized their skill sets and found better lines of work in various forms of industrial espionage or other criminal activities. For instance, in 2010, U.S. officials arrested and deported members of a large Russian spy ring in Washington and New York. But there has also been some skullduggery in Canada by Russians. In 1998, a company listed on the Toronto Stock Exchange, YBM Magnex International, whose board boasted blue-ribbon American and Canadian directors, turned out to be a billion-dollar fraud and a suspected money-laundering operation run by a shadowy Russian organized crime group.[55]

Many Americans and Canadians of eastern European origin flooded back to Russia, Ukraine and other former Soviet republics after the 1989 collapse of the Soviet Union. Most ended up having their financial heads handed back to them on a platter. For instance, in a high-profile incident in August 2004, Russians seized the Aerostar Hotel, a Moscow landmark, which was 50 percent owned by IMP Group of Halifax, a conglomerate controlled by Nova Scotia tycoon Kenneth Rowe. The hotel's management and 150 guests were evicted by a phalanx of private "security" guards working for one of IMP's partners, Aviacity, which owned property rights to the building. The hotel's general manager, Andrew Ivanyi, told the *Los Angeles Times* "about 30 goons" accompanied Aviacity's legal team. "Their lawyer said, 'I would advise you to leave quietly. It would be better for you.' The words he used were, 'Or we'll carry you out.' We picked up the papers on our desks and left."[56]

Canadian ambassador Christopher Westdal took up the cause at the Kremlin, suggesting the Aerostar events could cloud the investment climate in Russia.[57] But the hotel was sold by the "new" owners in 2007.

In 2006, the Canadian Security Intelligence Service (CSIS) used its website to alert Canadians to the dangers of Russian gangs who had infiltrated the country's diamond mining industry in the Northwest Territories. "Since the 1998 opening of Canada's first diamond mine, Canada has become the third-largest producer of diamonds in the world after Botswana and Russia. CSIS has determined that individuals associated with eastern European organized crime have demonstrated their interest in the Canadian diamond industry. This poses a potential threat to the level of government revenue accrued from the industry, the stability of the NWT [and beyond as exploration and production expand] and consequently, to Canada's national security."

Russian investors, using Swiss fronts, have taken major positions in mining companies and their suppliers. Perhaps coincidentally, in 2008 Quebec police warned the operators of mines in the province to tighten up security measures at their operations and offered to help. Russia's interest in controlling parts of Canada's resource businesses is somewhat counterintuitive, because Russia is more blessed with resources than Canada. But Moscow sees its future as a resource giant, benefiting in a world of looming resource and food scarcity, and has been busy capturing pieces from the chessboard or being tough with customers.

Another victim of Russian ruthlessness was a Canadian uranium company called Khan Resources, which had a joint venture in Mongolia with a Russian government-owned entity called Atomredmetzoloto (ARMZ). In 2009, ARMZ made an unsuccessful hostile takeover bid for Khan. Then, due to disagreement and damages involving a joint venture, Khan sued ARMZ for $300 million.

The Russians, in their legal defense in a Canadian court, used a section of the Hague Convention, a treaty, to stymie the lawsuit. Khan's lawyers asked the Russian Ministry of Justice to serve the litigation papers, but it refused, citing Article 13 of the Hague Convention, which allows a government to refuse documents "if it deems that would infringe its sovereignty or security." In March, a Canadian judge agreed that if the Russians were not served papers, the case would be on hold. No service of documents, no case. Khan appealed that decision but faced years of expense and delay, which occurred after Sinopec's refusal to be served Canadian court papers in China.

Khan's CEO, Grant Edey, put his company's predicament in context for me in a series of emails. On October 26, 2012, I wrote in the *Financial Post*: "Khan believes it unfair that ARMZ can come into Ontario and avail themselves of our capital markets through actions such as initiating a takeover bid in 2009 for Khan and acquiring a controlling 51 percent interest in Uranium One, but now hide behind the Russian government and thereby avoid having to defend their conduct before an Ontario court."

An article by Toronto lawyer Ken MacDonald in the Canadian journal *Advocates' Quarterly* corroborated this serious precedent. "A Russian lawyer with Baker and Mackenzie gave evidence that success would be unlikely because the Russian government owns 80 percent of the defendant companies and would likely interfere in the proceeding. The Ontario Superior Court of Justice has effectively stymied a Canadian company's attempts to sue two Russian government-owned companies in Ontario. Canadians with claims against defendants in countries whose courts are subjected to political interference and/or corruption can thereby be denied access to justice."

The Russians and others used the Hague Convention to frustrate justice in the U.S. and U.K., but their courts ignored the gambit and the cases continued. As Khan's Edey wrote to me: "If the [Russian] company is successful in avoiding service, it reinforces the position that state-owned companies can avoid the Canadian justice system even while being able to carry on business here in Canada."

In 2010, Russia quietly overtook Saudi Arabia as the world's biggest oil producer, at 10 million barrels a day, giving it leverage in Europe and Asia. The country is also the world's largest producer of natural gas, and as energy prices jump, Russia's economy will grow. Controlling energy interests is its weapon to keep China, India, Europe and its "near-abroad" neighbors in line.

The country afforded everyone a preview of its business model by using its monopoly position to hold eastern, central and western Europe hostage over the years. Premiums for its natural gas have been extracted by bullying Ukraine, Belarus, Bulgaria, Hungary, Italy and others. These countries have found supplies suddenly disrupted only because Ukraine's government balked at paying transmission prices higher than were agreed to in contracts.

The Kremlin's capo, President Vladimir Putin, is not above meddling in the internal affairs of neighbors and customers. In 2006, Russia interfered in Ukraine's political affairs, and still does, even after the Orange Revolution, when protestors worked to overturn a rigged election won by a Russian-supported candidate by taking to the streets in large numbers. By 2012, Ukraine's Orange Revolution leaders had fought one another so fiercely that the Russian-supported candidate they unseated took power again.

In 2008, Russia frightened all of its customers by invading the republic of Georgia without provocation. Moscow occupied, and has yet to return, the two Georgian provinces of South Ossetia and Abkhazia. Russia's not-so-hidden agenda in Georgia was to dampen enthusiasm among those companies and countries that intended to enlarge or extend the Baku–Tbilisi–Ceyhan (BTC) pipeline. Not coincidentally, the 1,100-mile line opened just before the invasion, pumping a million barrels a day of oil from offshore Azerbaijan to Turkey via Georgia. The $3 billion pipeline was a partnership involving Azerbaijan and corporate partners BP, SOCAR, Chevron, Statoil, TPAO, Elf, Total, Itochu, Inpex, ConocoPhillips and Hess. Moscow's underlying concern has been that the BTC pipeline is capable of being expanded to carry 10 million barrels daily from Central Asian republics to the Middle East and Europe. This would allow the neighbors to bypass Russia's oil pipeline and supply customers directly.

Likewise, Russia has waged a "proxy war" in Syria, where it has supplied diplomatic support, United Nations vetoes and advanced missile or weapons systems to the violent Assad regime. This is simply an extension of the Georgian intervention by Russia, on behalf of Gazprom, in order to control or block the export of natural gas to the European Union. Natural gas could come from gigantic offshore fields in the Levant Basin, shared by Cyprus, Israel, Turkey, Syria and its client state Lebanon.

In a sense, Russia, China and OPEC producers like Saudi Arabia have been behaving like nineteenth-century robber barons, ruthlessly eliminating competition, exploiting customers or workers and using their own government power to unfairly extract commercial or geopolitical advantages. A merger of the U.S. and Canada would rebalance their control over resources and exploding economic clout. Too many American and Canadian business leaders and politicians assume that all countries adhere to the rule of law, to World Trade Organization requirements or to guidelines advanced by organizations such as the World Bank, the International Monetary Fund or the Organisation for Economic Co-operation and Development. But many do not.

Moscow is a notably ruthless economic player, even though it professes to uphold free enterprise and the law and has become a member of the World Trade Organization. American money manager Bill Browder lost hundreds of millions and was kicked out of Russia in 2006 after he objected strenuously to stock market manipulations. (The case is ironic considering that his grandfather had been leader of the Communist Party of America.) Browder felt comfortable in Russia and raised $25 million in 1996 to invest in Russian privatizations. His problem was success. His fund became the largest foreign investor in the country, and his outspokenness cost him everything. He exposed management malfeasance and corporate corruption in corporations partly owned by the Russian government. He explained that this was necessary despite risks and told *The New York Times,* "You had to become a shareholder activist if you didn't want everything stolen from you."[58]

His criticisms and objections provoked severe actions against him by Russia. He was denied entry to Russia in 2006 for being a threat to national security. *The Economist* said Browder was punished for interfering with the flow of money to "corrupt bureaucrats and their businessmen accomplices." Unknown persons beat and robbed his associates and lawyers, then stole documents.[59]

In June 2007 police raided his offices and removed documents and equipment. During the raid, the police beat an employee so severely that he was hospitalized for two weeks, according to *The New York Times.*[60] Browder told a reporter his predicament reminded him of the Soviet saying his Communist grandfather used to repeat: "It's not whether you love the party; it's whether the party loves you."[61]

Another high-profile event occurred on July 23, 2008, when BP's current CEO, Robert Dudley, fled Moscow by private jet in the middle of the night. A terse press release issued later that night from London stated that he would run the company "temporarily" from outside Russia. At the time, Dudley was chief executive of BP's oil

71

venture with Russian shareholders, called TNK-BP, and had fallen victim to an "orchestrated campaign of harassment." The pattern was
well worn. Managers were dogged by interventions from a phalanx
of Russian state agencies and recruited by BP's Russian shareholders,
and BP was parted from its control and assets. Dudley resisted, only
to be denied a visa.[62]

The BP fiasco illustrates how Russia, like other countries, is
undaunted by the size of the victims it punishes. BP is bigger than
most nation-states, and yet Russia pushed it around publicly with
impunity because Putin will stop at nothing in his pursuit of global
supremacy over the United States and Europe. BP's Dudley openly
criticized Russia's tactics. "In light of the uncertainties surrounding
the status of my work visa and the sustained harassment of the company and myself, I have decided to leave and work outside Russia,"
he said in the media, adding that his personal working conditions
were "intolerable."[63] Despite mistreatment, Dudley, who became BP's
CEO in 2010, re-entered Russia to explore an offshore venture with
Rosneft, another Russian oil giant. But again, BP's other Russian partners intervened and the scheme dissolved with more money lost.

Russia should be a no-go zone for businesses, Canadian lawyer Robert Amsterdam told me. He was part of the legal team that
attempted to defend jailed Russian oligarch Mikhail Khodorkovsky,
who infamously sat in court in a cage. Once the richest man in
Russia, Khodorkovsky was arrested in 2003 for tax fraud. Six days
later, Putin's government froze ownership of the shares of his company, Yukos, because of alleged tax violations, and then undertook
actions against the company that caused its stock price to collapse.
In 2004, Yukos' assets were sold off to various Kremlin oligarchs.
Khodorkovsky was eventually sentenced to nine years in a Siberian
prison for many crimes he did not commit, according to Amsterdam.

Yukos was not Putin's only target. "One large coal company was verbally attacked by Vladimir Putin, when he was prime minister, which shaved about $6 billion off its stock market value," said Amsterdam. "Putin's attack drove the stock down, then another set of comments drove it down further, which is very important for foreign investors to understand. There is a confiscatory attitude, called corporate raiding—a willingness for the state to literally raid companies. Not only the state, but people who have connections to the state."

Interestingly, Putin's power began to be tested after he announced changes to the constitution in 2011, then said his sidekick, Dmitri Medvedev, would swap jobs with him so Putin could be president for another twelve years. In late 2011, Putin was booed in public, and fifty thousand protesters mobbed the streets in December, demanding the overturn of an election marred by voter fraud. Putin ignored their demand, but was put on notice that a newly confident Russian opposition would oppose him vigorously. As if to underscore the wobbliness of Putin's regime, a Russian billionaire immediately announced he would oppose the president in an upcoming election.

In 2012, Russians began to make high-profile entries into Canada. Russian oligarch Oleg Deripaska and his company, Rusal—the world's largest aluminum company, with 10 percent of global output—announced a joint venture with a Montreal company to develop a mining project. Years before, he had bought 20 percent of the control block of auto parts giant, Magna International (one of Canada's largest corporations), but lost the stock in a margin call in 2008.[64] Then Russia's largest oil firm, Rosneft, formed an alliance with Exxon Mobil to buy 30 percent of Exxon's stake in a large shale oil play in Canada in return for Exxon's partnership in offshore Russian projects in the Arctic and Black Sea.[65] For years, Russia's largest corporation,

Gazprom, has had agents in Canada scouting for energy and mining opportunities, but approaches have usually been rebuffed amid concerns about Russian practices.

THE ARCTIC: MOTHER OF ALL WARS

The Arctic is Russian.

—SCIENTIST ARTUR CHILINGAROV

In 2008, Moscow threw down the gauntlet and made it clear it intends to control the Arctic and its immense resources. The incident, widely reported, embarrassed Canada, exposed its impotence and revealed North America's strategic vulnerability. In February of that year, Russian President Vladimir Putin staged a ceremony at the Kremlin to honor scientist Artur Chilingarov as a "Hero of the Russian Federation." Months before, Chilingarov, also a politician, had led an expedition of two research ships to the North Pole. He piloted a small submersible to the seabed, 14,000 feet below, to collect samples and data, and then, before surfacing, he planted a titanium version of the Russian flag. The mission was completed on August 7, 2007, and a jubilant Chilingarov boasted over the world's wire services: "The Arctic is Russian."

Canada's Arctic coastline is enormous, but its officials knew nothing of the expedition or its purpose because their military presence in the North is negligible. A cabinet minister in Ottawa immediately labeled it a "stunt," yet three days later small projects were announced designed to establish Arctic sovereignty. These included a second, small deepwater port in an abandoned mining town and a research center.

The Americans responded by dispatching a research icebreaker out of Seattle days later, and a spokesman with the U.S. State

Department sneered, "I'm not sure whether they've put a metal flag, a rubber flag or a bed sheet on the ocean floor. It certainly to us doesn't represent any kind of substantive claim and I certainly haven't heard anyone else make the argument that it does."

The Russian incident underscored two geopolitical tenets: the region's ownership will be contested because of its massive resource and shipping potential, and Canada was clearly in no position to protect its interests at sea or on land. Canada's northern defense consists of a militia called the Canadian Rangers—some 4,400 volunteers equipped with Enfield rifles who conduct "sovereignty patrols" on a part-time basis across an expanse of treeless tundra the size of western Europe. In 2011, Canada spent $22.8 billion on defense, which ranked it fourteenth in the world in expenditure but seventy-fourth in manpower. The United States spent thirty-one times as much, or a total of $711 billion.

Canada is vulnerable, which exposes the United States, too, Canada's foremost military historian, Jack Granatstein, told me in an interview in 2010. "The fear is that someone can enter Canada and set up a base to mount attacks on the U.S. We have huge borders and we don't have the capability to know who could do this or to do anything about it. For example, a few years ago there was a Chinese ship in the Arctic, and Canadian officials didn't find it, much less track it. The ship was discovered only because it stopped in for food and supplies and someone asked what they were doing there. What if it had been carrying five hundred dope smugglers or five hundred terrorists? They could just drop them off in the Arctic and get into the U.S. by merging with the general population."

Canada's reliance on the United States for defense, without paying for it, will be an issue, if it has not already become one, behind closed doors. In 2010, it sort of burst out. The issue of Canada's military shortfall, and the future ownership of the Arctic, was raised sternly and publicly by U.S. Secretary of State Hillary Clinton at a conference in Montreal sponsored by the Canadian federal government. She was responding to the guest list for the conference and was also angry about recent cuts to the Canadian defense budget. Canada, along with Russia, Norway and Greenland, had been invited to participate at the conference because each borders the Arctic Ocean. But Clinton uncharacteristically scolded her host for not inviting Iceland, Finland, Sweden and aboriginal representatives to the conference. She then chided Canada for its intention to pull out of Afghanistan in 2011. Her blunt, and unusual, pronouncements abruptly ended the conference and cast a cloud over what Canadian officials hoped would lead to solidarity over the future of the Arctic. But she straightened them out.

"Significant international discussions on Arctic issues should include those who have legitimate interests in the region," said Clinton, "and I hope the Arctic will always showcase our ability to work together, not create new divisions. We need all hands on deck because there is a huge amount to do, and not much time to do it. What happens in the Arctic will have broad consequences for the earth and its climate. The melting of sea ice, glaciers and permafrost will affect people and ecosystems around the world and understanding how these changes fit together is a task that demands international co-operation."

Her anger shocked Canada's leadership and sent two clear signals: the United States expects a more significant military presence from its neighbor to the north, and the United States, not Canada, will set the agenda concerning the Arctic's land claims and future. This was a dramatic signal that Canada would have to pull its weight in terms of defense spending or face conflict with the United States that would adversely affect the relationship, both politically and economically.

(After the incident, in 2010, Canada announced a $16 billion deal with Lockheed Martin to buy dozens of F35 jets, without going through a competitive international tender-bid process. The Auditor General of Canada condemned the contract, and estimated the true cost at $25 billion, but the government denied this and won re-election in 2011. Then, in December 2012, after estimates by consultants that costs would actually be $40 billion, the Canadian government postponed final approval. This underscored Canada's proclivity to equivocate about defense spending and unwillingness to do much heavy lifting.)

The significance of defense, in the Arctic context, is that energy will be produced there as it is in Norway. By 2035, world oil demand is forecast to increase from 87 million barrels a day in 2010 to 99 million (and the number of cars is forecast to double to 1.7 billion), according to the International Energy Agency, a Paris-based offshoot of the OECD that monitors energy production, alternatives and policies worldwide for its members. Oil will still be needed, it concluded, because the only valid replacement, nuclear fusion, is decades away. Alternatives such as solar and wind will be helpful, but are not economically viable except at the fringes. They certainly cannot make up for declining oil production or increasing demand. The reality is that the only known deposits of oil big enough to meet additional future needs are in Canada's oil sands, Russia and the Arctic, which contains an estimated 13 percent of all undiscovered oil and one-third of all natural gas, according to the U.S. Geological Survey.

The Middle East will remain an important source, but production may decline due to instability or the diversion of energy toward building their domestic economies. Whatever scenarios are assumed about the future growth of Canada or Russia, the fate of the Arctic is sure to become a tug of war between those two countries, other nations and environmentalists, who want a ban on any development there whatsoever.

The legal ownership of the Arctic presents another challenge. Under international law, no country owns the North Pole or the Arctic Ocean region. But the five countries that border the ocean—Canada, Russia, the United States, Norway and Denmark (via Greenland)— "own" an exclusive economic zone that extends 230 miles from their coastlines. Those countries, under the United Nations Convention on the Law of the Sea, have ten years from the time they ratify the law to make claims beyond this economic zone. If they can prove their claims, their exclusive rights to resources would extend the boundaries of their underwater land claim.

Four of the five countries have ratified the convention; only the United States has not. All four have launched scientific projects to prove claims beyond their exclusive economic zones. Not surprisingly, the most aggressive country is Russia, claiming that its Siberian continental shelf extends beneath most of the Arctic Ocean all the way to the geographic North Pole itself. In 2002, the UN looked at Russia's claim and asked for additional research to back it up—in particular, scientific evidence of the extension of the continental shelf beneath most of the Arctic Ocean.

There is also the issue of Greenland, which, according to a 2007 cable from the U.S. State Department exposed by WikiLeaks, is "just one big oil strike away from economic and political independence." The leaked document reveals the concern about Chinese, Russian and European efforts to control the Arctic's resources and shipping lanes as well as Greenland. The cable continues: "American commercial investments, our continuing strategic military presence, and new high-level scientific and political interest in Greenland argue for establishing a small and seasonal American Presence Post in Greenland's capital as soon as practicable . . . Chevron and Exxon Mobil are part of an international consortium exploring off Greenland's western coast, and the U.S. Geological Survey is completing an assessment of Greenland's potential oil and gas reserves. Its initial findings suggest Greenland might have reserves to rival Alaska's North Slope."[66]

LATIN AMERICAN TROUBLEMAKERS

I hereby accuse the North American empire of being
the biggest menace to our planet.
—HUGO CHÁVEZ

American and Canadian investments have been routinely disappearing into other black holes, including Venezuela, Ecuador and Bolivia, sometimes in cahoots with Russia and China. The spiritual leader of this group was Venezuela's unhinged president, the late Hugo Chávez, who made no pretense as to what he was up to with his latter-day communist revolution.

On October 14, 2009, in Caracas, Chávez staged a press conference to announce a government action. He explained that he didn't like the attitude of the management at the Hilton hotel located on Margarita Island, off Venezuela's coast. He had recently stayed there to attend a government conference.

"To hold the conference we had to ask for permission," he told Agence France-Presse, "and the owners tried to impose conditions on the revolutionary government. No way. So I said, 'Let's expropriate it' . . . and, now it's been expropriated."[67]

Venezuela already owned a majority of the hotel's shares, but likely wouldn't pay for the rest. In fact, Chávez also renounced the hotel's debts owed to banks and suppliers. This was the second Hilton to be confiscated by the president, and was simply another asset added to a long list of stolen items. Even so, the American assistant secretary of commerce, Walter Bastian, was quoted as gamely clinging to the free-enterprise, rule-of-law model: "We have no problem with expropriation as long as those affected are paid."

Venezuela had no intention of paying, because it has no rule of law. Its judiciary has been politicized or frightened. So, between 2006 and 2009, Chávez expropriated $23.3 billion in corporate assets and hundreds of thousands of acres of land, according to Ecoanalítica, a Caracas economic consulting firm. Of this amount seized, $14.65 billion remained unpaid for.[68]

Venezuela's confiscations are sometimes orchestrated with co-conspirators like the Russians and Chinese. They are not restricted to shaking down the Big Gringo, the United States, but have also included companies owned by Europeans and Canadians. Two Canadian mining companies became high-profile victims: Crystallex International and Gold Reserve. Listed on the Toronto Stock Exchange, they each spent millions exploring in Venezuela and found world-class ore bodies. Then, suddenly, in 2009, Crystallex was denied an environmental permit. An attempt at international arbitration went nowhere. Gold Reserve also suddenly had permit difficulties. Its shares fell in value, allowing Rusoro Mining of Moscow to make a low hostile takeover bid.

It was a Venezuelan–Russian partnership, according to a blog post sent to investors by a Chinese official who attended a meeting where the matter was discussed: "Venezuela said it will offer a joint venture to Russian-owned miner Rusoro to operate the Las Cristinas [developed by Crystallex] and Brisas [developed by Gold Reserve] gold projects, currently under contract to two Canadian companies, Mining Minister Rodolfo Sanz said on Thursday. He told a Russian delegation that a memorandum of understanding would soon be signed with Rusoro. It appeared that Sanz intends to replace the Canadian companies who operate the projects that contain some of Latin America's largest gold deposits, with Rusoro." Sanz confirmed that leak to Reuters in 2008.

Chávez trampled human rights as well as property rights. In the summer of 2010, forty-three brokerage firms were seized and twelve brokers jailed. He jailed business leaders and judges who opposed him. And if his successors' planets align, he will posthumously damage the region by leading dozens of countries in South America, Central America and the Caribbean into a protectionist regional trading bloc with its own currency, the *"sucre."* He had some allies, but not enough. Bolivia, Peru and Ecuador have embarked on his agenda: politicizing central banks or seizing them; nationalizing key industries; confiscating property without compensation; eliminating or severely trimming press and political freedoms; booting out foreigners; defaulting on foreign loans; and supplementing revenues by signing long-term oil and commodity deals with China.

In 2012, Argentina shocked the world by expropriating the 51 percent controlling share block, owned by Spanish oil giant Repsol, of Argentinian oil company YPF. The value was estimated at about $5 billion, but the Spanish are demanding $10 billion. The oil company had been owned by Argentina until 1993, when it was privatized and, in essence, it has been renationalized. The Argentinian president, Cristina Kirchner, said her country will pay Repsol for the shares but will decide the amount. International outrage and condemnation were unanimous, but the government was adamant about its seizure. Speculation was that the compensation would be reduced or eliminated by massive fines for environmental and other infractions concocted by the government. (Interestingly, China, which wanted to buy Repsol, bought two large energy companies in 2012 and is Argentina's largest trading partner, mostly of foodstuffs.)

Various Latin American regimes have also perpetrated some "kangaroo court" schemes to manipulate American courts. Lawsuits making outrageous claims are filed against American companies, evidence and witnesses are uncorroborated, and local judges award huge damages. American lawyers then attempt to get these cases heard in American courts to enforce the judgments or arrive at out-of-court settlements.

In 2007, Dole Food was ordered to pay $1.58 million in damages to a group of Nicaraguan plantation workers who claimed the company's use of a pesticide had rendered them sterile. Two years later, Judge Victoria Chaney of the Los Angeles County Superior Court dismissed two similar suits against Dole, saying, "What has occurred here is not just a fraud on the court, but it is a blatant extortion of the defendants." Judge Chaney cited evidence that Nicaraguans had been "recruited and coached by lawyers, outfitted with false work histories and falsified medical lab reports, and promised payouts to pose as pesticide victims."

More than forty related cases, involving plaintiffs from Nicaragua, Honduras, Costa Rica, Guatemala, Panama and the Ivory Coast, were pending in her court, while a federal judge in Miami was being asked to enforce a $98.5 million judgment handed down in Nicaragua. *The Wall Street Journal* referred to such cases as a "torts-for-import game," and they follow a similar pattern: "U.S. tort lawyers travel abroad, join with local lawyers to manufacture claims, and then engage in client recruitment practices that are blatantly illegal in the U.S. In essence, the tort bar's goal is to import lawsuits from foreign countries where it's nearly impossible to challenge claims on factual grounds because evidence is hard to come by."[69]

When Chevron acquired Texaco in 2001, it inherited a massive lawsuit accusing the oil company of causing $27 billion worth of damage to the environment and the health of locals when it operated in northeastern Ecuador between 1964 and 1990. The allegations made no mention of Texaco's longtime partner, the state-owned oil company Petroecuador. In 2011, the company was ordered to pay more than $17 billion in damages, plus $860 million in compensatory damages to one of the plaintiffs, the Amazon Defense Front. Both sides announced their intention to appeal the ruling: the plaintiffs because they felt the judgment should have been much larger, and Chevron because it alleged the ruling was "the product of fraud" and accused the plaintiffs' lawyers of a plan to "coordinate with corrupt judges."[70]

In 2012, Ecuador pursued a strategy to bypass U.S. courts, and attack through the Canadian back door, by filing a lawsuit against Chevron in Canada. A group of forty-seven Ecuadoreans have asked the Ontario court to seize Chevron assets in Canada, ranging from an oil sands project to offshore wells, to satisfy the 2011 ruling in the Latin American nation. The attempt was an irritating precedent that enmeshes Canada, by virtue of the fact it hosts hundreds of foreign-owned branch plants and subsidiaries with assets, in any and all serious disputes abroad. In May 2013, an Ontario Superior Court justice ruled that the Canadian courts have no jurisdiction to enforce the controversial award handed down by an Ecuadorian court against Chevron, because the judgment was levied against the parent, not the Canadian subsidiary. The matter is being appealed on the basis that the subsidiary's and parent's assets are one and the same. If fully pursued through the courts and successful, Canada may be considered off limits to some multinationals.[71]

But in 2007, Ecuador invented another form of state-sanctioned shakedown. President Rafael Correa announced his Yasuni–ITT Initiative before the UN General Assembly—a proposal by his government to refrain from exploiting oil reserves in its Yasuni National Park rain forest if the international community gave his country half the value of the oil reserves, or $3.6 billion. The scheme has not gotten any traction, but could mark the beginning of future attempts by developing nations to hold the environment for ransom.

By far the most insidious tactic deployed by some Latin American leaders, led by Chávez until his death, is to aid, or turn a blind eye toward, their region's most lucrative export: cocaine. The Andes region of South America, in Colombia, Peru and Bolivia, is the world's only source of coca leaves, which are refined into cocaine. The major distributors, or traffickers, are Mexican and Colombian, and the wholesale value of these exports to the U.S. is estimated at as much as $39 billion a year, or roughly the size of Luxembourg's economy, according to the Drug Enforcement Agency's 2010 report to Congress.[72]

In 1999, Chávez expelled American drug agents shortly after taking over the country. In 2007, Ecuador closed down an airport listening post run by the Americans. In 2008, Bolivia asked American drug officials to leave the country. And in 2011, Peru's new government suspended anti-coca operations. The United Nations issued a report in 2010 stating that 40 percent of cocaine shipments to Europe, and 51 percent of all cocaine shipments worldwide, were going through Venezuela. In 2009, the U.S. Government Accountability Office accused Chávez and his government of direct involvement in the trade.

State Capitalism Outperforms Free Enterprise

Instead of trying to prevent—or worse, dismiss altogether—the rise of state-capitalist systems, U.S. and European companies and governments would do better to learn from them.

—BLOOMBERG BUSINESSWEEK

Clearly, state capitalism has served China and many other countries, including Canada and European nations, well. This is because it is more effective than traditional capitalism for lots of reasons. The story of Zhu Gongshan, a solar-energy magnate in China who had gone from rags to riches, exemplifies the superiority of entrepreneurship leveraged with state support. In 2007, foreign suppliers of polycrystalline silicon were holding to ransom Zhu, and other manufacturers. Shortages had sent prices soaring worldwide, and the Chinese buyers had been unable to get any supplies and were being gouged, according to a story in *The Wall Street Journal* in November 2010.

The material is made in refineries and consists of many small silicon crystals. It is a key component needed by manufacturers such as Intel for integrated circuits and central processing units. It's also used in the manufacture of solar panels. Zhu and the others were being run out of business. Beijing was alerted and decided to become involved in their plight and in trying to find a solution. Financing and expertise were put in place quickly because the government declared domestic development of this type of silicon to be a national priority. China needed solar power domestically, and wanted to cash in on interest in the green movement by exporting solar panels around the world.

The government encouraged state-owned companies and banks to get into the game. They financed new plants, and the federal and local governments expedited approvals. Within months, facilities were up and running. In the United States, by comparison, these large chemical plants would have taken years to build because of zoning, political and financing obstructions.

"In just a few years, he [Zhu] created one of the world's biggest poly silicon makers, GCL-Poly Energy Holding Ltd. China's sovereign wealth fund bought 20 percent of GCL-Poly for $710 million," wrote the *Journal.* "Today, China makes about a quarter of the world's poly silicon and controls roughly half the global market for finished solar-power equipment." The piece concluded with the obvious: "China's national economic strategy is detailed and multifaceted and it is challenging the U.S. and other powers."[73]

Stories like this illustrate the competitive advantages of government and business collaboration. These are the norm in China and other emerging economies, especially in Asia. Government is not considered to be the enemy, as is often the attitude in the U.S., but is regarded as an ally. This is also, in part, because these governments employ bright people and technocrats who are as capable of identifying and developing niches and opportunities as are entrepreneurs in the West.

In Singapore, for instance, civil servants are held in high esteem and are among the world's highest paid. They are routinely recruited by headhunters from the private sector, and are paid as much as their private-sector counterparts, upward of $1 million a year plus bonuses. This practice results in smart public-private partnerships and, in a sense, more efficient allocation of resources in terms of people and capital. This turns traditional American capitalist thinking on its head. The Asians have shown that competition is a wasteful system that often results in duplication and oversupply. They have also demonstrated that fire must be fought with fire: monopolistic or market oppression by foreigners entitles them to deploy government interference or involvement, particularly in a strategically important sector.

Another justification for government involvement is that these countries sometimes have no track record with the world's commercial banks or investors. They have not enjoyed the luxury of being able to build relationships over decades, as have the Americans, Canadians and Europeans. So their governments compensate for that by creating sovereign-owned enterprises that may or may not eventually be replaced as their businesses become freestanding and are listed on world stock markets.

Canada's governments did the same. In the past, they created many sovereign-owned enterprises, such as Air Canada, Petro-Canada, Canadian National Railways and other Crown corporations. They were launched with government funds to compete against gigantic American or European companies. Eventually, most were privatized once their training wheels could be removed. But as long as they were sovereign-owned, they enjoyed enormous advantages over foreigners and even domestic private-sector firms. This was unfair, but was exactly why they were created in the first place, to level the overall playing field.

So Asia's army of state-owned enterprises and government investment agencies is not a new mousetrap. And American and Canadian enterprises must reflect on how they can collaborate with their governments when necessary to match foreign corporate power involving state-owned enterprises or partnerships. During the 2008 and 2009 financial crisis, the U.S. and Canadian governments indulged in some serious state capitalism by jointly investing in Chrysler and General Motors to stave off their bankruptcies. But the American government was upset that it had to do so and sold its shares in GM as soon as it could. Canada, on the other hand, took a different view and held on to some of its shares—if only to ensure that the two companies did not shut down their existing plants in Canada.

Such state-owned, or hybrid, enterprises may end up being the new normal. And they are winning the race for riches. In 2000, seven of the world's ten biggest oil companies were American or European multinationals. By 2010, the world's largest oil corporation was Saudi Arabia's Aramco, and twenty-eight of the fifty biggest oil companies were government-owned, according to industry bible *Petroleum Intelligence Weekly.* This was because four countries—Iran, Iraq, Venezuela and Saudi Arabia—contained 50 percent of the world's conventional oil and gas reserves, and their national oil companies owned 85 percent of these reserves.[74]

"Not only do they [countries and their companies] shut privately owned competitors like Exxon out of their own oil patches, but they compete aggressively, often with few market constraints, for access to other countries' oil resources. The big oil companies are rapidly running out of real estate to operate in," wrote economist Jeff Rubin in his 2009 book *Why Your World Is About to Get a Whole Lot Smaller.*[75]

The same story applies to the mining sector. Nearly one-third of global mining is held in the hands of corporations owned or controlled by governments. These include Brazil's Vale SA (the government holds protective golden shares that can veto any takeover by foreigners), as well as large entities in Russia, Morocco, India, Chile and Botswana. Two of the world's ten largest diversified mining companies in 2008 were government-controlled.[76]

Canada has lost four of its most successful iconic private-sector mining companies, Inco, Noranda, Falconbridge and Alcan, to foreign interests. Even so, Canada is still home to more of the world's "top 100" mining companies than any other nation, with nineteen—China has seventeen; Australia and the United States eleven each; and South Africa nine, according to a study in 2010. But American and Canadian mining outfits are finding that their opportunities and profits are evaporating as governments and sovereign-owned enterprises scoop up ore bodies and promising exploration acreage or co-opt prime ministers and potentates to become their allies.

These companies also play rough and dirty. They not only have more access to capital, exploration opportunities and oil fields, they are aided and abetted because their governments are partners, or owners. This enables them to benefit from side deals or sweeter terms as a result of diplomatic pressure, foreign aid, market access, cheap loans, weapons or bribes. They are also protected from take-overs themselves and establish global beachheads in friendly countries to make further acquisitions elsewhere, as TAQA's seduction of Canada's federal government illustrated.

Emerging economies also break the rules whenever possible. In early 2011, European and American technology manufacturers went to the World Trade Organization after China slashed exports and raised taxes on its "rare earths," seventeen elements critical to making such high-tech products as iPods, wind turbines and missiles. China produces more than 90 percent of these minerals. In July of that year, the World Trade Organization ruled that China's actions transgressed commitments it made when it joined the organization. But China denied this vigorously and said it would appeal. Its strategy from now on—just a guess—is that it will drag its feet and continue to hoard strategic materials for years to come.

The case revealed another danger the West faces: the hoarding of raw materials to benefit local manufacturers. As European Trade Commissioner Karel De Gucht said, China was obliged to ensure "free and fair access to rare earth supplies," as well as other elements such as bauxite, coking coal, fluorspar, magnesium, manganese, silicon metal, silicon carbide, yellow phosphorus and zinc. All are key inputs used in producing steel, aluminum and chemicals. Hoarding promises to be a new technique to damage rivals.

Such cheating obstructs free markets and free trade. Worse yet, enforcement and compliance are difficult when so many sovereign players indulge in these misdeeds. There are no global police in the international economic space, nor are there many early-warning systems. Even those entrusted with policing economic activities, such as the World Trade Organization, have no means of punishing or stopping members such as China or others, even when they abuse, jail or damage investors, corporations or fellow WTO members.

There is also little recourse to another egregious practice, that of influence peddling by members of multilateral organizations. For instance, the permanent members of the United Nations Security Council can veto anything the organization wants to do. And China and Russia have used this to commercial, as well as strategic, advantage.

"China continues to crassly trade the power of its UN veto in exchange for energy, raw materials and access to markets," writes Professor Peter Navarro of the University of California, Irvine, in his 2006 book *The Coming China Wars*.[77] In return for commercial contracts, China has shielded Sudan, Iran and various corrupt African leaders from Angola to Zimbabwe by executing its Security Council veto on their behalf to prevent sanctions or disciplinary actions against them.

Another threat to global capitalism is the existence of sovereign wealth funds that operate outside the law. Their operations and assets are hidden. This allows them to trade clandestinely in jurisdictions that do not require disclosure, the payment of taxes or adherence to trading rules that govern private-sector Western mutual and pension funds. Their size and ability to buy billions of dollars' worth of government securities also give their government owners special access and inordinate political leverage.

"Chinese purchases of Costa Rican government bonds, for example, were closely linked with Costa Rica's decision to switch allegiance from Taipei to Beijing as the legitimate representative of the Chinese people," noted economist Stephen D. King in his book *Losing Control*.[78] And China's intransigence, despite repeated requests by the U.S. to stop manipulating its currency downward, is a bilateral standoff in large measure due to China's gigantic investment in U.S. government bonds.

In 2007, the G7 finance ministers asked the International Monetary Fund and the World Bank to examine the structures, transparency and accountability of the world's gigantic sovereign funds. The request was unmet, but a scorecard by the independent think tank the Peterson Institute for International Economics in Washington confirmed that sovereign wealth funds, or pension pools, in rich countries scored high in terms of ethics and disclosure while Middle Eastern and Asian entities did not.[79]

Essentially, the new cold war is being fought on economic grounds and divides the world into players who are open and those who are secretive. This represents a grave threat to capitalism, whose tenets include transparency and full disclosure. The Sovereign Wealth Fund Institute, a consulting and advisory service that compiles statistics, calculated that the sovereign capital totals for its members in 2012 was $5.019 trillion,[80] with China, Japan and Gulf regimes each investing hundreds of billions annually. That amount is more than three times the size of the Canadian economy. If they pooled or coordinated their efforts, any two or three of these funds, or countries, would be able to destroy the free-market system altogether by secretly manipulating stock and bond markets, commodity prices, currencies and, ultimately, geopolitical decisions.

The U.S. and Canada Must Adapt to Succeed

Countries will increasingly be forced to operate like South Korea or China—as gigantic holding companies armed with a series of "soft economic weapons" such as national champions, state-owned enterprises, subsidies, protectionism and sovereign wealth funds. This will eventually apply to the United States and Canada, who must realize they are playing checkers while their competitors are playing chess, thinking several steps ahead and using board pieces that adhere to variant rules. If they do not, the two will end up being outmaneuvered and recolonized by bigger, smarter, faster nation-states or regional blocs.

Currently, the U.S. and Canada are boy scouts among nations. The Americans, for instance, have picked up the tab for military protection everywhere, including in countries such as Japan and South Korea that have blatant protectionist policies toward U.S. goods and services and can afford to protect themselves. Canada fetes competitors such as China that do not believe in a level playing field.

In January 2011, the Bank of Nova Scotia hosted a cocktail party in its posh offices in downtown Toronto to celebrate the opening of the China Investment Corporation's first office outside China. The gigantic sovereign wealth fund had $200 billion in assets and opened shop in Canada in order to target every Canadian resource or resource-related company in the country. Some attendees of the party were privately furious. They attended because the party was a "command performance" invitation by a major bank for a major competing investment group.

"When CIC opened their new office in Toronto, they emphasized that they expected to be treated like any other investor in the country," said a Canadian pension fund manager who spoke anonymously with me in 2011. "The reaction from a couple of Canadian institutions in the back of the party was that's great for them, but a Canadian has to go through a one- or two-year process to become a Qualified Foreign Institutional Investor in China, just to be able to purchase A-shares of domestic Chinese companies on the stock exchange."

Beijing's stock markets are closed to foreigners, as is resource ownership, except in certain token cases designed to keep Western accusations of protectionism at bay. Foreign investors must qualify and apply for permits to become Qualified Foreign Institutional Investors to buy Chinese stocks. The approval process is complicated and lengthy and, even if approved, these lucky few investors are restricted to so-called A-shares, which may be the least desirable companies available.

Ironically, at the time of the Bank of Nova Scotia party welcoming China's funds to buy Canadian stocks, the blue-ribbon Canada Pension Plan and Ontario Teachers Pension Fund, among the world's most qualified investors, had been waiting months for these same Qualified Foreign Institutional Investor permits, suggesting that Chinese approval had nothing to do with being "qualified," but was political in nature. The China Investment Corporation (CIC) showed it could pick up a telephone, rent office space in Toronto and start snapping up resource companies without extending reciprocal investment privileges.

A few months after that cocktail party, the Chinese gave the Bank of Nova Scotia permission to buy part of a Chinese bank.[81] The Chinese also bought a stake in the Canadian auto parts industry to gain its technology secrets, invested in small Canadian mining companies and by 2012 pulled off the huge $15.1 billion oil buyout, followed by the inordinately beneficial "free trade" deal with Canada. The CIC and its thousands of sister companies in China are directed by Beijing. They share information among themselves but not with the rest of the world, unless required to do so legally. So the extent of the CIC's influence and ownership in Canada remains unknown. Clearly, the Toronto and Hong Kong offices are two of China's back doors into the United States.

Such one-way globalization has been greatly damaging to the United States and Canada. Trade has been lopsided, as have, increasingly, foreign-ownership figures. By 2010, foreigners of all kinds owned 19.7 percent of all Canadian business assets and 28.9 percent of Canadian business revenues. In the U.S., foreign ownership had jumped to 13.9 percent of total corporate assets in 2005, up from 1.3 percent in 1971, according to the latest U.S. tax data analyzed by accounting firm Grant Thornton. Again, like farmland, these figures were badly out of date and incomplete, as China's secret FDI figures illustrate.[82]

Americans and Canadians must examine their place in the sun before it's too late and invest in one another's success more than is already the case. They need to realize the games that are underway. They need to undertake thoughtful planning. Right now, they are wedded to a form of bake-sale capitalism and globalization that few others adhere to. The two countries, and their 347.4 million residents, are no longer the chosen ones; their sixty-year head start has been whittled down by others and will eventually disappear.

Becoming bigger by merging will give the U.S. and Canada the power to face down bullies or push aside rivals, force China and others to stop manipulating their currencies, protect jobs and workers, raise capital, force payment by deadbeat customers, extract cooperation, impose laws and afford the research and innovation that can help people and the planet. Without dramatic change, Canada will remain a massive Madagascar, somewhat sleepy and vulnerable. The United States will continue to go broke buying foreign oil and cheap goods from Asia, then guarding countries that could and should pay for their own protection and, while they are it, "buy American."

CHAPTER TWO

Bilateral Threats: Terrorism, Immigration and Drug Smuggling

Canada? I don't know what street it's on.

—AL CAPONE

T HE UNITED STATES AND CANADA HAVE DONE BUSINESS
together forever. Chicago gangster Al Capone "sourced" much
of his alcohol from Ontario, but denied he even knew that
Canada existed, much less that he was a bootlegger. The American
federal government and police forces knew differently and were furi-
ous about Canada's complicity, but they were powerless: Canada's
provinces forbade consumption of alcohol, but the federal government allowed the production of alcohol and for it to be shipped to
the border. Prohibition was responsible for what has been, apart
from the War of Independence and War of 1812, the only public
border dispute between the two countries that involved violence.
For decades, Canadians have proudly described the boundary as the
world's longest undefended border. That is no longer true.

The 9/11 attack changed everything. Border controls have since
tightened. Since 2006, Americans have begun to militarize the border. Drone aircraft, and several thousand border, drug-enforcement
and customs officers have begun to patrol the divide. Americans
began to expropriate strategically located properties just inside the
U.S. border as listening posts. In 2010, Homeland Security expropriated 4.9 acres of a farm in Vermont owned by Clement Rainville.
He was, like most Americans and Canadians, oblivious to the border

situation. He told *The Globe and Mail:* "We're not at war . . . I have no problem with Canadians and with my neighbours."[1]

Most Americans and Canadians have been unaware of the seriousness of border issues, noticing only the increasingly long lineups and added security at crossing points. In 2011 and 2012, President Barack Obama and Prime Minister Stephen Harper held joint press conferences to announce their intention to negotiate a "perimeter security" deal. Each press conference was long on homilies and smothered in nice statements about neighbors, but short on details or definitive agreements. Talks were to take place behind closed doors among officials from both governments, with two stated (and mutually exclusive) objectives: to create jobs by expediting travel and trade and, simultaneously, to block undesirables and dangerous or illicit goods at the border.

Canada and the U.S. said they would blend and harmonize standards and regulations, a goal announced in 1996 but one that has not been accomplished. The countries would foster "cooperation" and the sharing of information between police, customs, border and national securities officials. They would streamline border crossings for people and goods. While it sounded neighborly, the facts were that the militarization on the U.S. side continued.

The Bridge Fiasco

The Ambassador Bridge, which links Detroit and Windsor, Ontario—and the two countries' auto industries—is in itself a symbol of an increasingly dysfunctional relationship. Detroit is the capital of North America's "Auto Alley," which consists of five thousand auto assembly plants, parts suppliers, small shops, engineering firms and makers of components or accessories from Southern Ontario to the Gulf of Mexico. One in fifteen jobs in the United States and Canada is dependent upon auto manufacturing, which remains North America's economic cornerstone.

Windsor is home to Chrysler Canada and several car plants. Municipalities across southern Ontario are host to Ford Canada, General Motors Canada, Toyota Canada, Honda Canada and hundreds of parts suppliers and manufacturers. The reason the border point is critical is that the industry is integrated on both sides of the border. This means that thousands of components, auto parts or even *parts* of parts cross the border dozens of times as they are gradually incorporated into portions of a vehicle, then eventually the final product. The Ambassador Bridge has become a choke point, harming exporters in both countries after years of failure on the part of dozens of governments, agencies and regulators.

The border stretches 3,987 miles from east to west, and the crossing at Detroit is by far the busiest. A quarter of all merchandise trade and 40 percent of all truck traffic between the two countries travels across this dilapidated bridge. Most days, between 7,500 and 10,000 tractor-trailers haul automobiles, parts, drive shafts, steering wheels and tires in both directions. Despite the importance of the bridge, access is inadequate, causing costly delays, which have become commonplace. In 2010, a fire in a factory a mile from the crossing caused a traffic backup for hours, forcing trucks to drive hours out of their way to another crossing.

The 9/11 attack created chaos. The bridge was closed and placed under heavy guard because of its strategic importance. When it was reopened, enhanced security measures caused fifteen-mile backups and twelve-hour waits. At one point, truck drivers became so angry that they swarmed the one hundred customs and immigration inspectors on the bridge, and the Michigan Army National Guard had to be summoned to protect them.

Delays became routine in the weeks that followed the terrorist attacks as inspections became more time-consuming. Additional booths and customs officers were needed, and the U.S. General Services Administration, in charge of such operations, approved an expansion plan, but nothing happened for weeks as officials bickered with the bridge's owner, a businessman named Manuel Moroun, over lease terms on his land.

Moroun went ahead and built his own tollbooths on the American side. The city of Detroit sued him, arguing he needed building and zoning permits. The case was tied up in the courts for more than three years until a Michigan judge ruled that the bridge was exempt from local law on the U.S. side. Since then, federal, provincial, state and municipal governments have been unable to collaborate with the owner, so they have sought to build an alternative crossing. And that, thanks to Moroun's litigiousness and lobbying, has become all but impossible despite a decade of effort. In February 2012, Moroun, an elderly man, was briefly jailed for being in contempt of a court order to cooperate with highway authorities to finish work that would provide trucks with direct access to the bridge.

In 1979, Moroun, a Detroit truck company owner with Teamster union backing, bought the Detroit International Bridge Company for $30 million. He outbid Warren Buffett and immediately began jacking up tolls and playing all three levels of government off one another to protect his monopoly. He collects an estimated $100 million a year in tolls and has built a trucking and logistics empire by giving customers who hire his trucks or rent his warehouses throughout the United States special access to his bridge ahead of other truckers. The bridge has made Moroun a billionaire, according to *Forbes*.[2] He has effectively held the continent's most important industry hostage ever since.

For years, Moroun has turned down efforts by the Canadian government to buy the bridge, reportedly demanding more than $1 billion for its purchase. Washington has refused to expropriate the bridge. Moroun has balked at expansion or improvement requests and has successfully lobbied, advertised against or sued every level of government on both sides of the border to stop construction of a nearby, alternative bridge. "The bridge could have been expropriated years ago by the two federal governments, but it hasn't for some reason. The border itself should disappear. This is not working at all," Eddie Francis, the mayor of Windsor, told me in 2010.

The bridge has not been expropriated because truck traffic delays are not important in Washington; the narcotics trade and security concerns are. In 2009, the U.S. Department of Homeland Security instituted strict passport requirements for Americans returning from Canada that has contributed to a collapse of tourism to Canada. The Drug Enforcement Agency has added to red tape in its attempts to plug the increasing flow of narcotics from Canada. U.S. Customs now holds up products for weeks. "We call it a thickening of the border," said Michael Wilson, the former Canadian ambassador to the U.S.

In 2008, the U.S. and Canadian chambers of commerce weighed in on the issue and published a joint report from members about "increases in border costs due to increased wait times; fees to cross the border; additional border programs; higher fees to participate in 'trusted' shipper and traveler programs and increased inspection times."[3] The Vancouver think tank the Fraser Institute estimated that the waiting, processing and security measures cost the equivalent of two to three percent of total trade, or between $6.6 billion and $9.9 billion a year, based on 2007 figures.[4]

The threat to the Canadian auto industry was defined by Sergio Marchionne, the CEO of the Fiat Group of Italy, which owns Chrysler: "Unimpeded access from Ontario's highway to Michigan's interstates [is essential]. Each day, Chrysler moves more than 1,300 shipments, some 2,000 cars and trucks, and makes 1,600 entries per day at the Detroit–Windsor border. Hundreds of our employees cross the border to work in the U.S. or Canada. Smooth crossing is essential to our just-in-time manufacturing enterprise. For example, engines made in Trenton or stampings from Warren or Sterling Heights cross the border daily for use at assembly plants in Ontario . . . The need for an additional crossing to handle current and future trade flows is widely acknowledged, and it is imperative that this new crossing be completed as soon as possible."[5]

By 2012, American authorities appeared to be close to finally approving a second $1-billion bridge-and-road system, to be financed with $550 million from Canadian taxpayers. But new obstacles may arise that would add years to any completion date. These decade-long delays and other issues have damaged all Canadian export and tourist industries. The recession, Detroit's troubles, passport requirements for U.S. citizens traveling to Canada and the increasing value of the Canadian dollar have also contributed to the problem. But red tape and bureaucratic meddling were the biggest causes, according to the Fraser Institute. Whatever the causes, Canada's economic well-being and the gains from free trade have been slipping as American law enforcement officials gradually close the border. The Chrysler–General Motors bailout of 2008–09, along with increasing border strangling, provided the impetus behind Canada's willingness to enter into talks to create a new perimeter security agreement.

The 9/11 Effect

The Americans had different reasons for requesting a perimeter deal. Their concerns about the Canadian border began after 9/11, when Canada was identified as a problem country, mostly due to the attempted terrorist attack by an Algerian refugee living in Canada, Ahmed Ressam. He did not participate in the 9/11 attacks, but was a member of al-Qaida and a prime example of Canada's inadequate immigration and law enforcement efforts. He had eluded deportation for years until December 14, 1999, when, on his way to commit an act of terrorism, a U.S. border guard caught him.

Ressam's story was not unusual. He had first arrived in Canada in 1994 and lived in Montreal with others, having successfully conned the loose Canadian system by falsely claiming refugee status, obtaining a passport under an assumed name and then being granted health care, a work visa and even welfare payments. It turns out Ressam and his housemates were members of an al-Qaida cell that had established itself in Canada, awaiting instructions.

He supplemented his income by shoplifting and committing other crimes. He was arrested four times but never jailed or deported, even though there was a warrant out for his arrest. His fingerprints were never taken. He even defied Canadian refugee laws forbidding asylum seekers from leaving the country. He traveled to Afghanistan to learn bomb-making techniques at least once.

In 1997, Interpol tipped me off about the existence of Ressam and other terrorists who had been allowed into Canada as refugees. The leak came from an official who was shocked that Canada would accept these people as refugees, because they were known Algerian terrorists. "'At least two dozen Algerian terrorists have been allowed to immigrate to Quebec,' a source in France told me in a recent interview," I wrote in the *Financial Post* on September 23, 1997. "'These are very dangerous people and they have been hiding in Montreal for some months,' he added."[6]

After the story was published, I forwarded the list of names Interpol had given me to appropriate Canadian federal authorities. They were supposed to be monitoring these criminals, but they obviously were not, or else they had been given the slip. On December 13, 1999, Ressam arrived in Vancouver, where he met an accomplice and the two rented a dark green Chrysler. They drove to an isolated location to load equipment and explosives into the trunk of the car. The next morning, Ressam took a ferry on his own to Victoria, British Columbia, and then another to Port Angeles, Washington, to enter the United States. He arrived at 6 p.m., on the last ferry to arrive that day, and breezed through U.S. immigration with a fake passport.

But as he drove through, U.S. customs inspector Diana Dean decided to search his car. She later described his behavior as "hanky," or strange. When asked to get out of the car, Ressam bolted and fled six blocks before customs officials wrestled him to the ground. He had been on his way to Los Angeles to blow up the city's airport during New Year's celebrations marking the turn of the millennium.

The American press dubbed him the Millennium Bomber. He was tried and convicted and received a 135-year sentence, and then he began cooperating with the U.S. government. His information about al-Qaida's structure, and its sleeper cells awaiting commands to launch attacks, was transmitted to the newly elected president, George W. Bush, in a memo dated August 6, 2001.

On September 11, 2001, another sleeper cell succeeded where Ressam's had failed. Nineteen al-Qaida terrorists hijacked four planes, an act that changed the course of history. At 8:46 a.m., American

Airlines Flight 11 slammed into the World Trade Center's north tower; at 9:03 a.m., United Airlines Flight 175 hit the south tower; at 9:37 a.m., American Airlines Flight 77 flew into the Pentagon; and at 10:03 a.m., United Airlines Flight 93 plunged into a farm field as passengers and hijackers fought for control. It had been aimed at the Capitol building.

Fortunately, none of the nineteen terrorists had arrived in the United States from Canada, or with help from Canada, but many American officials still didn't believe that, because of Ressam's case and others. In 2005, there was a flap in Canada after a *New York Times* editorial repeated the "urban myth" that the route for the 9/11 hijackers led through Canada. The 9/11 Commission determined that none of the terrorists came via Canada, but it cited the fact that two Canadian immigrants, one a pal of Ressam's, had just missed out on starring roles in the attack.

Canadians have tended to view terrorism as a phenomenon aimed at Americans, but they are wrong about this. If Canada has been a staging ground for U.S. attacks, as it was in Ressam's case, then terrorism is also a Canadian problem. Many forget that, before 9/11, the largest aviation terrorist attack in history originated in Canada and killed 280 Canadian citizens. In 1985, Sikh terrorists blew up Air India Flight 182, killing all 329 people on board, including 280 Canadians, mostly of Indian birth or descent. Three of those on board were my neighbors: my daughter's Girl Guide leader, as well as her thirteen-year-old daughter and eight-year-old son.

The Air India investigation and prosecution in Canada took twenty years and cost $130 million, and only one person, Inderjit Singh Reyat, was convicted of manslaughter. He was sentenced to fifteen years in prison for building the bombs and another nine years for perjury. In 2010, a Canadian judicial commission concluded that the federal government, Royal Canadian Mounted Police and Canadian Security Intelligence Service (CSIS) had all failed to prevent the attack and had then botched the investigation and prosecution.

In addition to these high-profile cases, evidence supports the view that domestic terrorism exists in Canada among certain immigrant communities. In 2006, police jailed the "Toronto 18," a group of terrorists who planned to blow up the CBC headquarters and CN Tower, then kidnap and behead the prime minister. Ringleader Zakaria Amara pleaded guilty in 2009, and by 2011 eleven of the eighteen plotters had received life sentences. Another terrorist plot in 2009—to blow up the New York subway, which involved members of an al-Qaida cell working out of Winnipeg—was foiled. In 2011, arrest warrants were finally issued for two conspirators—university students with families in Canada—but they had disappeared. And in 2013, just days after the Boston Marathon attack, two Canadian residents, believed to be al-Qaida operatives, were arrested in Canada by the RCMP for plotting a major terrorist attack in downtown Toronto.

Canada's weak anti-terrorist efforts became public in 2010. Newspapers published a withering attack by Canada's former master spy about the country's poor attitude and feeble efforts. In a U.S. State Department memo disclosed by WikiLeaks, Jim Judd, former director of CSIS, accused the Canadian government, leaders and courts of having an "Alice in Wonderland" attitude toward the terrorists in their midst. He blamed Canadian judges for "tying in knots" attempts by police to detect and prevent terrorist attacks in Canada or from Canada. He cited "knee-jerk anti-Americanism" and "paroxysms of moral outrage, a Canadian specialty" for the resistance among politicians, civil servants and courts toward cracking down on terrorists.

After publication of the WikiLeaks cables, Canadian politicians heavily criticized Judd, but that ended when his successor, the then-current top CSIS chief, Richard Fadden, followed suit, albeit in more temperate language. He uncharacteristically came out of the espionage shadows to be interviewed on CBC Television to warn Canadians about another foreign danger in their midst. He said some Canadian politicians were under the influence of foreign governments, along with some immigrant groups, and acted in the best interests of foreign countries rather than Canada's. He said that China and Middle Eastern nations were involved. "For a G8 member and important middle power with a long history of positive engagement in the world, debate about national security in Canada is, for the most part, fairly sparse," he told a security conference in 2009. "Our elites tend to ignore it altogether. I suggest we have a serious blind spot as a country." He was clearly frustrated with the level of denial in Canada about people who had been allowed into the country and had hidden agendas not in the nation's best interests.[7]

The cases of Ahmed Ressam and the others illustrate why Canada and the United States must share law enforcement and terrorism efforts. Ressam slipped through the cracks of a weak refugee and law enforcement system in Canada and poor police and court systems. Even after being arrested a few times, he was released. This situation would be unacceptable to Canadians if the reverse were true, and the incident has sullied Canada's reputation among law enforcement and border officials in the U.S.

In addition, Canada has been in the hot seat over its immigration and refugee system. To placate Washington, and to enact overdue reforms, the Conservative federal government, after winning a clear majority in 2011, began announcing new immigration rules and more national security measures. It pledged to buy new fighter jets and enact an omnibus crime bill to toughen laws and increase jail sentences against terrorists. But another, bigger bone of contention existed, and led the government to crack down on drug usage and drug smuggling.

Prohibition Redux

The Ambassador Bridge, and the Detroit River that passes beneath it, had been a hotbed of smuggling activity in the United States during the 1920s and 1930s. By the time Prohibition ended, many fortunes and empires had been built on both sides of the border. But smuggling has remained big business and become even bigger since 9/11. Lax law enforcement and immigration laws have allowed foreign drug traffickers to set up operations in Canada as an alternative to Mexico, which has become a slightly tougher place to smuggle drugs from, due to crackdowns at the U.S.–Mexican border. But a home-grown drug industry had developed in Canada too.

In 2002, I spent weeks researching a series of articles about marijuana production in British Columbia and learned that B.C. exported more marijuana to the United States than exports of forest products. The information shocked many, and in 2004 U.S. officials launched a two-year pilot project at the Washington State–B.C. border called Operation Outlook. Military-grade radar and predator drones were deployed for months and were able to detect and document significant numbers of low-flying aircraft from Canada carrying high-grade marijuana and other narcotics.

The Drug Enforcement Agency initiated a second drone program to monitor activity along the Manitoba border. The results revealed that huge amounts of marijuana, methamphetamine and ecstasy were being smuggled into the U.S. by land and air. In fact, the lack of enforcement and punishment in Canada, plus lax immigration laws that allow drug smugglers into the country, has metastasized the production and export of all types of narcotics across Canada from indoor meth and ecstasy labs in Manitoba to marijuana grow-ops in rented houses, factories, farms and on large acreage everywhere.

On December 17, 2010, the General Accountability Office in Washington issued its report "Border Security: Enhanced Department of Homeland Security oversight and assessment of interagency coordination is needed for the Northern Border." The report disclosed huge gaps in border controls and widespread wrongdoing. For instance, immediate arrests were only possible along less than 1 percent, or 32 miles, of the 3,987 total miles of border.

The report cited Department of Homeland Security sources who concluded that the risk of terrorist activity was higher from Canada than from Mexico because of the existence of Islamist extremists in Canada and the openness of its border. This was followed, on February 1, 2011, by a strong statement from Senator Joe Lieberman, chair of the U.S. Senate's Homeland Security and Governmental Affairs Committee: "The numbers speak for themselves. These findings should sound a loud alarm to the Department of Homeland Security, the Canadian government and our committee. The American people are grossly underprotected along our northern border. We've got to work together with our neighbors in Canada to raise our guard. We should at the very least be able to detect all illegal entries from Canada into the U.S. so we can get this information into the hands of law enforcement agencies that are well situated to make the necessary arrests."

Not coincidentally, three days later the two governments announced their joint perimeter agreement talks. The timing was unusual to announce what simply amounted to an agreement to make an agreement after the next U.S. federal election. But it was damage control on Canada's part for two reasons: Congress and the Obama administration were about to make huge public announcements about their crackdown on the Canadian border, and Harper needed to hold an election and get a majority in order to placate the Americans by toughening drug laws, hiring police, building jails and buying U.S.-built fighter planes. He called the election and ran successfully on this "jails and jets" platform to address a border crisis involving marijuana and narcotics that the Canadian public knew virtually nothing about.

But Americans certainly did. Just before Canada's 2011 election was called, U.S. Secretary of Homeland Security Janet Napolitano bluntly told the Senate about her tough new, and permanent, border controls. "Over the past two years, we also have made critical security improvements along the Northern border, investing in additional Border Patrol agents, technology, and infrastructure. Currently, we have more than 2,200 Border Patrol agents on the Northern border, a 700 percent increase since 9/11. We also have nearly 3,800 CBP [Customs and Border Protection] Officers managing the flow of people and goods across ports of entry and crossings. We have continued to deploy technology along the Northern border, including thermal camera systems, Mobile Surveillance Systems, and Remote Video Surveillance Systems. We also successfully completed the first long-range CBP Predator-B unmanned aircraft patrol that extends the range of our approved airspace along the Northern Border from Washington to Minnesota."[8]

Press attention in Canada was scant during the election about this and other American initiatives, including the launch of the Northern Border Counternarcotics Strategy Act, targeting Indian reservations along the border noted for large-scale smuggling activities. "Law enforcement in communities along the northern border can rest a little easier tonight knowing that resources they need to stop the flow of drugs should be on the way soon," said New York Senator Charles Schumer after the act passed. "As I travel the state [of New

York], one of the first things I hear from law enforcement is how they're stretched thin trying to fight the drug trade. This bill will ensure that federal law enforcement officials are working hand in glove with cops on the ground to fight drug trafficking."[9]

Canadian politicians have no excuse for ignoring the marijuana issue; by doing so, it has become worse: the drug trade will proliferate and the effects will damage our relationship with our neighbor to the south. To me, the problem has been obvious whenever I have visited Vancouver, half a dozen times a year. People smoke dope on the streets and in bars. British Columbians are making fortunes in the marijuana industry. For instance, in 2002 I met two Australians who were living illegally in Canada and were each making $100,000 a month transporting marijuana in backpacks to wooded border points for pickup, then couriering the cash home. I traveled with marijuana activist Marc Emery, an entrepreneur who had made millions selling marijuana seeds by mail order to the United States. In 2010, he was finally extradited to the U.S. after years of failed attempts. He had financed the Marijuana Party, which supported legalization, and the Americans demanded his extradition.

RCMP drug squads in British Columbia have been frustrated with the courts and immigration system for years. In 2003, an undercover officer took me on a tour of Vancouver's seedy east end of flophouses and opium dens, where dozens of young Peruvian drug dealers openly sold drugs of all kinds on street corners. They worked for Colombian cartels that began transporting them to Canada in the late 1990s. They posed as refugees, and established a supply line into the U.S. and Canada. I wrote about it for Canada's news magazine, *Maclean's*. Nothing happened.

Vancouver has been nicknamed "Vansterdam" and has become Canada's epicenter of narcotics smuggling. Vancouver is where "B.C.

Bud"—a high-octane version of cannabis that fetches premium prices everywhere—was developed. It is grown on farms, on remote B.C. islands, on Native reserves and in remote mountainside clearings accessible only by forestry roads, and it has also been grown in thousands of homes called marijuana "factories" or "grow-ops" using hydroponic farming methods. Planeloads, and truckloads, leave routinely from Nelson, Trail and other towns hidden away in mountain valleys. People talk openly about being "vegetable salesmen."

And the legal system is lax. I went on a bust with a Vancouver drug squad called the "Grow Busters," who were focused on shutting down these grow-ops. They had a search warrant to enter the premises, but rang the doorbell first, then hesitated before entering so that the workers inside could flee out the back entrance. "We don't arrest them because you have to fill out all this paperwork and nobody goes to jail. Maybe they get a sixty-dollar fine, somebody pays it and they go back to work," explained the officer in charge.

The bungalow measured about 1,000 square feet. It had been rented, and a hydroponic farm with hot lights was built in its basement. Windows had been tightly sealed to retain humidity for the plants. In the living room was a Buddhist shrine for the Vietnamese workers (a candle was still burning during the bust), and videos from Vietnam were strewn on a bed. The workers had been stripping off marijuana leaves, cutting and microwaving them, and placing them into plastic bags for market. There were scissors everywhere. The squad found prescription narcotics in a medicine chest, but the names had been carefully removed from the labels. A stolen car with Ontario plates sat in the driveway.

Hundreds of marijuana plants were under hydroponic lights in the basement. The police pulled them out by their roots and stuffed them into garbage bags for incineration. The street value of that crop in New York City would have been roughly $250,000, and the annual profits from that house would amount to as much as $1 million. This was organized crime, and the police raid was simply part of the cost of doing business for these criminals. At the time, I estimated that British Columbia's marijuana crop alone was worth $6 billion, or bigger than its softwood lumber export sector.

The RCMP's 2006 Drug Situation Report proved my estimate to be shy of the potential total. "Smuggling of Canadian-grown marijuana to the United States continues to be a concern for both countries. Annual Canadian marijuana production is estimated at between 1,399 and 3,498 metric tonnes."[10] The estimated street value of that crop in 2011 would have been about $4,000 per pound, or $8 million per tonne. That made the Canadian cannabis cash crop worth between $11.2 billion and $27.98 billion annually, nearly equal at the high end to Canada's exports of vehicles and auto parts in 2011.[11]

A 2009 update of the Drug Situation Report added another issue: "Canada remained one of the primary global source countries for MDMA [ecstasy] and methamphetamine. Organized crime groups not only produced synthetic drugs for domestic markets, but also provided significant quantities for international markets such as the United States. And Canada has become a major exporter of ecstasy and meta-amphetamines to Japan and Australia as well as of cocaine and heroin."

About 750 organized crime groups were operating across the country, said the police report. Outdoor cultivation took place mostly in B.C., Ontario and Quebec, while indoor cultivation was the primary method in the Prairies and Maritimes. Meth and ecstasy labs proliferated in houses and garages, smugglers had infiltrated airport staff in most airports, and smuggling to the U.S. had become relatively easy by foot or vehicle.

There is little doubt that Canada's failure to stop smuggling has damaged its reputation. This is not a sovereignty issue; this is about respect for neighbors. It is also about the threat to Canadian society. Roughly 17 percent of all murders in Canada are gang-related, involving drug smuggling.[12] They are rarely solved. Biker gangs are heavily involved and visible everywhere as drug couriers or as organizers of grow-ops across the country. Natives are also heavily involved in, or turn a blind eye to, trafficking on their reserves, and Ottawa is reluctant to enforce federal laws on First Nations' territories. This reluctance to enforce the law does not exist south of the border, Native reserve or not, and a merger would certainly help eliminate smuggling through First Nations' lands along the border.

While both sides are negotiating their "perimeter" deal to combine police efforts, make no mistake: the border is closing anyway. Canadians now need passports to enter the United States. Lineups at crossings, to enter the U.S., grow longer. The Detroit–Windsor bottleneck will not be remedied unless the border disappears. There has been serious slippage in the U.S.–Canada relationship, and a "perimeter deal," if it is ever negotiated, will be only a temporary bandage. But Canada's reputation and economy will be damaged if another Ahmed Ressam slips across the border to attempt a terrorist attack or if drug interdiction efforts continue to be limp. The border would shut indefinitely and the Canadian economy would come to a halt. My guess is that the Americans, frustrated with Canadian law enforcement inaction, have deliberately been tightening the border to keep out contraband and undesirables, and then used that to insist on the "perimeter" talks.

Quietly, Canada has been put on notice. A new, tougher crime bill and more jails may come about, but a Vancouver newspaper estimated that one out of every eight British Columbians is somehow involved in growing, distributing or smuggling narcotics. It's accepted. Canadians are indifferent. When jail sentences for marijuana possession of more than two plants were proposed by the federal Conservatives in the 2011 election, all hell broke loose among under-thirties, who voted in the much more liberal-minded New Democrats as the official Opposition. The First Nations and the United Church of Canada also opposed jail sentences for possession.

Canadians may want to legalize marijuana, as I do, but the border would become an armed camp unless the Americans legalized it simultaneously. What's interesting, however, is that change in the United States began in November 2012, when referendums to legalize marijuana for recreational purposes passed handily in Washington, Oregon and Colorado. These states will be at the forefront of removing marijuana from the federal government's list of illicit substances because they will be challenging, to the Supreme Court, the right of states and voters to legalize cannabis. This could lead to its legalization nationally in the United States.

All these border issues underscore the worrisome disconnect between the two countries and the lack of long-term strategy. This is not the way neighbors and friends should behave—or have behaved in the past. As things now stand, the two countries are simply inconvenienced and somewhat at odds over the issue of border clog. They are trying to come up with a "perimeter" plan, something that has eluded them for years but won't solve the issues. The only solution is to erase the border completely through a comprehensive treaty that involves a customs union agreement or through an all-out merger. Failing either, the two will continue to clash and damage the relationship.

Oil

Formula for success: rise early, work hard, strike oil.
—J. Paul Getty

On November 10, 2011, Canada's best-laid plans for its future prosperity received a major blow when the U.S. State Department announced that a permit would not be granted for the Keystone XL pipeline project. The line was expected to deliver up to 830,000 barrels a day of gooey, unrefined oil from Alberta's oil sands to Texas refineries. Canadian oil companies needed the pipeline, and others, to meet their objectives of increasing oil and petroleum product exports from 2.815 million barrels daily in 2012 to 5 million per day by 2035.[13] (As of September 2012, Canada's oil exports to the U.S. accounted for 26.7 percent of that country's total imports of 10.533 million barrels per day.[14]) Estimates were that the oil sands would add $1.7 trillion to Canada's GDP between 2012 and 2037, an increase 21 percent larger than Canada's total economic output in 2011.[15] They were seen as the underpinning of Canada's economy over the next quarter-century. It was a vast resource, the second-largest petroleum reserve in the world after Saudi Arabia but more expensive to produce and refine.

The Keystone decision was a major setback. In Calgary, Peter Tertzakian, like others in the oil business, remembers exactly where he was when he heard the news. Tertzakian was perhaps more shaken than most because, as an economist and advisor on energy matters to major oil corporations, banks, investors and governments, he understood the consequences. Canada had invested decades and tens of billions of dollars banking on the oil sands as the cornerstone of its growth. But without the Keystone pipeline, a nation's plans were

placed in jeopardy as the world's biggest oil deposits appeared stranded as a result of the efforts of the world's environmental

Synthetic crude oil from oil sands is expensive to produc raw material is found in tar-like deposits that are mined fro open pits, or melted below ground with steam, and then ported to "upgrading facilities" where water, sand and imp are removed, leaving behind the key ingredient, bitumen. Thi: then be further processed into crude oil, and then refined int line, diesel fuel and other products. By contrast, conventiona ready to refine into fuel once it's brought to the surface from t ground deposits.

The Keystone pipeline was intended to transport bitum refineries in Texas that had been retrofitted to handle the v and viscosity. It was to be the second-largest pipeline dedica transporting oil sands products to the U.S. The first, called the A Clipper, was designed to carry the same volume of oil per day, ar been approved in 2009 by President Barack Obama to link oil plants with refineries in the Chicago area.[16] By 2013, it was opera

Beginning in 2010, Canada's oil patch, or oil industry, si to meet resistance on a number of fronts. Environmentalists lated their fight against further oil sands production and att: the Keystone pipeline. Obama's decision not to grant the p for the Keystone pipeline project, billed as a delay and not a tion, appeased the environmental lobby, which had moun mass protest against the pipeline. Human chains formed ar the White House. Thousands protested along the route an Capitol Hill. Lobbyists were out in full force in Washingtor at the state capitols along the pipeline's route. The most left-Democrats pressured the president, worried that he would i don Al Gore's tough green agenda.

Obama caved, thus undermining the integrity of the environmental and regulatory review process he had helped to reform. He said more study was needed, even though the project and its route had been scrutinized for three years and passed all environmental tests. The decision was odd, considering that Obama had previously approved the Alberta Clipper pipeline. This time, however, environmentalists were better organized and a looming U.S. election worked in their favor. The president faced reelection and could not risk alienating any portion of his voter base. So he handed a victory to Al Gore. Quietly, however, some Obama officials indicated that the pipeline would be approved after the election. But Canadians took no comfort from that, nor should they have. The energy world was changing.

"Oil and [natural] gas is the biggest product this country exports, or $115 billion in 2011, and I worry that the Americans won't want our stuff. This is twice the value of our auto and parts exports," Peter Tertzakian said to me. "This is worrisome. Canada has built tremendous living standards off the backs of the Americans. We get our capital from them to develop oil and natural gas, then sell it back to them. We have skimmed prosperity from the United States since World War II. This setback, and what we are going to do about it, is the most important question facing this country."

Even worse, a new technology known as "fracking" had resulted in massive reserves' estimates of natural gas and soaring production levels. This led to dramatically lower prices and a cut in export volumes from Canada to the United States. Both oil sands opposition and fracking were threatening Canada's oil industry. Fracking, or hydraulic fracturing, was a "disruptive" technology, the energy industry's equivalent of the invention of the laptop or the telephone. The technology was even being applied, with great success,

to finding light, or high-quality, crude oil, thus posing another threat to Canada's oil sands sector. This technology causes fractures in deep shale rock, through the use of water pressure and chemicals, and releases natural gas, oil and coal seam gas previously thought to be economically unviable to produce. By 2012, estimates were that the United States now had a century's worth of "shale [natural] gas" in reserve. Prices collapsed to 100-year lows.

"This is a megatrend in the making, with profound implications," said Tertzakian. "The real price of [natural] gas, adjusted for inflation, is lower than it was a hundred years ago. Our gas exports to the U.S. have been cut in half. Effectively, our natural gas industry [geared toward exports for decades] is going out of business."

Then the oil companies began fracking for oil and producing top-quality crude in impressive amounts. By 2012, drilling in North Dakota and Texas had begun to yield dramatic results. This meant that another treasure house of oil reserves, in deep shale rocks or spent oil fields, could be produced, thus endangering Canadian oil sands exports to the U.S. The only saving grace was that the break-even cost of fracking for oil required a relatively high oil price of $50 to $80 a barrel, similar to that required for oil sands production. Both were expensive to produce, but the danger associated with fracking was that, if extensively successful, it might begin to cause the price of oil to drop below break-even levels for the oil sands as well as for other oil producers.

"North Dakota produced 100,000 barrels a day for decades, but since 2006 production has jumped and in 2012 was 650,000 barrels a day, with estimates this will reach one million barrels a day shortly," said Tertzakian. "In Alberta, light [shale] oil reached 150,000 barrels a day in 2012 in just two years, which is equivalent to the output of two oil sands plants. The issue is that even if Keystone is built, this light [American] oil may fill it, rather than Alberta oil sands oil."

Cheap natural gas also led some U.S. power utilities to switch from dirty coal to natural gas to generate power. This brought about environmental benefits, and the International Energy Agency said that greenhouse-gas emissions in the United States declined by 8 percent between 2006 and 2012.

In 2012, the International Energy Agency forecast that, as a result of its shale oil revolution, the United States could overtake Saudi Arabia as the world's largest producer by the mid-2020s and, when combined with expected increases in Canadian oil sands production, North America would be self-sufficient in energy by 2035.[17] But these developments, plus the pipeline setback, worried Canada's oil industry and politicians, convincing them more than ever of the need to find markets for oil sands output in Asia as quickly as possible. Weeks after the Keystone postponement, the Canadian government led a trade mission to China. But other geopolitical trends were bearing down on Canada's oil future.

NON-STATE PLAYERS CONTROL AGENDAS

Canada's oil sands strategy was under attack by the world's environmental movement, which had reorganized in the lead-up to the United Nations Framework Convention on Climate Change in Copenhagen in 2009. Environmental transnationals such as Greenpeace, the Sierra Club and the World Wildlife Fund joined forces with others to lobby for changes. But the convention's failure to impose an enforceable set of guidelines and laws to stop environmental degradation required their continued vigilance. These networks felt they were armed with a planetary mandate and became financially capable, politically linked, media-savvy and sometimes violent.

Canada and the United States, in general, and the oil sands, in particular, became their principal targets. "The effort to stop Keystone is part of a broader effort to stop the expansion of the tar sands. It is based on choking off the ability to find markets for tar [oil] sands oil," admitted Michael Brune, executive director of the Sierra Club, in an interview with *The New York Times* after Keystone was set aside.

Critics of the oil sands used the same tactics as used by opponents of Canada's controversial seal hunt. That battle had lasted for decades and turned the world's animal rights activists and environmental organizations against Canada. In 2007, celebrities Pamela Anderson, Brigitte Bardot and Sir Paul McCartney organized a global protest against the bloody bludgeoning of helpless, doe-eyed baby seals. Many Canadians, including me, believe the hunt should be banned, but obstinacy has dragged the country's image through the mud and led to consumer boycotts in Europe and the United States.

The baby seal campaign is the template for this crusade: aerial photos of the oil sands, with gigantic tailings ponds and dead ducks, have provided visual fodder for the media and for environmental groups' fundraising efforts. This money has financed mass protests, lobbying efforts and negative press.

Star power is added to the mix. After the Keystone affair, actor Robert Redford waded into the fray, attacking not just this pipeline but another one planned to take oil through British Columbia to the Pacific coast for export to China. Redford wrote in an op-ed piece in *The Globe and Mail:* "Where spruce and fir and birch trees once rose and waters ran fresh and clean, tar-sands production has left a lifeless scar visible from outer space. Crossing the territories of more than 50 First Nations groups [in British Columbia], slicing through rivers and streams that form one of the most important salmon habitats in the world and putting at risk the coastal ecosystem of British Columbia?

Americans don't want to see that happen any more than Canadians do, and we'll stand by you to fight it."[18]

The Sierra Club, Greenpeace and others are convinced that the oil sands, which they label "tar sands," are dangerously hazardous to water, people and wildlife. But that's untrue. The deposits are located in a high-income, sophisticated jurisdiction with government officials who impose some of the toughest environmental standards in the world. Oil sands emissions are roughly equivalent to California's heavy oil production (roughly 17 percent higher than average oil emissions)[19] or ethanol. And the burning of coal in the United States, the world's single biggest emissions problem, gets a virtual pass compared to the oil sands. Canada has been an easy scalp because it is not an American-based asset and is not a constituent.

After Keystone, environmentalists stepped up their attacks by intimidating potential customers. The Sierra Club sued the U.S. Department of Defense to stop it from using oil sands output. The case was dismissed in 2011. In December that year, environmental groups convinced the United Fruit Growers to boycott oil sands–based transportation fuels. Others making similar commitments are cosmetics giant Avon and drugstore chain Walgreens. Pressure to boycott Canada's oil is widespread and a threat to its economy as a whole.[20]

THE FIRST NATIONS THREAT

The world's environmentalists and some First Nations bands also formed an alliance to impede resource development in Canada. The strategy has been to block an export pipeline to the Pacific Ocean as well as the Keystone XL pipeline to the United States. "I'm going to stand in front of bulldozers to stop this project, and I expect my neighbors to back me up," declared Chief Jackie Thomas of the Saik'uz First Nation at a 2011 press conference in British Columbia. She represented First Nations who control more than 25 percent of the territory along the proposed pipeline route. "I have news for you, Mr. [Canadian Prime Minister Stephen] Harper: you're never going to achieve your dream of pushing pipelines through our rivers and lands. We will be the wall that Enbridge [the pipeline company] cannot break through."

For the environmental movement, opposition to the oil sands has been one of many battles in their global war against fossil fuels. But it's an important one because the oil sands are the world's biggest reserves in a politically safe jurisdiction, and environmentalists intend to shut down their production. But for Chief Thomas and other First Nations leaders, the B.C. oil sands pipeline represented a tactic in a larger war to extract land claims settlements from Canada.

The outstanding claims in British Columbia, for instance, add up to more than the landmass of the province itself, and the amounts being sought are significant. For example, a small tribe in B.C. turned down a $350 million deal in 2011 to build a portion of the proposed oil sands pipeline through a minuscule portion of their territory.

Concerned about protecting its oil strategy, the Canadian federal government waded into the fray to try to win approval for the pipeline to the Pacific. It expedited an environmental hearing into the line, then banned foreign-financed environmental groups or individuals from appearing as interveners. In early 2012, one cabinet minister in Ottawa suggested that the federal government could simply declare the pipeline in the "national interest" and force it to be built. That, however, would be challenged by the provinces on the basis that such a move was commercial and abrogated their jurisdictional rights under the Canadian constitution.

If force were applied, violence would result on the part of First Nations and their allies. This has happened before in dozens of disputes about resource development and/or aboriginal claims. And such confrontations, if escalated to attract American involvement, would create serious conflict. In 1995, during the Quebec referendum on separation from Canada, the Cree and Mohawk First Nations chiefs, both U.S. and Canadian citizens, fiercely opposed separation. They publicly threatened actions—against power transmission lines and the St. Lawrence Seaway—that would have been designed to provoke the United States to invade Canada to help their cause.

Cree Grand Chief Matthew Coon-Come granted me an interview just before the 1995 referendum. I asked him what the Cree would do if the separatists won and unilaterally seceded from Canada as planned. He said he would ask the Canadian federal government to send in troops to protect their right to remain part of Canada. When I suggested that would not happen, he said he would petition the United Nations to do so. When I said *that* would fall on deaf ears, he said that some "warriors" might take a little "target practice" on hydroelectric transmission towers in Quebec and plunge most of the American Eastern Seaboard into darkness. This would bring the U.S. Marines into Quebec within hours, he speculated.[21] Likewise, Mohawk Chief Billy Two Rivers hinted that his band would halt traffic along the St. Lawrence Seaway, which runs through his reservation in Quebec, and said, "We won't back away from war if need be."[22]

More Oil Sands Enemies

Besides environmentalists and First Nations, oil exporters from foreign countries have also opposed the oil sands and the Keystone XL pipeline. This became obvious in 2011 after a shipment of oversized equipment from South Korea traveled through the U.S., destined for an oil sands operation in Alberta. The equipment had been barged up the Columbia River close to the Canadian border, where it was to be hauled by special trucks able to carry wide loads. But American officials detained the equipment at the border.

The customers, oil giants ConocoPhillips and Exxon Mobil, were told that their trucks could only travel at night because they presented a potential hazard to others on the road. They spent $25 million providing road "turnouts," or places where these wide loads could pull aside to make room for motorists. But permission to travel was denied amid a huge, orchestrated protest campaign waged by environmentalists and foreign entities.

"Somehow some entities got mobilized about the extra-size equipment and got organized to stop the shipment on the basis of highway safety," said Matt Morrison, executive director of the Pacific North West Economic Region.[23]

The local newspapers picked up on the issue, environmentalists rallied, and Idaho and Montana authorities invited public input. Not surprisingly, a flood of letters and other communications opposing the transport streamed into the Department of Highways in Montana, said Morrison.

"We were shocked that only 37 percent of those who wrote complaining [about the equipment going to the oil sands] lived in the state and the rest were from places like Nigeria, Venezuela. Most were international," said Morrison. "The equipment was held up for quite some time."

Nigeria and Venezuela, like Saudi Arabia, supply oil to the United States and, as such, are in competition with the oil sands. Such geopolitical lobbying and interference is not new. Russia spends millions opposing and supporting opposition to fracking in Europe, alleging that it causes environmental damage. In 2012, the United Arab Emirates (UAE), a member of OPEC, spent millions to finance an anti-fracking film called *Promised Lands,* directed by and starring Hollywood actor Matt Damon.

The Russian and Arab strategy is obvious. Europe buys most of its natural gas from Russia and pays three or four times more than North Americans do. Moscow's concern is that huge potential deposits of shale gas have been identified in Poland, Ukraine, France and elsewhere. If that gas goes on stream in huge quantities, as appears to be possible, the Russians would see European gas prices tumble and would lose their stranglehold on the market. Likewise, the UAE is the world's fifth-largest exporter of liquefied natural gas, mostly to Europe, and realizes that shale gas will drive down prices and affect its exports.

In 2011, the Saudis leveled a legal attack inside Canada against an organization called Ethical Oil that questioned the importation of Saudi oil because the regime abused the human rights of women and others. The group launched television commercials in Canada labeling Saudi and other OPEC exports as "conflict" oil, like conflict diamonds. The advertisements showed footage of females being mistreated in Saudi Arabia.

The kingdom hired lawyers to tell the Television Bureau of Canada—the advertising review and clearance service funded by Canada's private broadcasters—to ban the ads. Ethical Oil responded by raising funds to run the ads on CTV, a national network with a large audience, but the network responded: "As the ad in question is the subject of a legal dispute between Ethical Oil and the Kingdom of Saudi Arabia, at the advisement of our legal department we will not accept the order until the matter is resolved."[24]

Industry sources confirmed that the Saudi government also approached Canada's oil industry to express its concerns over the

Ethical Oil campaign, just in case it had a role in it. The controversy attracted the attention of Canada's minister of immigration, Jason Kenney, an Albertan, who was outraged and told a newspaper, "Canada is a country that is a champion of freedom of speech. That is a constitutional right. And we don't take kindly to foreign governments threatening directly or indirectly Canadian broadcasters or media for giving voice to freedom of speech."[25]

CANADA'S SELF-INFLICTED CHINA THREAT

The Keystone XL decision particularly upset Canadian politicians who were pro-American. Some reacted like jilted lovers. "The White House wimped out on us. The president caved," was how one of Canada's most powerful leaders privately described the decision. Without new pipelines to the U.S., the country's trade strategy was in shambles and its faith in Americans was shaken. So in February 2012, a disappointed and angry Prime Minister Stephen Harper led a high-level mission to China to line up another customer for Canada's oil sands production.

The optics made American politicians take notice, and that had been the intention. The announced trip to Beijing became an issue for several Republican presidential candidates, and the day before the Canadian prime minister left, Republican front-runner Mitt Romney raised Keystone XL to the top of his agenda and said, "Canada, don't sell your oil to China." He later promised to approve the pipeline the first day he assumed office if he won the presidency. (Not coincidentally, some of the refineries to be supplied by the Keystone Pipeline were owned by Koch Industries, whose owners were backers of the Tea Party rump of the Republican Party.)

China welcomed the Canadians with open arms. Its companies

had been circling Canada and investing in minority positions in the oil sands. So Beijing rolled out the red carpet, even announcing that Canada could have enough pandas for two Canadian zoos for a decade. Publicly, the Chinese agreed that the two countries should launch negotiations to formulate a free-trade agreement. Despite the dangers of trading with a country like China, the opening of talks was announced in September 2012 and a deal was quickly negotiated.

Shortly after the visit, CNOOC made its $15.1 billion bid in Canada, testing Canada's willingness to return China's hospitality. The gambit won and the deal was approved in December 2012. At the time of the announcement, the Prime Minister said that another would be denied, but the Canadian government left the door open for more of the same in future and was putting the finishing touches to a trade deal that would open the floodgates. The decision was strange given that public opposition was considerable, that Canada's spy agency, CSIS, had issued a warning about such transactions[26] and that an international expert had revealed that Canada's infrastructure and energy industries had been attacked and targeted by Chinese hackers.[27]

Even if the U.S. was indifferent to such coziness, or threats, the special bilateral agreement with China amounted to flirting with danger in terms of the U.S. relationship. I raised this specter, as well as the fact that China's behavior in the SSEC/Canadian Natural Resources incident in Alberta made it an unacceptable special partner. In October 2012, Americans warned about China's involvement in a Canadian telecommunications subsidiary, and days later the Canadian government admitted it was aware that a report accused China of a security breach at a firm that makes software used by the North American oil industry.[28]

Frankly, Canada should have built a pipeline to its west coast years before and sought customers in Asia and South America. But

Canada behaved like a colonial offspring, reliant upon the Americans, as it was toward Britain decades ago, then when disappointed by the U.S. immediately rebounded into the arms of another giant to rely on. Instead, Canada should have established trade relationships with every Asian nation.

The Canadian Conundrum

Canada finds itself between a rock and a hard place when it comes to its American relationship. The country cannot live easily with, or without, the United States. And it has only itself to blame for this predicament. The facts are that since 9/11, and due to lax law enforcement and questionable attitudes in Canada, the border has been slowly closing and opportunities disappearing along with it. Without Keystone, a west coast pipeline, or other transportation infrastructure, such as rail links between the oil sands and U.S. destinations like Alaska's Valdez supertanker port, Canada's future oil sands projects will be stranded and canceled.[29] This represents a disaster to a country with declining manufacturing, high living costs and an increasingly frayed relationship with its most important trading partner. It also represents a disaster to an energy-starved United States, which will need the oil sands to become energy and oil independent by 2035.

CHAPTER THREE

Why a Merger Makes Sense

When everything seems to be going against you, remember that the airplane takes off against the wind, not with it.
—HENRY FORD

ON August 15, 2011, Google announced a bombshell bid to buy Motorola Mobility, the phone division of the storied U.S. electronics pioneer, for $12.5 billion. The offer was 63 percent above the company's market capitalization, and payable in cash, in a declining stock market. The strategy was bold but essential. Google was girding for an epic battle against Apple to capture the lucrative market for smartphones and tablets, which many believe will eventually replace cell phones and laptops. The struggle, wrote *Businessweek,* was "between Silicon Valley's two superstars that would change the future of mobile computing."[1]

Motorola had been the Google of its day. The company, founded at the advent of the Depression, invented the car radio, the walkie-talkie, the portable television set, the portable phone and cell phones with extra features. The brand became synonymous with innovation and trustworthiness, and the company remained a technology leader for three generations. But corporate excesses, innovation fatigue, marketing missteps and the onrush of rivals such as Samsung, Nokia and Apple dragged it downward. In January 2011, the company spun off its phone division after losing $4.3 billion between 2007 and 2009.

Apple, on the other hand, has been on fire, producing the iPod, iPhone and iPad to much acclaim and huge sales. Google was also a home run of a company, harnessing its superior search technology to become the world's foremost advertising agency, while also acquiring Skype and YouTube. Google entered the smartphone market late by creating a software system it called Android. By 2010, Motorola, Apple, Microsoft and others had launched thirty-seven Android-related patent-infringement lawsuits. To stanch the claims of the lawsuits, Google bought Motorola and its 17,500 patents in August 2011.

Larry Page, Google's CEO and founder, elaborated at a press conference on why he acquired Motorola: "We recently explained how companies including Microsoft and Apple are banding together in anticompetitive patent attacks on Android. The U.S. Department of Justice had to intervene in the results of one recent patent auction . . . Our acquisition of Motorola will increase competition by strengthening Google's patent portfolio, which will enable us to better protect Android from anticompetitive threats from Microsoft, Apple and other companies."[2]

This was a classic merger, both offensive and defensive. The offer generated speculation and much handwringing on the part of Nokia, Samsung, Microsoft and Canada's Research in Motion, maker of the BlackBerry. But Motorola shareholders were certainly happy. They could cash out, at a profit, from an intensely competitive sector that Apple, America's biggest corporation, had been dominating.

Google's entry into the smartphone market with Motorola was a coup for the little PhD research project that grew. Google's Larry Page and Sergey Brin met in 1996 at Stanford University. Their search project became a company that grew meteorically, and its acquisition of Motorola, while gigantic, represented only sixteen months' worth of Google operating profits. Once Motorola was digested, the two companies would go head to head against Apple and all the others.

Such software and technology companies know that recalibrating their businesses is a constant requirement because nothing stays the same. They are in the business not just of trying to stay ahead of the curve, but of *being* the curve. Software, for instance, can take years to develop but has a shelf life somewhere between those of yogurt and a bestselling book. Google is enormous, but is not guaranteed its place in the sun, any more than Apple, Microsoft or Motorola are. The reality of business is that algorithms and business models work until they don't. Innovators lead until others overtake them. The smartest guys in a room win until a smarter one comes along.

The same Darwinian swap-out applies to the economic development models of nations. Today's China can be tomorrow's Greece. And the United States and Canada are no different. They share the same challenges, externally and bilaterally, but also have some problems internally.

America Inc. and Canada Inc.

Since the crisis of 2008, the United States and rest of the developed world have been "marked down" in living standards. Unemployment will remain high because their aging populations won't consume as much as before and because high-value American, European and Canadian products are likely going to be manufactured by robots, which will take away jobs, or, alternatively, be made by five workers in Asia at the cost of one worker in the West. The downgrading of America's credit rating to AA+ from AAA in August 2011 was simply a warning that continuous public borrowing to artificially stimulate demand, where there isn't any, cannot continue forever. Now the tough stuff begins: raising taxes, slashing entitlements and chopping government services.

The European Union, with its thirty-two-hour workweek, six-week vacations and retirement age of fifty-five, is in even worse shape. The twenty-seven EU members have similarly crossed the economic Rubicon. Their credit has been maxed out after spending trillions to bail out and stimulate their economies and governments. And, as they postpone tough decisions about dismantling their welfare states and growing their economies, the stock, bond, currency and debt markets correct to account for their discount in living standards.

The "markdown" is as immutable as gravity and a correction that will wreak havoc on nest eggs and governments alike. Managing the fallout and reducing expectations will be difficult for politicians and leaders, causing many more to lose their positions. If America and Canada were corporations, more of its shareholders, employees, suppliers and directors would be heading for the exits.

In 2011, the U.S. had a gross domestic product, or GDP (based on purchasing power parity), of $15.08 trillion, gross governmental debts of 80 percent of GDP,[3] a current account deficit of $465.9 billion and reserves of foreign currency and gold of $148 billion.[4] The current account deficit measures how much more America buys than it sells, in goods and services, to the rest of the world. Canada had a GDP of $1.395 trillion, gross public debt of 75 percent of GDP,[5] a trade deficit of $48.91 billion and reserves of foreign currency and gold of $65.82 billion.[6]

GDP figures are compiled differently, and for the purposes of comparison I am using purchasing power parity, a metric based on relative price levels in two countries to avoid distortion caused by volatile currency or market exchange rates. For instance, the U.S. GDP based on purchasing power parity was $15.08 trillion, but nominal

GDP based on the official exchange rate was lower, or $14.83 trillion. More significant are the discrepancies between the two methods of measuring GDP in poor countries. For instance, China's GDP (PPP) was $11.3 trillion in 2011, but its nominal GDP was $7.181 trillion. Comparing U.S. and Canadian figures, apples to apples, to China's performance is depressing. China's revenues in 2011 were $11.3 trillion, its public debt was 43.5 percent of that (including local government debts), its current account *surplus* was $201.7 billion, and its reserve of foreign currency and gold was $3.213 trillion, or nearly two and a half times the size of Canada's economy.

These figures do not include Hong Kong, which, although considered independent, is a city-state controlled by Beijing. In 2011, Hong Kong's revenues were $351.5 billion, debt was 39.8 percent of GDP, its current account surplus was $12.91 billion, and its reserve of foreign currencies and gold was $285.4 billion. Added together, China and Hong Kong in 2011 had a current account surplus of $214.6 billion and reserves of foreign currencies and gold totaling $3.498 trillion.[7] Those are impressive numbers, and the rest of the world has taken note.

A merger of the U.S. and Canada would improve their financial situations. About 19 percent of U.S. exports are destined for Canada, and 73.7 percent of Canada's head to the U.S. These would become interstate or interprovincial transfers, not current account deficits, and would be secure transactions not subjected to possible tariffs, sanctions or protectionist legislation. Even better, if the two merged they could easily become not only energy self-sufficient but major energy exporters to Asia and other regions. Energy independence would give domestic manufacturers a pricing advantage at home and the current account balance a boost because trade deficits would be diminished. The two would enjoy market dominance in key resource areas, thus allowing them to bargain harder to reduce the currency manipulations that China and other Asian nations utilize.

Eliminating trade deficits, mostly due to oil imports by the United States, would result in benefits similar to the synergies that will be realized by combining Google and Motorola. A merger would go a long way toward reversing America's slide on the trade side. The annual current account surpluses posted by the United States ended in 1976. Between that year and 2011, small surpluses occurred in 1980, 1981 and 1991, but the cumulative total of current account deficits, or losses, was $8.68 trillion, according to the U.S. Bureau of Economic Analysis.[8] That represents an outflow of wealth equivalent to 57.5 percent of the U.S. economy in 2011, or nearly 6.5 Canadian economies.

So, like Google and Motorola, the U.S. and Canada could combine to better meet competition and cope with shrinking markets. Unfortunately, Americans and Canadians don't quite understand that their markets are shrinking and that they cannot beat their competitors independently. They don't understand that their troubles are not temporary and may become permanent unless they devise new strategies. They don't understand that they are at the beginning of a long, slow slide downward unless they change their attitudes and behavior. Worst of all, the U.S. and Canada are at a major disadvantage because they consider themselves superior after being on top for so long. (Remember how Rome once ruled the world, and how the sun always shone on the British Empire?) The truth is, to borrow a baseball analogy, each country was born on third base, but they both think they were there because they had hit triples.

Canada is gradualist. It thinks small—even though it is big—and lacks strategy, capital, population and self-protection. America is a slowly fading powerhouse and a narcissist—long on pride, short on introspection, unaware of other models and sometimes revisionist. Neither country realizes how dependent it is on the other for its future success.

The U.S. has many serious shortcomings, yet it enjoys many more competitive advantages than most nations, including Canada. Canada has serious policy and economic challenges, but also has vast, untapped resources.

America's Competitive Advantages

In Britain, prior to the mid-nineteenth century, those unable to pay their debts were locked away in debtors' prisons. Creditors ruled because the land-owning and wealthy elites controlled the country and passed laws to protect themselves, creating a huge underclass and serious social problems. Many avoided prison by agreeing to work off their debts as indentured workers, serving for years as house servants or laborers in steamy or frigid colonies. These were the "lucky" few.

In 1869, Britain passed the Debtors' Act, which helped to slowly reform the system by eliminating the ability to jail debtors indefinitely. But the Americans, on the other hand, who were often British debtors or indentured, began instituting reforms immediately after their independence. One of the U.S. Congress's most significant laws was the Bankruptcy Act of 1800, which leveled the playing field between creditor and debtor. By mid-century, the United States had become the first nation to allow voluntary bankruptcy, and in 1898 Congress—in a forerunner to chapter 11 of the Bankruptcy Code—gave companies the option to seek protection from creditors in order to reverse their fortunes or to work out repayments and compromises.

The decriminalization of indebtedness encouraged risk-taking, but the groundwork for economic achievement was laid in May 1775, when the Second Continental Congress met and adopted the Declaration of Independence, then repudiated Britain's feudal concept of Crown land and Crown estate; as a result, the ownership of all the lands in the thirteen British colonies belonged to the people of America. These lands were placed in trust as "public domain" and were eventually ceded to settlers, states and territories to colonize the country. In other words, America's Founding Fathers "privatized" the lands. Americans were able to buy land outright with clear, or freehold, title. This right to own property was unprecedented, and as revolutionary as the right to representative democracy.

Title to land allowed people to buy and sell property, accumulate and mortgage land, and bequeath it to their children. They could form partnerships, or companies, to do the same. In other words, they could accumulate capital through land ownership, which sparked unprecedented economic activity. The Second Continental Congress had, in effect, democratized wealth creation. The direct result was the migration of millions of landless persons from Europe to the United States to get their piece of the American rock.

Peruvian economist Hernando de Soto credited this innovation for America's economic preeminence in his bestseller *The Mystery of Capital: Why Capitalism Triumphs in the West and Fails Everywhere Else.* "The recognition and integration of property rights was a key element in the United States becoming the most important market economy and producer of capital in the world. The efficiently crafted legal right to have their property integrated into a formal legal system . . . allows them to use it to create capital. Americans built a new concept of property. American property changed from being a means of preserving an old economic order to being, instead, a powerful tool for creating a new one."[9]

A CULTURE OF ENTERPRISE

These were transformative measures. The United States liberated individuals and companies and psyches. Individuals could get assets, or land, and with them a second chance to succeed, while at the same time creditors were protected, within reason. This helped create a real economy, along with a formidable financial system with risk capital to bankroll agriculture, mining, energy and ideas.

Americans are more resilient and more comfortable with risk than most nationalities. Even today, ordinary Americans invest in stocks and bonds or mutual funds to a greater extent than others around the world. In 2011, the average household wealth included 68 percent in these financial instruments compared to Canada's 56 percent or 35 percent in Australia and most other developed countries, according to Credit Suisse's Global Wealth Research Institute.[10]

America's greatest competitive advantage is this culture of risk-taking and entrepreneurship. American attitudes de-stigmatize setbacks and even failures by entrepreneurs operating in good faith, while other nations or cultures punish any failure. In some countries, bankruptcy leads to family ruination, exile or even suicide.

In Silicon Valley, for example, bankruptcy is treated as one of the rites of passage, and what some call "failure" is regarded as the economic equivalent of the scientific method or engineering process: try, fail, learn and keep trying. Steve Jobs is celebrated, even though he was a college dropout, was fired as an executive and was, initially, an unsuccessful businessman, because he just kept trying.

The Americans, in essence, have internalized the attitude of most successful people: a person, organization or nation is only as successful as one's ability to handle setbacks or failure.

This can be attributed, in some measure, to the fact that the United States overtook Britain economically in just five generations. This achievement was even more amazing given that the fledgling country waged many wars, including a devastating civil war, during this period. Throughout their history, Americans have shown that they can pick themselves up off the mat quicker than most.

Silicon Valley is not the only cluster of unmatched global excellence that rooted itself in the United States because of its unique economic climate. New York City, Hollywood and the Boston-Cambridge region are unique ecosystems that attract talent from around the world. China and others covet this wealth-creating machinery, but will never replicate it by definition. These are freewheeling, libertarian petri dishes, and China, like most countries, is a hierarchical, authoritarian, bureaucratized ecology.

Americans also work harder than people in most other developed countries. They have half as many statutory holidays as—and fewer vacation days than—Canadians, Australians or Europeans. They are also more productive. Only three nations—Norway, Luxembourg and Ireland—have higher rates of productivity in terms of GDP per hour worked than does the United States.[11] All others lag, including Canada.

The United States remains the greatest wealth-creation machine in history. Others, such as China, are gaining ground by gaming the system, keeping currencies artificially low, counterfeiting, maintaining slave wages, running a dictatorship and instituting protectionism. But these methods are not sustainable.

America's government debt is concerning but is only half the story. America's borrowing grows, but so does the other side of its balance sheet. In 2011, the United States represented 25 percent of the world's household wealth of $231 trillion in assets (Canada accounted for 2.8 percent). By contrast, China's overall wealth was 8.7 percent of the total, or equivalent to America's in 1968; Brazil's wealth was comparable to America's in 1948 and India's to America's in 1916, according to Credit Suisse's Global Trends analysis. By 2016, the bank forecasts that the United States will remain the world's wealthiest nation, with 23.5 percent of the world's total household wealth of $345 trillion, while China will still be a very distant second.[12]

An article in *The Economist* in July 2012 described the American economy as "The Comeback Kid" and pointed out the resilience the U.S. enterprise culture has demonstrated since the 2008 collapse, compared with Europe and others. By 2012, its banks had recapitalized, household debt had been chopped, its houses were undervalued, exports flourished, oil and natural gas production from shale deposits boomed because of fracking technology, innovations such as the "app economy" employed hundreds of thousands and made sales globally, and manufacturers were recapturing some markets.[13]

These developments indicated that alarms about America's impending collapse had been hyperbolic. The country's unbridled, adversarial media and acrimonious political process, which is perpetually in election-campaign mode, is noisy and alarmist. But Americans unite when they must; witness the massive bipartisan government rescue mounted in 2008 after Wall Street collapsed. As Winston Churchill, whose mother was American, once famously observed during the Second World War, "You can always count on Americans to do the right thing—after they've tried everything else."

Canada's Competitive Advantages

Canada's best assets include its resources, stability and banking system, its strong relationship with the United States and an educated, law-abiding people. Canada's culture, while entrepreneurial, is more British and more cautious in execution. For example, Canada never had a Wild West era; rather, it had a "Mild West," where the British made peace deals with the aboriginals and dispatched police to keep the peace before pioneers were allowed to settle. Since that time, the country has continued to slowly and deliberately build a stolid and secure socioeconomic system.

Canadians, like Australians, spend more proportionately on social services than do Americans. Some Americans regard this as a competitive disadvantage, but it has, arguably, enhanced economic development. Low-income or disadvantaged individuals and families have access to housing, health care, drug rehabilitation, psychiatric services and the same quality of schooling as richer citizens. In the United States, slums and inadequate schools perpetuate a cycle of poverty for millions, contributing to crime rates. For instance, most people who declare bankruptcy in the U.S. are forced to because they incurred exorbitant medical costs. And most prisons are filled with people from impoverished backgrounds.[14]

THE BANKS

Nowhere is Canada's slow-but-steady style more evident than in its banking system. Five dominant banks have been allowed to share an oligopoly, thanks to government protection from foreign ownership and competition, in return for following rules that ensure their solvency. The result is stability. No major Canadian financial institution

146

went out of business during either the Great Depression or the Great Recession of 2008.

Solvency remains the watchword. In the early 1990s, Canadian financial institutions were allowed to acquire risky investment banks or brokerage firms, as happened in the U.S. But banks and their brokerage subsidiaries were regulated by different agencies and their capital was sequestered. This was not the case in the United States.

Likewise, the Canadian banks asked for permission to merge from five entities into two bigger banks, but were refused on the basis that each conglomerate would be too big to fail, or bail out, in a country the size of Canada. So in 2008, Canada's five banks sailed through the crisis without much of a bailout.

In 2011, the five banks, plus the Quebec credit union Caisses Desjardins, were among the fifty safest banks in the world.[15] That same year, six American banks finally made it back onto that elite list, but only after most of them—and the sector as a whole—had received hundreds of billions of dollars in bailouts. Also in 2011, three of the Canadian banks were among the world's fifty biggest.[16] Only five American banks made the cut, and each of them had been rescued.

The nature of Canada's regulatory system is superior to America's because it is modeled along traditional British lines, according to Prem Watsa, chair and CEO of Fairfax Financial. He is one of the few individuals in the world who saw the U.S. crash coming. Watsa made billions and catapulted his company into one of North America's five biggest property and casualty insurers. He explains the difference: Canadian institutions are asked to justify their investment choices to regulators while Americans impose rules.

"The U.S. rating agencies created the [real estate] asset bubble," Watsa told me in 2010. "Bankers looked at what Standard & Poor's or Moody's said, and as long as they said a credit was AAA, you said it was AAA. This crept in. [The bankers] were in charge. That's what's happened. In Canada, like Britain, we have the 'prudent man rule.' This means you must judge the quality of your assets, and strategy, in terms of what a prudent man would do. This is a principles-based system, as opposed to a rules-based one, which is in the U.S."

As Americans have learned a few times the hard way, the governance of a financial system is critical to sustaining wealth creation. Banks are like a nation's bloodstream: they must remain intact to bring nutrients and oxygen so the rest of the body can function. If the system collapses, the patient is threatened. If collapse is permanent, the patient dies.

THE RESOURCES

But banks did not build the Canadian economy; resources did. The country's undeveloped endowment represents its greatest asset. The scale of magnitude is difficult to quantify, but it's fair to say that Canada's unrealized potential is mind-boggling. I interviewed Wayne Goodfellow of the Geological Survey of Canada, a petrologist (a geologist who specializes in the origin, structure and location of resources). He has edited the Survey's annual publication for several years and offered a guesstimate of Canada's mining potential. "If you added up all the metals and minerals ever found and produced in Canada historically, plus the [known and proven] reserves yet to be produced, we have three to five times more than that left. It's huge."

Goodfellow estimated that, up to 2009, $1 trillion worth of metals had been produced in Canada's history, along with another $1 trillion worth of industrial minerals such as potash, coal, clays, phosphates, limestone, asbestos, sulfur, sodium and salt. In addition, there was another $1 trillion in known and proven reserves. That brought his estimate of produced resources and known reserves to $3 trillion. Using Goodfellow's math, three to five times as much is between $9 trillion and $15 trillion worth of metals and minerals still to be found and produced in Canada. The multiplier effect of economic activity to find, build and operate mines, then build infrastructure or add value to the commodities—this would be in the form of exploration, engineering, construction, financing, refining, smelting, fabricating, manufacturing and transportation—could be even more significant.

This does not include Canada's energy potential in oil and natural gas. Just one Prudhoe Bay–sized find, with 16 billion barrels, would be worth $1.6 trillion at $100 a barrel—bigger than Canada's total economic output in 2011. Estimates are that 25 percent of the world's total energy—and mineral—resources exist in the Arctic offshore, including significant amounts in Canada's Beaufort Sea and Baffin Island offshore regions.[17]

In 2008, the U.S. Geological Survey estimated that the area north of the Arctic Circle contains 90 billion barrels of undiscovered, technically recoverable oil; 1,670 trillion cubic feet of technically recoverable natural gas; and 44 billion barrels of technically recoverable natural gas liquids (propane, butane, ethane, pentane, hexane and heptane) in twenty-five geologically defined areas. That's roughly 13 percent of all of the world's undiscovered oil, 30 percent of the undiscovered natural gas and 20 percent of the undiscovered natural gas liquids. Of these, about 84 percent will be found offshore.[18]

A recent study carried out by Scottish consultant Wood Mackenzie said most of the energy potential in the Arctic will be found in four basins: the Kronprins Christian Basin off Greenland, which belongs to Denmark; another southwest of Greenland; Baffin Bay (shared by Greenland and Canada); and Laptev (off the northern coast of Siberia).[19] The Beaufort Sea is another promising region. There have been huge finds on the Alaska North Slope and in Canada's Northwest Territories, both on and offshore. A portion of the Beaufort Sea is at the core of a dispute between the U.S. and Canada over 8,000 square miles that, both sides claim, fall within their nautical-mile territorial limits.

There is also onshore potential. "There are vast areas in this country where boots have never been on the ground," said Goodfellow. "The Howard's Pass deposit in the Yukon is probably the largest reserve for lead and zinc in the world. It is a belt that is twenty to thirty kilometers long [twelve to eighteen miles], and this area is continually mineralized. There is no access, only an airstrip—no roads, no power grid, no rail. It could be the biggest lead-zinc mine in the world."

The concentration of mining effort in Canada has been in its more populated south, or along coastlines where tidewater provides logistical support to bring in, and ship out, materials and people. Elsewhere, development has been nonexistent, including the Arctic as well as the northern portions of most provinces. "These lands are virtually unexplored," said Goodfellow. "It's a staggering asset base."

What Ails the USA

The Great Escape, the iconic 1963 Hollywood movie starring Steve McQueen, James Garner and Charles Bronson, portrayed cheeky and courageous American prisoners of war who stage a brilliant and daring breakout from a German POW camp. The movie was based on the March 25, 1944, escape from Stalag Luft III by seventy-six Allied air force personnel. Three got away; the rest were captured, and most were executed. The story was a compelling example of invention and moxie on the part of six hundred prisoners who forged tools, counterfeited documents and built a 330-foot tunnel beneath the prison's barbed-wire fence—under the noses of its guards.

But the movie should have been called *The Great Misrepresentation.* The truth was that only a handful of Americans were involved, and they played minor roles. Months before the escape took place, the Americans had been relocated to another camp. The real heroes were Canadians and British. The two masterminds were a British pilot named Roger Bushell and a Canadian pilot named Wally Floody, a mining engineer from Ontario who devised the tunneling operations. Bushell, on whom the character Roger Bartlett, played by Richard Attenborough, was based, escaped but was caught by the Gestapo and was executed along with forty-nine others. Floody, thought to be the inspiration for Charles Bronson's tunnel-king character, survived because the Germans suspected he was up to something, but could never figure it out, and transferred him to another prison just days before the escape. After the war, Floody testified at the Nuremberg Trials about camp conditions and torture.

"By Hollywood's account, you would never know Canadians played a prominent role in the construction of the tunnels and the escape itself," says an essay on the website CanadaAtWar.ca. "Wally Floody . . . had a major role in the construction of the escape tunnels, while 9 Canadians escaped, 6 were murdered by the Gestapo. Of the 1,800 or so POWs in the compound, 600 were involved in the escape, 150 were Canadian."[20]

Floody became a technical consultant to the film's director and never complained about the Americanization of the story. Most Canadians, and the rest of the world, know that Hollywood, the dream factory, has never let the facts get in the way of a good

"American" story, whether it's about wars, hoisting the flag at Iwo Jima, Custer's Last Stand, the Wild West or the deification of historical figures. Other countries do likewise, mythologizing or romanticizing their pasts, but the Americans are better at it than most.

The issue is that the dream factory and political revisionism appeal to audiences that are isolated, undemanding or uneducated. They want entertainment, heroism and happy endings. This makes them vulnerable to phony narratives on the screen and in politics. They love war movies, rags-to-riches stories and tales about good and great America. Americans are just plain better at storytelling and salesmanship or marketing than other nationalities. Many Americans believe they are exceptional, that theirs has always been the best country in the world and has always stood for such tenets as "all men are created equal," despite the stain of slavery. It borders on self-delusion and has perpetuated bad practice and impeded the search for, and adoption of, better ideas. And it's changing, slowly.

"Let America realize that self-scrutiny is not treason. Self-examination is not disloyalty," said the late Cardinal Cushing of Boston.[21] He and other activists helped African-Americans finally gain equal rights a century after the Civil War ended and two centuries after the phrase "all men were created equal" was penned by the Founding Fathers.

Delusion, inflexibility and exaggeration did not turn America into the richest and most innovative economy in the world; facts, risk-taking, hard work and innovation did. Americans didn't just imagine a world with horseless carriages; they created mass production and invented the car culture. Americans invented airplanes, phonographs, transistors and the Internet. And they are inventing the future in Silicon Valley, Cambridge and other centers of research excellence.

Delusions certainly have not helped America's best corporations remain at the top of their game. But gullibility or ineptness has contributed mightily toward the waging of unsuccessful wars in foreign countries, where intelligence was baseless, without exit strategies or where cultures were misunderstood or ignored, as well as toward the unquestioned support of America's gigantic military machine. The country cannot afford delusion or its monolithic military any longer.

In 2011, the United States spent six times as much on military defense as the next highest spender, China. Its budget represented 43 percent of the world's total spending, according to the Stockholm International Peace Research Institute. "The USA has increased its military spending by 81 percent since 2001. At 4.8 percent of GDP, U.S. military spending in 2010 represents the largest economic burden [of any nation] outside the Middle East," wrote Dr. Sam Perlo-Freeman, head of the institute's Military Expenditure Project.[22]

By 2010, the U.S. controlled 5,113 nuclear weapons, or two-thirds of the world's arsenal, with several thousand more scheduled to be retired and dismantled. Russia, by comparison, had 2,200 warheads in 2010, according to Reuters, and pledged under the New Strategic Arms Reduction Treaty to lower that number to 1,550 active nuclear weapons. The U.S. base defense budget in 2010 was $533.8 billion, with another $130 billion earmarked for the War on Terror; Veterans Affairs, Homeland Security, nuclear weapons maintenance and the State Department accounted for $262 billion. None of those figures included the tens of billions more dollars, allocated most years, to develop and buy new weaponry.

America has become Sparta, the powerful Greek city-state with an oversized military culture. The subculture involved directly and indirectly with the Pentagon is one of the country's biggest political constituencies. By December 31, 2011, there were 1,456,862 active personnel in the military,[23] along with 1,079,355 in its reserves[24] and roughly 21,500,000 living veterans,[25] for a total of 24,036,217—two-thirds the population of Canada. This means that one in twelve Americans had been in uniform.

Roughly one dollar out of every five spent by Washington is ear-marked for the care and feeding of its armed forces.[26] If the Pentagon were a nation, it would have an economy as big as Turkey's. Millions work for the military or its suppliers, and sociologists have identi-fied hundreds of clusters of ex-military personnel who live and work around military facilities. In 2010, Dante Chinni and James Gimpel, co-authors of *Our Patchwork Nation,* identified a subculture they called "military bastions," located near bases and filled with soldiers, mili-tary base workers, veterans and their families.

Hopkinsville, Kentucky, for one, is a town of about 31,577, but 20,511 army and air force personnel—and 40,491 of their family members—are living on the Fort Campbell base nearby. Most of the region's population consists of active-duty military, veterans, their families and relatives, and others directly tied to the military. The *Patchwork Nation* authors designated fifty-seven such U.S. counties as military bastions.

With so many millions affiliated with the armed forces, it's hardly surprising that pro-military boosterism and flag-waving proliferate. For instance, Senator John McCain strongly criticized President Obama in August 2011 for letting NATO forces liberate Libya instead of having the American armed forces do most of the heavy lifting. McCain boasted that American military superiority would have been preferable to letting France and Britain shoulder a large burden. "It would have been finished faster," he claimed on CNN.

That mentality has financially damaged the country, senior Congressman Barney Frank, a Democrat, told me in 2010. "America is spending the equivalent of the level of expenditures in 1946 after the Second World War. Iraq cost $1 trillion and was a Vietnam-scale mistake, not in terms of lives lost, but as a geopolitical disaster that destabilized the region, encouraged the worst kind of radicalism and made us hated around the world. It is one of the single worst decisions in the history of the U.S. We are defending the Czech Republic and Poland against an Iranian missile attack. We have expensive bases all over the world that are not needed.

"There is no threat to the U.S. in the sense of the Soviet Union," continued Congressman Frank. "China is decades away from being a military issue if it ever does become one. We should have a policy only of going to the defense of countries that are attacked. As for our own home defense, tell me what a Trident [nuclear] missile does against a shoe bomber. You could cut $250 billion a year from our military budget and take 5 or 10 percent of that to put into increased security at home and we would be a safer country. More airport security and more magnetometers would be more effective. Also more cyber security."

SPARTA

America's military burden continued to cost the country its economic pre-eminence even after the Cold War ended. In 2000, America's public debt was $9.5 trillion, or 56 percent of GDP, and by 2011 it was climbing toward 100 percent.[27] But old habits, and the emotional investment in perceived past glories, have not disappeared. Even as debate raged in Washington in the summer of 2011 over the deficit crisis, Congress handily approved massive military expenditures without much debate. On July 8, 2011, Reuters reported: "A $649 billion defense spending bill for next year easily passed the U.S. House of Representatives on Friday after four days of debate. The measure, approved 336–87 in the Republican-dominated House, would raise the Pentagon's base budget for the 2012 fiscal year beginning on October 1 by about $17 billion over current levels, despite intense pressure to slash the $1.4 trillion U.S. deficit."[28]

The rest of the summer of 2011 was a disaster as Congress clashed over the rest of the budget, how to cut the deficit in future and, having addressed neither issue, whether to raise the debt ceiling. The endless debates went down to the wire, and the raising of the debt ceiling was approved just twenty-four hours before the U.S. would have ended up technically in default. But nothing was resolved. The nation's credit rating was downgraded, costing the federal government more to borrow funds, and a "super committee" of three Democratic and three Republican Congressional representatives was formed and given a November 2011 deadline to agree on deficit cuts.

They failed, and by the end of 2012 the U.S. stood at the edge of what Federal Reserve Chairman Ben Bernanke had dubbed the "fiscal cliff": the expiration of tax cuts introduced by former president George W. Bush in 2001 and 2003, combined with automatic and deep reductions in spending on Medicare and national defense. These measures—set to take effect on January 1, 2013, unless Congress passed legislation to abrogate them—would reduce the deficit by about half a trillion dollars, but the Congressional Budget Office also estimated they would cause the economy to contract by 4 percent, causing recession. The deadline passed without a solution, but within hours a bill was passed in both the Senate and the House of Representatives to increase taxes, and it was signed into law the next day. The problem was not completely solved, however, but astounding spending cuts (and tax hikes) began in April

2013 and effects were positive. Markets boomed, and the federal government posted a fiscal surplus that month.

The country's defense costs still threaten the balance sheet. In 1961, President Dwight Eisenhower warned that the biggest danger to the country was its "military–industrial complex," or the link between politicians and defense contractors. He had been Supreme Allied Commander Europe and orchestrated the D-Day invasion, then served two terms as president. His words were prescient then and remain relevant now.

"Our military organization today bears little relation to that known by any of my predecessors in peacetime, or indeed by the fighting men of World War II or Korea," Eisenhower said. "We have been compelled to create a permanent armaments industry of vast proportions. We annually spend on military security more than the net income of all United States corporations. In the councils of government, we must guard against the acquisition of unwarranted influence, whether sought or unsought, by the military–industrial complex. The potential for the disastrous rise of misplaced power exists and will persist."

Since Eisenhower's time, Americans have remained in a perpetual state of war readiness, even after the dismantling of the Berlin Wall in 1989, which brought about a brief peace dividend. By 2000, the military budget had declined to 3.7 percent of GDP, compared to 7 percent during portions of the Cold War.

Then 9/11 happened.

The tragedy traumatized the world and launched President George W. Bush's War on Terror. In October 2001, he invaded and occupied Afghanistan to find Osama bin Laden, then decided to try to turn the place from a tribal society into a mature democracy. He convinced the United Nations Security Council to create the International Security

Assistance Force (ISAF) to prop up Hamid Karzai's Afghan administration. By 2011, nearly half a trillion in U.S. tax dollars had been spent and nothing much had changed. Afghanistan was still tribal and still ungovernable.

"Victory in Afghanistan is impossible," said former Soviet leader Mikhail Gorbachev in 2011. "Withdrawing troops will be difficult, but what's the alternative—another Vietnam? Sending in half a million troops? That wouldn't work." Gorbachev knew a thing or two about Afghanistan. The Soviet war in that country has been credited, in large measure, with bankrupting the Russian treasury and undermining its credibility among its citizenry.

The next target of the War on Terror was Iraq, because intelligence reports, later found to be wrong, linked its dictator to bin Laden's al-Qaida terror network as well as to nuclear and chemical weapons. Despite skepticism, and protests in the U.S. and around the world, the Americans invaded Iraq on March 19, 2003. They never found nuclear or chemical weapons, and the intervention became another Vietnam, with troops mired until 2012 in guerrilla warfare. On May 1, 2003, President Bush infamously and inaccurately trotted out the traditional American triumphalism when he stood on the deck of an aircraft carrier before a banner that read, "Mission Accomplished." But it was another great misrepresentation. By 2011, when the last American troops left behind a fragile, vulnerable, democracy, the cost of the war in Iraq had reached more than $1 trillion.

The wisdom of either invasion is debatable, but that's not the point. The invasions and occupations were simply unaffordable. Worse yet, the Americans did not do their homework, militarily or culturally. Both military interventions were monstrously expensive miscalculations. In October 2007, the Congressional Budget Office estimated that the Afghan and Iraqi invasions and occupations would end up costing taxpayers $2.4 trillion by 2017 if interest payments on debt to pay for combat were included. Some estimates, which included post-war health care and support for veterans, were higher, at $4 trillion.

Eisenhower foresaw the dangers of the military-industrial complex, but, even so, its durability has been surprisingly resilient in a country built on thrift, collaboration and efficiency. If Americans spent half as much, they would likely be just as safe and secure as they are now. The Pentagon budget is unsustainable.

ISN'T THE PENTAGON A GOVERNMENT DEPARTMENT?

Interestingly, the blind allegiance of American conservatives to the Pentagon flies in the face of their belief in fiscal rectitude or their unquestioning belief in the superiority of the private sector and the mediocrity—even, possibly, evil—of the public sector. Slandering government—the non-military portion—and praising the troops was a specialty of the late President Ronald Reagan. He embodied that American distrust of institutions and saw a "red," or something dead, under every government bed.

An example was his demonization of President John F. Kennedy in 1960. At the time, Reagan was a political activist and a Democrat about to switch his support to Kennedy's opponent, Richard Nixon. He joined the Republican Party in 1962, and in 1966 became governor of California. "Under the tousled boyish haircut [of John Kennedy] it is still old Karl Marx—first launched a century ago. There is nothing new in the idea of a government being Big Brother to us all. Hitler called his state 'State Socialism,' and way before him it was called 'benevolent monarchy.'"

Government bashing and dismantling prevents the United States from deploying an arsenal of economic weapons, such as sovereign-owned enterprises or sovereign wealth funds, that are used successfully by other nations to enhance growth, expansion, investment at home and abroad, and trade. These governments, led by China, and their state-owned enterprises attain dramatically better outcomes than do their American private-sector counterparts. And this is not about Saudi Arabia, China or Russia only. Countries such as Singapore, Canada, Norway, Australia, France, Sweden, Brazil, Mexico, Germany, Switzerland and others have grown their economies by using such state-owned instruments and government tools.

There are many American conservatives who would privatize everything in the U.S. except, presumably, the military. Their mantra is Reagan's famous line: "The nine most terrifying words in the English language are 'I'm from the government and I'm here to help.'" He also dismissed the attitude of the state in the economy as nothing more than "If it moves, tax it. If it keeps moving, regulate it. And if it stops moving, subsidize it."

Such anti-government tension is rooted in American history ever since the chaotic thirteen states tried to fend off federalism after the War of Independence. But disdain for government ignores the fact that governments have played a key role in creating the country's culture of innovation, wealth and economic development. As such, history has been revised.

For instance, from the beginning Washington expropriated, then distributed, the landmass, a type of cataclysmic land reform that facilitated the creation of a national economy. In the past century, governments commissioned and/or subsidized several of the most important technological advances in the world: commercial aviation took off after the federal government mandated that its postal service transport the mail by air; the electronics revolution that launched Silicon Valley was a Department of Defense war initiative during the Second World War; and the invention and subsequent commercialization of the Internet began as a Defense initiative that has changed everything. More recently, fracking, a technique to tap deep underground deposits of natural gas and oil, has been funded in part by governments and has reversed the country's declining supplies of energy.

America's competitive advantages have also flowed from its embrace of public education in the late nineteenth century, ahead of other nations, and the education of tens of millions under the GI Bill. Public education created America's middle class and underpinned a meritocracy where the best and brightest have been able to contribute to national prosperity and the common good.

Governments paid for Eisenhower's postwar infrastructure megaprojects, which transformed the economy, and for the Marshall Plan, which transformed Western Europe. And, finally, government social security schemes in the U.S., and around the world, have stabilized incomes for disadvantaged and elderly residents, propped up their middle classes and ring-fenced their societies from the rich-poor divide that creates chaos, desperation, lawlessness and social instability, thus impeding wealth creation and democracy.

History shows that governments, even American ones, underpin civilization—not Wall Street bankers or industrialists or good intentions. As U.S. jurist and Supreme Court justice Oliver Wendell Holmes said in 1935, when asked about taxation: "Taxes are what we pay for a civilized society."

Clearly, the role of the state in society is debated in every democracy, but the difference is that in the United States there are millions who believe there is no role for government, with the exception of a military one. But as American historian Francis Fukuyama wrote: "[Alexander] Hamilton foresaw that a centralized state would be necessary to create a national market, and an economy based on manufacturing. [Franklin Delano] Roosevelt understood that the industrial economy had unleashed forces that needed to be tamed. They [Hamilton and Roosevelt] saw national power as a tool to achieve their ends, something to be nurtured and built rather than demonized as something to be drowned in a bathtub."

AMERICA'S HEALTH-CARE BLIND SPOT

Another example of anti-government bias involves America's other unsustainable overhead: its hybrid system of health care. American health care is run by the private sector, with the result that costs are twice as high as the average expenditure among the thirty-four other rich countries in the Organization for Economic Co-operation and Development (OECD). Their systems are principally nationalized, and run as not-for-profit organizations. This template reduces costs and inefficient duplication resulting from competition. Worse yet, American health care is not only unnecessarily costly, but medical outcomes are no better than the European, Canadian or Japanese models.

In 2009, the health-care expenditures of developed nations in the OECD averaged 9.5 percent of GDP, or $3,265 per person (adjusted for purchasing power). America's represented 17.7 percent of GDP, or $7,990 per person. Canada's health-care cost was 11.4 percent of its GDP, or $4,317 per person; Germany's was 11.7 percent, or $4,225; Japan's 9.5 percent, or $3,035; Australia's $3,670; South Korea's $1,864; and Switzerland's $5,135 per person.[29]

Government-managed systems are cheaper because they have lower administrative costs. In Canada or Norway, health-care facilities collect their fees from their governments. In the U.S., hospitals and clinics may be faced with collecting fees from hundreds of insurers. This paper burden alone, according to a study by the McKinsey Global Institute in 2008, cost Americans an additional $150 billion a year in medical costs.[30] That added cost is interesting and is roughly the amount that Canadian governments in 2009 spent— actually $140 billion—providing complete health care to Canada's total population of 34.4 million people that year.

Government-managed health care saves money by negotiating volume discounts for pharmaceuticals and equipment, and by operating hospitals as nonprofits, so excessive fees are eliminated. Government-managed health care, with universal coverage, eliminates the need to sue to recoup medical costs, thus reducing medical insurance costs for practitioners and facilities. A Canadian surgeon pays as little as one-eighth the amount of insurance as does his or her American counterpart. These savings are reflected in lower doctors' fees, also mandated by governments. And without universal government health care, people die, remain sick or lose their life savings. In 2007, unaffordable health-care costs caused 62.1 percent of personal bankruptcies in the United States.[31]

The U.S. system of health care is indefensible from an economic as well as a business standpoint. Imagine if Americans had the same system as Canada or Germany: the savings would total $1.079 trillion per year, more than Washington collected in social insurance payroll taxes. (Social Security and Medicare payments totaled $934 billion in 2011.)[32] But the U.S. health-care lobby is as formidable as its defense lobby. Both have inordinate influence over the political system through campaign contributions derived from profits.

But the 2012 presidential election was a de facto endorsement of universal health-care coverage, in the form of a piece of legislation nicknamed "Obamacare." The law requires uninsured Americans to buy insurance, a controversial aspect that was contested, then upheld, in the U.S. Supreme Court. Obamacare is the first step in health-care reform and will give governments greater control over the costs of the system.

In summary, the United States' federal government, as it is currently operated, resembles a mature corporation with good assets and reasonable prospects, but without any control over its two biggest cost centers: its military and its health-care system. This inhibits investments in education, research and infrastructure. The United States, with its dynamic economy and hardworking people, clearly must repair its political system, or it will become like General Motors before its 2009 bailout, not after.

What Ails Canada

Canada has better health-care and banking systems than America's, but its living standards are headed lower. As of 2007, American productivity rates, as measured in terms of GDP generated per hour worked, were 26 percent higher than in Canada, according to the Organization for Economic Co-operation and Development.[33] This hurts manufacturing and exports and is worrisome.

Of greater concern, however, is that Canada has trade deficits at a time of record commodity prices—unlike Russia or other resource-rich nations that have posted trade surpluses as commodity prices began rising in 2003. Canada's performance lags because the country is sandbagged by three problems: the size and complicated nature of the Canadian political structure; government ownership of resources, and the investment of little effort to develop them; and the brain drain and capital outflow to the United States.

Fortunately, Canada is in better shape than before. In 1980, the country was in trouble. Inflation, triggered by the oil price shocks of 1973 and 1979, had reached 13.5 percent. In July 1981, a severe recession hit the United States and Canada. By 1982, unemployment had hit 10 percent in the U.S., and was even higher in Canada. The U.S. Federal Reserve increased interest rates to 21.5 percent; Canada's central bank followed suit, because it always follows the Fed, so Canada was also damaged by high interest rates and a collapse in commodity prices.

Canadian unions were as militant as Britain's and constantly on strike. Prime Minister Pierre Elliott Trudeau became embroiled in battles against separatists in Quebec and oil companies in Alberta. He was also uninterested in economics. In a brief interview, he once said that economics were not his *"métier."*

Trudeau's Transformation

Trudeau was a social democrat and bon vivant who dated famous women such as Barbra Streisand and maintained close friendships with Cuba's Fidel Castro and Jamaica's socialist leader Michael Manley. He was mainly elected to repair Canada's French–English divide. He brought in bilingualism, thumbed his nose at the Queen of England and stood up to Washington. He was also a trailblazer, and in 1970 he officially recognized Communist China, two years before President Richard Nixon's visit there.

Most significantly, he charted a course that rebranded Canada from a British-style colony to a bilingual social-democratic haven. Along the way, he borrowed heavily from France's welfare, statist and protectionist policies, imposed foreign-investment restrictions and created many subsidized state-owned enterprises, led by his centerpiece, Petro-Canada.

By 1982, he was preparing to leave politics, after sixteen years off and on as prime minister. But he realized that the country needed new solutions or it was headed toward disaster. A former academic, he assigned a research project to a former finance minister, Donald Macdonald, and asked him to examine all the country's policy options. The report was called the Royal Commission on the Economic Union and Development Prospects for Canada and was a sweeping, thorough undertaking that took three years to complete.

Macdonald was, like most Canadian leaders, a sophisticated and well-traveled professional. "The country was in dire straits, and Trudeau's instructions to me were to look at anything and everything. He said, 'We have to see what others are doing,'" Macdonald told me. "He did not exclude free trade with the Americans, but he warned me against it by saying to me 'open our markets to them and they'll eat our lunch.'"

Macdonald's Commission included twelve other persons, drawn from different regions, speaking different languages and selected from business, labor, government and all political parties. They crisscrossed the country, eliciting comments and briefs. They commissioned original research and tapped into academic studies from around the world. By September 1985, Macdonald was ready to publish the findings, and his Royal Commission published seventy-two volumes of research. But his report had reached a shocking recommendation that changed the country's course permanently: after examining all options, the Macdonald Commission concluded that Canada's best, and only, choice would be to approach the Americans and convince them to undertake a free-trade agreement.

The reasons, published in 1985, still apply today when it comes to approaching the Americans with a full-fledged merger: "As we peer into the future, there is only one central fact about which we can be reasonably certain: there are powerful forces loose around the

166

globe that will profoundly affect the lives of all of us here in Canada. The global outlook is full of danger signals; a majority of the world's citizens are facing very troubled prospects. . . . [e]conomic growth is critically dependent on secure access to foreign markets. Our most important market is the United States, which now takes up to three-quarters of our exports. More, better and more secure access to the U.S. market represents a basic requirement, while denial of that access is an ever-present threat. We are extremely vulnerable to any strengthening of U.S. protectionism. . . . Commissioners recommend that the Government of Canada . . . open negotiations with the Government of the United States to reach agreement on a substantial reduction of barriers, tariff and non-tariff, between Canada and the United States."[34]

Trudeau had left office by the time the Macdonald Commission completed its work, and he never commented publicly on the recommendation. Privately, he opposed free trade with the Americans, as did many other influential and powerful Canadians. Polling showed that Canadians were divided on the issue. Organized labor, protected industries and economic nationalists feared an outright hostile takeover by the Americans. Only the business community was in favor of such a deal, and as luck would have it, their preferred candidate, Brian Mulroney, had become the prime minister.

Mulroney had rejected free trade during the 1984 election contest, but after Macdonald's compelling recommendations in 1985, he embraced the policy and immediately approached President Ronald Reagan to start negotiations. The president welcomed the initiative, and Congress gave him the authority to sign a free-trade agreement with Canada, subject to it being presented for Congressional review by October 5, 1987. In May 1986, Canadian and American negotiators began to work out a trade deal.

Free Trade Finally

The agreement between the two countries removed most remaining tariffs and guaranteed access to one another's economies. Cultural, agricultural, softwood lumber and water issues were left out of the deal. The debate in Canada was emotional and raised fears of the country becoming the fifty-first state or that health care would be eliminated. Mulroney was accused of being "too American," so he called an election to decide the matter after polling showed support.

On November 21, 1988, Mulroney squeaked through with only 43 percent of the vote, due to his personal unpopularity and the fact that the opposition was divided among two other parties. Reagan, on the other hand, easily guided the deal through Congress in September, perhaps partly due to the fact that polls showed that 40 percent of Americans were unaware of the agreement.

The benefits were immediate. Trade between the two countries more than tripled, to $596.235 billion in 2011 from $166.761 billion in 1989. Even so, Canada's credit rating was downgraded from AAA to AA+ in April 1993, and another such cut was threatened in February 1995 because of overspending, the collapse of the Mexican peso and a looming referendum on secession in Quebec.

As Thomas Friedman writes, the Canadian Department of Finance, on the eve of releasing its 1995 budget, issued an uncharacteristically frightening statement designed to let the world's investors know it understood the seriousness of its situation: "The sheer magnitude of Canada's foreign debt in relation to the size of the economy means that Canada has become excessively vulnerable to the volatile sentiments of global financial markets. We have suffered a tangible loss of economic sovereignty."

"For those Canadians who might not have gotten the point," Friedman continued, "Finance Minister Paul Martin put it more bluntly: 'We are in hock up to our eyeballs.'"[35] Martin announced deep cuts to spending, as well as tax increases, which calmed the currency and debt markets. Boom years, and fiscal discipline, followed. Trade increased, the economy grew and the federal government balanced its budgets for twelve years in a row until the meltdown and recession of 2008. The debt rating was upgraded back to AAA in 1999.

A generation later, Canadians have grown to accept free trade. Opponents warned that there would be mass unemployment or the loss of entitlements such as health care or pensions, but none of that proved true. Canada's economy was back on track, anti-Americanism had abated, governments cut taxes, and many state-owned enterprises were closed or privatized. A larger share of the so-called mixed economy became privately held as trade boomed. Air Canada began flying directly to dozens of smaller U.S. cities due to increased trade, travel and business demand.

By 2000, an average of $2 billion worth of goods and services crossed the border every day. Canadian investment poured into the United States—in the first decades of the Free Trade Agreement, Canadian foreign direct investment in the U.S. nearly matched, in absolute dollars, American totals in Canada. The Canadian dollar began to move up from a low of 60 cents U.S. toward parity. So did incomes. In 1988, Canadian per capita incomes were $18,298, compared with $20,280 in the U.S. By 2012, Canadian incomes were slightly ahead of American incomes because of the higher value of the Canadian dollar.[36] But this, without accompanying productivity, could be unsustainable.

The Dutch Disease and the Brain Drain

The rise in the Canadian dollar has infected the country with a dose of the "Dutch Disease," an affliction caused when a booming resource sector drives up the value of a country's currency, which in turn drives costs so high at home that its export, manufacturing and tourism sectors cannot compete. In 2011, a report by Macro Research Board, a consulting firm in London and Montreal, described the national predicament.

"A severe case of Dutch Disease has dramatically reduced the breadth of the Canadian business sector over the past decade, hollowing out manufactured-goods exporters and making the nation increasingly reliant on commodity demand. Canada has often been referred to in jest as the 51st state, due to its historical reliance on the U.S. as a key export market. However, it is becoming more accurate to regard Canada as another Province of China," wrote Macro partner Phillip Colmar. Colmar was basically stating that Canada had become dependent on high commodity prices, which had been largely caused by China's economic boom, for its economic well-being.

"When China stumbles in the years ahead," pointed out Colmar, "and the commodity bull market comes to an end, Canada will suffer through a painful economic contraction. The fallout at that point will be prolonged due to the fact that the Canadian business sector is uncompetitive and the household sector has accumulated substantial leverage [debt] to live beyond its means."

By 2012, Canadian household debt had become higher than American levels—and than those in most rich nations—according to the OECD. And its two biggest provincial governments, Ontario and Quebec, were soon to match the federal government in indebtedness. The country was losing money, in trading terms, because it was deindustrializing but not capitalizing on its resource wealth to the extent that was possible. In the first decade of this new millennium, commodity exports had increased from 20 percent of total exports to nearly half, but this was because prices had jumped and also because manufacturing exports had tumbled from 32 percent to 17 percent. "Canada runs a substantial trade deficit. This presents a significant longer-term risk for the economy, and is shocking given the natural resource boom [around the world]," warned the Macro Research Board report.[37]

The brain drain has also taken its toll. Estimates are that between 1820 and 2002, about 4.5 million Canadians immigrated to the United States. "But statistics prior to the United States census of 1910 and the Canadian census of 1911 are estimated, as Canadian movements were treated as internal migration rather than international immigration, and there were almost no regulations before 1965."[38]

Homeland Security published tables that showed that 3,573,626 Canadians left between 1910 and 2011.[39] This shows that for much of its history Canada has served, in a sense, as America's farm team, initially supplying cheap labor for its Industrial Revolution and then, more recently, furnishing brainpower for its wealthy universities, endowments and clusters of excellence in the world of finance, the arts, science, technology and entertainment.

Significant numbers of Canadians populate America's world-class clusters of excellence, such as Silicon Valley, New York City and Hollywood. Another loss is apparent in the facts surrounding winners of the Nobel Prize. By 2011, Canadians had received twenty-one Nobel Prizes, but ten laureates had moved; and Americans had racked up 331, but eleven of these recipients had been born in Canada.[40]

It would be difficult to quantify these expatriates' contributions to the GDP, but the expatriate Canadian nation might even be generating more economic activity than Canada itself. The brain drain is damaging, and new immigration to date has not replenished the talent being lost.

CANADA'S FIRST NATIONS PROBLEM

Canada has failed to reach settlements involving 1,300 land claims with its over 630 First Nations, the Inuit and Métis (or persons with mixed European–aboriginal heritage). Australia has done a better job, which is why, partially, its resource boom and incomes began outpacing Canada's at the beginning of the twenty-first century. The U.S., which mistreated its aboriginals more than did Canada or Australia, established a process after the Second World War that finally dealt with some grievances and compensation claims.

Large-scale Canadian mining and energy projects, or even exploration initiatives, will continue to be difficult until claims are settled and land titles cleared. Inuit leader Nellie Cournoyea, the former premier of the Northwest Territories, who pushed for development of the Arctic natural gas pipeline for decades, blames federal government bureaucrats. The Inuvialuit signed a deal with the Canadian federal government in return for hundreds of millions of dollars, infrastructure projects, fishing and hunting rights to a large territory and management oversight. They were hoping to benefit from the natural gas and oil in the Northwest Territories and a pipeline called the Mackenzie Valley Gas Pipeline, which has been delayed by governmental incompetence for thirty years.

In an interview in 2010, Cournoyea blamed governments for pandering to "professional environmentalists" at the expense of the national interest. "The environmentalists should want the Mackenzie Valley Gas Pipeline but have fought it all for decades," she told me. "Natural gas is cleaner [than oil] and should be considered to be more valuable. There are the special-interest guys who want us to save the polar bear and politicians who want us to look like, as a country, we're doing something. But this is more about coal plants than anything else. The environmentalists make it all about polar bears because they can't close the coal mines and coal plants. We're caught in a vicious cycle. It's demoralizing."

In recent history, the only comprehensive land claims deals struck were in Nunavut, with the Inuit, and in Quebec, with the Cree. Nunavut was turned into a territorial government controlled by the Inuit, and in Quebec the federal government gave some $1.4 billion to 16,700 Cree people to settle land claims, which doesn't include hundreds of millions more that Cree people received from the province of Quebec in return for permission to build the world's second-largest hydroelectric project on their lands, a project that covers an area the size of New York State.

Canada could adopt policies from other countries—notably Australia's, described fully in chapter 7—or adopt the U.S. post-war solution, which would be to set up the equivalent of the 1946 Indian Claims Commission in Washington, a joint government and Native American body to expedite compensation. But until the land claims situation is properly addressed and resolved, Canada is a country with a gigantic lien on its landmass that will continue to discourage development.

The U.S. and Canada Remain Lucky

The United States and Canada have internal issues to resolve, but most countries would gladly swap places with them. But, like Google and Motorola, they also face external issues. Other countries indulge in dirty tricks, sabotage, counterfeiting, information theft, cheating, surreptitious maneuvers and geopolitical skullduggery. To meet this dark and volatile future, the U.S. and Canada need a new playbook.

In the business world, corporations facing such deteriorating conditions hunt for complementary and compatible partnerships or strategic alliances. Most importantly, they look for synergies in terms of assets, people and organizations, to enhance shareholder value by reducing costs and boosting profits. In the world of enterprising nation-states, a partnership between two successful countries would be a logical strategy. Joining their talented populaces, their capital and their technology to develop an untapped resource-rich region the size of Australia represents one of the greatest business, and geopolitical, opportunities in history. The combination would be unbeatable.

CHAPTER FOUR

The Benefits of a Merger

Synergy is the highest activity of life; it creates new untapped alternatives; it values and exploits the mental, emotional, and psychological differences between people.
—STEPHEN COVEY, AUTHOR OF *THE SEVEN HABITS OF HIGHLY EFFECTIVE PEOPLE*

THE TERM "SYNERGY" COMES FROM THE GREEK WORD *synergos*, which derives from the phrase "working together." Colloquially, synergy is the combination of two or more things that can produce a preferable result that otherwise would not be possible if they remained independent from one another. Mergers and acquisitions are all about synergy.

Ideally, if Canada and the United States combined, they would be able to cherry-pick the best policies and practices from each economy and adopt what works best for both. For instance, Canada's banking and regulatory system would be a good match with the American work ethic and entrepreneurial spirit. The tax rates in some jurisdictions would be lower than they are in Canada, except for Alberta.

The most obvious synergy would be matching Canada's undeveloped resource potential with America's money, markets and workers. Canada is the second-largest country in the world and is virtually unexplored because of lack of government support, lack of capital and lack of technology to explore and develop. Canada is also described as "a human capital constraint country," with a workforce of 18.3 million but looming, and serious, skilled labor shortages. Canada needs millions more workers to develop its resource base, and the United States faces a chronic unemployment and underemployment situation. In March 2012, economists Michael Greenstone and Adam Looney estimated that the "jobs gap" totaled 11.3 million jobs, "5.2 million from jobs lost since 2007, and another 6.1 million jobs that should have been created in the absence of the recession." Even if the economy continued to create 208,000 new jobs per month—the rate in the best year of the 2000s—it would take until 2020 to close the gap.[1] Simply put, to lower unemployment from 7.7% in 2012 to optimal rates of 4.5% in years past, millions more jobs must be created.

Already Merging

A hook-up would not be difficult, because the two nations have been integrating for years, economically and otherwise. Canada's oil and auto industries comprise more than half of all exports, and most of the firms are U.S. subsidiaries or Canadian companies that have a large percentage of American shareholders.

As stated previously, by 2010, foreign-owned businesses in Canada controlled one-fifth, or 19.7 percent, of all business assets. Of this, U.S. companies dominated the foreign-owned portion of Canada's economy, according to Statistics Canada, controlling 52.5 percent of all foreign-owned assets and 58.1 percent of all revenues and profits, for a net total of 10.3 percent of all assets, 16.79 percent of revenues and 13 percent of profits.[2]

In the U.S., foreign and Canadian ownership figures are lower, but they are misleading because they out of date. As noted earlier, a study in 2008 estimated that foreigners controlled 13.9 percent of all large U.S. companies, up from 1.3 percent in 1971.[3] A 2010 report estimated that Canadians represented 8.8 percent[4] of total foreign investments in large U.S. corporations, or 1.2 percent of the total.

Canada and the U.S also have similar foreign direct investments in one another's economies, another sign a merger is underway. By 2010, Americans had directly invested about $306 billion, or 54.5 percent of all foreign direct investment (FDI), in Canada. That doesn't count the hundreds of billions, possibly more, that Americans have invested in Canadian bonds and equities. FDI consists of long-term investments that involve some control over a company, ore body or subsidiary, as opposed to real estate, passive, short-term stock or bond investments.

By contrast, Canada's foreign direct investments in the U.S. totaled $249.9 billion,[5] or 14.7 percent of all FDI there in 2010.[6] This amount was second only to Britain, level with Japan and ahead of Germany, France and the Netherlands. Added to that investment stake, Canadian individuals have outpaced all other foreigners in buying condos and other real estate, mostly for their own use, and in 2011 bought 24 percent of all U.S. real estate acquired by "foreigners"[7] for the third year in a row.

To repeat, the two countries are also one another's biggest customers. In 2011, 73.7 percent of Canada's exports were sold to Americans, and 19 percent of all U.S. exports were sold to Canadians. Canada is the biggest export customer for thirty-six of the fifty states, and its 34.4 million residents bought more goods and services from Americans than did the 340 million people who live in the European Union's twenty-seven countries.[8]

As many as one in ten Canadians, or more than three million people, live full or part time in the U.S., and an estimated one million Americans live in Canada. There are also 698,025 First Nations members, according to the latest Canadian census, who have U.S.

citizenship as well as Canadian. About 250,000 Canadians, including eBay founder Jeff Skoll, live in Silicon Valley, according to the industry website bible TechCrunch in 2010. In addition to the high-tech industry, one in nine of Canada's physicians, as well as nearly one in ten nurses, regularly cross the border or work principally in the U.S. (for instance, five thousand nurses living in Windsor, Ontario, commute to work in Detroit daily).[9]

In 2007, Canada's consul-general in New York City, Pamela Wallin, estimated that roughly 350,000 Canadians worked every day in Manhattan in the financial, arts, legal, real estate, advertising and media sectors, most prominently real estate and media tycoon Mort Zuckerman and Lorne Michaels, creator and executive producer of *Saturday Night Live*, *30 Rock*, *Late Night with Jimmy Fallon*, *Portlandia* and dozens of films and other TV shows. Another 250,000 Canadians work in Hollywood, on and off camera, including Jim Carrey, Martin Short, Mike Myers, Pamela Anderson, Ryan Gosling, Ryan Reynolds, Michael Cera, Seth Rogen, Keanu Reeves, Donald Sutherland, Michael J. Fox, Catherine O'Hara, Margot Kidder, Rachel McAdams, Eugene Levy, Howie Mandel, Dan Aykroyd, Kiefer Sutherland, William Shatner, Norman Jewison, David Cronenberg and two of the five 2010 Oscar nominees for best director, James Cameron and Jason Reitman. Famous Canadian singers include Justin Bieber, Neil Young, Leonard Cohen, Drake, Céline Dion, Bryan Adams, Alanis Morissette, Sarah McLachlan, Shania Twain, Anne Murray, Joni Mitchell, Gordon Lightfoot and Michael Bublé. Well-known American-Canadian journalists and commentators include David Brooks, Charles Krauthammer, David Frum, the late Peter Jennings, Morley Safer and Robin MacNeil. The drain of talent to American universities has been constant and is now at its highest levels. As of 2012, for example, Robert J. Birgeneau, former president of the University of Toronto, had become chancellor of the University of California, Berkeley; molecular biologist Shirley Tilghman was president of Princeton University; and Ronald J. Daniels, former dean and professor of law at the University of Toronto Faculty of Law, was president of Johns Hopkins University.

Naturally, border traffic has become enormous. In 2009, Canadians made 39,254,000 trips to the U.S. and Americans made 20,213,500 trips to Canada. In 2010, more than 15,700,000 travelers flew between the two.[10]

Financial markets are also integrated. American capital markets are the biggest in the world and critical to the well-being of Canadian business. In 2011, the American-based equity exchanges had a market capitalization of $15.635 trillion, not counting the Chicago Board Options Exchange, the world's largest futures market. Canada's stock market, TMX Group, had a total capitalization of $1.9 trillion, but the majority of trades involve only 200 of its 4,800 stocks, with most of those trades being executed in the United States because of U.S. investor interest.

A merger would complete this integration and create the world's foremost business, creative, energy and mining superpower. Besides the oil sands, both countries have enough natural gas, a dramatically cleaner fuel, to last indefinitely. There are also discoveries of large amounts of "shale oil," or oil contained in deep shale rock deposits, now producible in four western states and provinces.

Pierre Lassonde, a talented mining investor and former president of Newmont Mining in Denver, noted at an analysts' seminar in 2012 that major investments in scientific research, of the sort that led to fracking, must be undertaken in order to unlock and develop resources in Canada's vast, remote and unoccupied wilderness. "Canada's strategic advantage is that it has the second-largest landmass in the world, and another advantage is that it is 98 percent unoccupied. But it is unexplored because of its size. Generally speaking, there must be technological advances in mining exploration and extraction, such as 3D seismic [to find remote resources by satellite or heat sensors] or in situ leaching [separating the ore underground before bringing it to surface]. This R&D would cost billions and have to be done by universities and major corporations. It would involve research in physics and electricity. Have the last deposits been found in Canada? Nowhere near," he said.

Only the United States, through its federal government, universities, Silicon Valley and giant corporations such as Exxon Mobil, has the hundreds of billions to invest in science and technology. Canada's governments have made meager commitments to research and development. For instance, its federal government made a relatively tiny investment of $100 million over five years in geo-mapping to try to pinpoint mineralization in Canada's territories. But this is inadequate. Only full partnership with the United States, giving it a stake in co-development, will bring about technological advances and economic development of the North. This partnership would also lead to research into better environmental practices in the oil sands and mining, as well as investments in Canada's greener power prospects, such as hydroelectricity, wind, solar and tidal.

Lassonde also pointed out the competitive advantage of emptiness. Because Canada is uninhabited, development could be streamlined, in contrast to the delays and obstacles that occur in densely populated areas. These situations plague the power, transmission and resource industries despite public demand and the need for such projects to maintain living standards.

The Two Countries Could Remain
the World's Technological Superpower

The history of Silicon Valley—the Santa Clara Valley near San Francisco, which has become synonymous with high technology—is far from finished. Its denizens, who come from all over the world, are reinventing the world, and since 1912 the region has been a hub of innovation with an economic output that rivals most nation-states. That year, Lee De Forest headed a team that amplified sound through the vacuum tube. This technology led to the radio, radar, television, the tape recorder and the electronic computer. The team worked for the Federal Telegraph Company in Palo Alto, which had been enticed to the region by Stanford University associates. This startup led directly to the creation of Magnavox and Litton Industries.

But an electrical engineer and member of Stanford's faculty, Dr. Frederick Terman, is the one who became the father of Silicon Valley. He built the university's electronics and electrical engineering programs, but more important, he also encouraged faculty and students to create startups. Ownership of the intellectual property created as a result of their efforts would be shared with Stanford to encourage activity. Among the offspring of this entrepreneurial approach were Hewlett-Packard and, most recently, Google.

At a recent lecture in Silicon Valley, I learned how Dr. Terman played a geopolitically important role. In 1942, during the Second World War, he was tapped to help crack Germany's air defense and surveillance system, which used seven hundred radar installations and thousands of guns to track and destroy Allied bombers. Terman led a secret project at Harvard University, called the Radio Research Laboratory, with a staff of 850, and by 1943 had come up

183

with techniques that neutralized the German air-defense shield and helped turn the tide of the war.[11] Such "electronic warfare" allowed bombers to penetrate European airspace.

Terman returned to Stanford, and his startup model proliferated in the Valley, leading to world-shaping technologies that have benefited, and protected, the world since. The university has remained a center of excellence, and the region has prospered, even sailing through the U.S. recession and housing collapse of 2008–09. Property values skyrocketed in Palo Alto and local towns, even as values in the rest of the country cratered. Unemployment was considerably lower than the national average.[12]

Engineering, math, sciences and computer science drive innovation, and the United States remains the world's foremost player. Canada punches above its weight, due to the need for engineers in a resource-based economy, so a combination of the two nations would enhance the competitiveness of both. Canada had 250,000 engineers by 2011,[13] while the U.S. employed 1.5 million in 2006.[14] Canada graduates more in these fields—22 percent, compared with 15 percent in the United States.[15]

America leads the world in research and development investments, and Canada again punches above its weight. The Battelle Memorial Institute and R&D magazine forecast that the United States will spend a total of $423.7 billion on research and development in 2013 (based on GDP at purchasing-power parity). Second-place China is expected to spend $220.2 billion, while Canada, at $30.9 billion, would rank eleventh in the world, just behind Brazil ($31.9 billion) and ahead of Taiwan ($22.4 billion). At 2.1 percent of GDP, Canada's expenditure is about 20 percent higher than the world average.

The largest R&D spenders in the world will be U.S. private industry, at an expected $262 billion; the U.S. federal government is forecast to spend $129 billion, while academia is to account for $12.7 billion. Battelle projected that nonprofits and lower levels of government will spend $16 billion. Put another way, America's nonprofits and academia together invest nearly as much as Canada.

Energy research in the U.S. is expected to reach $5.83 billion, about 37 percent of the global total of $15.95 billion. Information and communication technology research was forecast to increase to $151.9 billion, compared with a worldwide total of $286.6 billion. The U.S. and Japan comprise 70 percent of all such spending, said Battelle.[16] The Americans will also increase investment in chemical and materials research to $10.7 billion, compared with the global total of $42 billion.[17]

These expenditures, and others in fields such as nanotechnology, robotics and biosciences, are critical to maintaining economic pre-eminence. And size matters. Currently, Canadian scientists and engineers, interested in pursuing underfunded new technologies, must emigrate to American clusters of excellence such as Silicon Valley or the high-tech region around Harvard and MIT.

America's universities and technology companies are at the forefront of technologies such as driverless cars; nanorobots to monitor bodily functions and administer medicines; virtual surgery stations that allow physicians to operate remotely; revolutionary 3-D "printing," or labor-free manufacturing that is able to print shoes for Nike and may one day produce simple organs like bladders for doctors; techniques to "hack" into the DNA of bacteria and enzymes to grow non-polluting fuels and speed up photosynthesis to increase food production; and other breakthroughs. The list reads like the stuff of science fiction, and no other country can, or will, keep pace.

This means that, whether it is a breakthrough in computers, medicine or energy recovery, a U.S.–Canada collaboration would benefit both countries, but would also provide research opportunities in all regions in order to better deliver diverse and future benefits to all the world.

The Two Countries Could Become the World's Energy Superpower

The U.S. and Canada already have enough reserves to become permanently self-sufficient in terms of energy. The United States still imports more oil than any other nation, and consumption began outpacing production in the 1970s. But around 2008, this began to reverse. By 2011, only 10 percent of natural gas was imported and oil imports had fallen to 10 million barrels a day, down from the peak of 13 million a day in 2007.

The reverse was due to increased oil and natural gas production, as well as a drop in demand triggered by the recession, conservation due to high prices, higher fuel-efficiency standards and the replacement of nearly 10 percent of gasoline with ethanol. In February 2012, Citibank issued a report, forecasting independence even earlier, called "Energy 2020: North America, the New Middle East?"

In November 2012, the International Energy Agency report agreed with these forecasts and gave them credibility. The United States was on track to become energy independent by 2035 with Canada's help. Historically, Canada's energy situation has been different. The country has been self-sufficient in oil and natural gas for decades and has become the largest exporter of oil, natural gas and electricity to the United States.

Obviously, if the two become partners they could freely use one another's energy and export the rest. They could export surplus natural gas in liquefied form, use natural gas to generate electricity, and convert vehicles to natural gas as a transportation fuel to reduce oil dependency and lower emissions. The gasification of vehicle fleets is beginning, and in 2012 Royal Dutch Shell and others announced plans in both Canada and the U.S. to provide long-distance trucks with liquefied natural gas.

Environmentally, a merger would also provide an opportunity to coordinate policies as well as to organize the financial and scientific backing to do research, build carbon-sequestration facilities and invent technologies to reduce or eliminate emissions. For instance, a concerted effort to switch to natural gas from coal and gasoline would clean up the environment dramatically. Natural gas emits 30 percent less carbon dioxide than oil and 45 percent less than coal.

Another synergy would be the creation of a binational electricity planning process to optimize efficiencies and reduce emissions by closing dirty plants and replacing them with clean hydroelectric, wind, solar, tidal and geothermal resources, located mostly in Canada. Roughly 42 percent of America's electricity comes from burning coal, and only 8 percent from hydropower. In Canada, 62.9 percent comes from hydropower and 16.1 percent from coal.[18] The Canadian Hydropower Association has estimated that Canada's untapped potential is 163,000 megawatts—more than twice the country's existing capacity—all of which could be exported to the U.S.[19] This power potential is seven times greater than China's Three Gorges Dam, and it's equivalent to 14 percent of all installed power capacity in the United States.

Wind and solar power could be generated where building them made the most sense. Canada has the greatest wind potential in the world: the world's second-largest (and largely empty) landmass; the world's longest coastline; the world's largest interior bodies of water, such as Hudson's Bay and the Great Lakes. Offshore wind farms, and farms on the vast tundra, could generate enormous amounts of power for the North as well as for populated regions to the south. Nuclear reactors could be built in remote regions, near uranium mines in northern Saskatchewan, and connected to the continental power grid. These sources could provide power to gigantic underground server farms, used by Google and others, to store information. Such facilities are best built in cold, remote areas. In essence, a merger would lead to the rationalization and remix of the continental grid to realize efficiencies and environmental benefits.

The existing political border makes exploitation of Canada's potential unattainable. Cross-border megaprojects are impossible to finance due to political risks as well as due to the rivalries and limitations of local utilities. For instance, a contract to develop and export power from Manitoba's Nelson River system fell apart in the mid-1980s when U.S. states such as North Dakota insisted on huge "wheeling" fees in return for permission to allow transmission lines to link Manitoba with its utility customers in Kansas. The project was never completed. A new proposal was initiated in 2012 by Manitoba, Minnesota and Wisconsin to develop the Nelson River, but it may take decades to iron out due to conflicting national interests.

Such barriers have stranded the world's most promising hydro-electric and tidal power prospects in Quebec, British Columbia, Manitoba, Newfoundland and Nova Scotia. The highest tides in the world are in Nova Scotia's Bay of Fundy, and the second highest are in British Columbia. The technology exists to harness these and other tides, but without guaranteed access to the American market these projects can never be designed, financed and built.

They Could Become the World's
Agricultural–Agribusiness Superpower

Former Canadian Prime Minister John Diefenbaker was elected in 1957 and intended to sell up to 10 percent of Canada's water to the Americans for billions, a concept endorsed at the time by the Canadian Association of Geographers. Interestingly, the United States has as many renewable water resources as does Canada, but the rain in both countries does not fall where the need is greatest. The misallocation of rainfall, if corrected, could dramatically increase the amount of arable land available in both countries. And a water megaproject, designed by a Canadian engineer in the 1950s, would have solved many problems in both countries. It never got off the ground, after being bogged down by financial and political concerns, but a scheme like it could succeed if there was a merger.

In 1959, a Canadian engineer named Tom Kierans unveiled a system of canals and rivers, based on the California Aqueduct and the Zuider Zee Works in the Netherlands, that variously generated power, moved water, reclaimed land and drained massive amounts of water. The Dutch finished their project in 1924 after damming the Zuider Zee inlet, on the North Sea, to improve flood control and create more farmland. The American Society of Civil Engineers cited it as one of the seven wonders of the modern world.

Kierans' project was even more ambitious. The problem in North America was not volume of water, but its location. The southwestern portion of the United States suffered from droughts, while the northeast had enormous precipitation. In 1959, Canada officially claimed that the Americans had expanded the "Chicago diversion" of water from Lake Michigan to meet their needs, and that this was adversely lowering water levels in Canadian lakes near the Great

Lakes. The government added that studies had shown there were no additional sources of freshwater available.

Kierans disputed this and unveiled a scheme that could solve the water issues for both countries. Some 60 percent of North America's rain falls in the northeastern portion of the continent, in Ontario and Quebec, where only 6 percent of the population lives. Kierans' concept was to use a series of outflow-only dikes to capture freshwater runoff from precipitation as it flowed into James Bay—before it mixed with the salty water of Hudson Bay. This water would be diverted into a reservoir and channeled through a series of canals into the Great Lakes. This excess water could be pumped to water-deficient areas of the U.S. or Canada.

He called it the Great Recycling and Northern Development Canal, or GRAND Canal.[20] In 1994, the project's estimated cost to build was $100 billion, and to operate and move the water—17 percent of Ontario and Quebec's freshwater—would cost $1 billion a year. The project caused quite a splash in newspapers and was endorsed in 1985 by Quebec Premier Robert Bourassa and major engineering firms. But environmentalists fiercely opposed the scheme.

"Unfortunately, their political influence continues to block Canadian government support for the urgently needed detailed studies of recycled runoff from James Bay. Until the government supports such studies, drought and freshwater quality in Canada and the U.S. will continue to worsen," said Kierans.

Objections could have been overcome, but the project's cost required commitments from both countries and local jurisdictions. Instead, two rivers in Ontario were diverted into the Great Lakes to compensate for the "Chicago Diversion" outflow. But the Kierans project in theory remains valid, and is another example of a project that can only happen if the two unite.

Canada has 1 percent of the world's population and 20 percent of its water, which includes half of the Great Lakes shared with the United States. Canada has 3,300 trillion liters of renewable water resources (replenishable by precipitation) and the United States has 3,069 trillion liters, according to the *World Factbook*. This ranks them third and fourth in the world in terms of water supplies.

To compare, China has 20 percent of the world's population and 7 percent of its global water supply. The Middle East has 5 percent of the world's population and 1 percent of its water. Bulk shipments and water pipelines within North America could overcome shortages and enhance agriculture. At a conference in Washington in 2010, a water consultant estimated that a link from Manitoba to Texas would cost $9 billion, but revenues would be $7 billion a year.

Manitoba, Newfoundland, Quebec and British Columbia would be in the best position to make bulk shipments, but the politics would be impossible without a merger. In 2010, American investment banker Mike Milken met with Prime Minister Stephen Harper to discuss a comprehensive and lucrative water deal for Canada that he told associates would eliminate the country's debt. But Milken's scheme was rejected out of hand. Even so, selling water to a thirsty world may someday become a lucrative business for Canada, the United States and others with surplus water resources, whether people desire it or not.

An increase in water supplies could enhance agricultural output in both countries. Already, the United States and Canada are two of the world's most important agricultural nations. The United States is self-sufficient and the world's biggest exporter of agricultural products. Canada is the world's sixth-largest exporter. The United States has 1,669,310 square kilometers of arable land with permanent crops, the size of Iran. Canada has 474,681 square kilometers of arable land with permanent crops, slightly larger than Sweden's total landmass. Some estimates claim that America could double its acreage devoted to agriculture if more irrigation were available. An alliance would create the world's breadbasket—a huge competitive advantage in an increasingly crowded, and prosperous, world.

They Could Become the World's Economic Superpower

About 89 percent of Canada, an area larger than Australia, is Crown land or is owned by governments and is virtually untouched. The ten provinces own 48 percent of the country, while the federal government owns 41 percent, mostly in the three Arctic territories— the Northwest Territories, Yukon and Nunavut. The Yukon is bigger than California; the Northwest Territories are twice the size of Texas. Nunavut, 17 percent of which is owned by the Inuit who live there, is as big as Alaska and Montana combined. Despite such vast territory, the population of Canada's three northernmost territories is roughly 100,000. Canada has thirteen subnational governments, and twelve are big enough, and rich enough, to be independent nation-states.

In the United States, 60.2 percent of the land is privately owned. The United States federal government, through various departments and agencies, directly owns about 31 percent for use as military bases or testing grounds, for parks and reserves and as Indian reservations. The other 8.7 percent is divided unevenly among the fifty state governments.

Vast public ownership makes exploration and development difficult. The fact is that Canada is already a mining superpower, as is the United States, but Canada's potential is greater. As estimated by Wayne Goodfellow, in chapter 3, up to $15 trillion worth of metals and minerals could be found—a sum more than ten times the size of Canada's economy—if governments got their acts together and paved the way so that industry had greater access to these untouched lands. This does not include the potential for oil and natural gas.

In Canada, development in these areas has been neglected because the lands are managed by government bureaucrats, while the United States has exploited its land in a much more effective way, as the private sector has been allowed to drive economic development.

The two countries' approaches to development diverged after the War of Independence. The Americans repudiated Crown lands and Crown estate and privatized. That never happened in Canada. The British retained the feudal rights and strategically meted out small amounts of land along the U.S. border to war veterans, mercenaries and loyalists who left the U.S. for Canada during and after the American Revolution. This allocation of land was remuneration for the loyalists' service, but it was strategic as well, as these men would become the shock troops necessary to repel an American invasion after the Revolution, as they did in 1812, when a few thousand U.S. militia invaded Canada. This ribbon of privately owned land along the border is where the country grew and where most Canadians now live.

The high degree of public ownership makes Canada one of the richest countries in the world. For example, the 4.5 million people living in British Columbia may or may not own private property in the southernmost portion of the province, which represents 6 percent of the province's landmass, but all of them indirectly and collectively own, in the form of provincial Crown lands, the other 94 percent of the province, an area as big as Texas and Colorado combined. In addition, British Columbians share, with other Canadians, ownership of the Arctic and the country's offshore rights through their federal government. Canada is like a gigantic trust fund run by risk-averse bureaucrats, generating no income—only losses—on behalf of 34.4 million people who have no idea they indirectly own the place. Put another way, Canada is the world's biggest real estate and resource opportunity.

The United States has taken a much different approach, as noted. In Asia, where government-controlled economies have left no stone unturned, the Canadian model of benign neglect would never have worked. (If Singapore's Lee Kuan Yew had been prime minister of Canada after the Second World War, he would have created an executive committee of technocrats and consultants drawn from many disciplines, with the power to optimize all of its resources and real estate.)

If the U.S. and Canada merged, the Canadian economy would become, in a handful of years, several times larger. Canada's GDP in 2011 was $1.385 trillion (spread across a population of 34.4 million), compared with California's $1.9 trillion in 2010 (with 36.9 million residents). To be fair, Canada is not exactly California. It may be bigger than Australia, but it has a hostile climate and probably fewer highways than Los Angeles.

But Alaska, for one, has overcome its hostile climate and remote geography and has had a booming energy and mining sector for two generations, with a population of 710,532 people. Alaska and Russia alike have put Canada to shame by overcoming identical obstacles. The Alaska Pipeline was built eight years after discovery and had produced 16 billion barrels by 2010, whereas Canada's Mackenzie Delta and Beaufort Sea region have been undeveloped for more than three decades due to Canadian government incompetence.

The Russians—whether czarist, communist or free market— have also built up the economy in their hinterland. By 2010, Siberia had a population of 36 million, bigger than Canada's, and was the world's biggest oil producer. In 1891, Nicholas II, the future czar of Russia, financed construction of the Trans-Siberian Railway to open up Russia's frozen hinterland to settlement and development. After the communist revolution, billions of rubles were invested in the territory to build cities, ports, shipping facilities, roads, power projects, dams, landing strips, airports, housing, infrastructure, exploration, oil and natural gas development, lumber and paper mills, smelters, steel mills, refineries, pipelines and mines. By 2010, seven Siberian cities had populations of 500,000 or more. The biggest, Novosibirsk, is nicknamed the "Chicago of Siberia," has a skyline of tall buildings and is home to 1.5 million people.

By contrast, Canada's Arctic was untouched except for a handful of French explorers who obtained financing from the British Crown to tap the fur trade in the region. Prospecting for gold led to the 1897 Klondike Gold Rush in the Yukon and some small settlements and mines. More gold was discovered in the Yellowknife Bay area around the same time, but remained untapped because the location was too remote. Several mines operated until the Second World War, when workers left to join the armed forces, and then an exploration program at the Giant Mine property discovered a sizable gold deposit. Staking resulted, and the population grew to about 1,000. Then, in 1967, the town became the capital of the Northwest Territories and its population grew again.

The gold ran out in 2004, but diamonds had been discovered for the first time in Canada in 1991, and several mines were built. By 2011, Canada had become the world's third-biggest diamond producer, after Botswana and Russia. Yellowknife became Canada's largest Arctic "city," with a population of 18,700 and one ten-story building.

In 2007, after the Russians planted their flag at the North Pole, Ottawa outlined a "Northern Strategy" and allocated money to build some infrastructure and invest $100 million over five years to geo-map its northern territories. Data would be made available to interested parties so that they could determine whether leasing lands for exploration was viable.

It was, as usual, a good idea executed poorly. The amount of investment was insignificant given the size of the North. By comparison, Geoscience Australia had been spending around $158 million annually to map and encourage resource development on lands one-quarter the size of Canada's Arctic. The allocation of $20 million a year to map the Arctic was minuscule by comparison, and even less than Canadian politicians spent every year building hockey arenas or roads to garner votes in southern cities.

The ultimate synergy would be to finally connect Canadian development prospects with American money and mining capacity. Canada is already one of the world's biggest mining export nations, but only the low-hanging fruit—deposits found near existing railroad or waterways—has been picked. The only mines that make sense in the hinterland involve commodities, such as diamonds and gold, that are hugely valuable and cost-efficient to transport.

Russia's construction of a transcontinental railroad opened up its hinterland to massive mining and energy development. Rail access was essential because most resources were inland and too bulky or heavy to transport to markets by any other means. Canada's transcontinental railroad hugged the U.S. border, but even so, it also opened up exploration and development. For instance, one of the world's biggest nickel deposits, in Sudbury, Ontario, was found after the railroad was finished in 1883 and the area became accessible. Interestingly, American inventor Thomas Edison came to the region in 1901 and made a significant nickel discovery there. (His father was Canadian, but left for the United States after he participated in an armed insurrection by colonials in 1837 in Ontario against British control led by the first mayor of Toronto, called William Lyon Mackenzie, who also fled south.)

Likewise, the commodity boom led to high prices for iron ore along the Labrador–Quebec border in a geological anomaly called the Labrador Trough. The ore is located along a band that measures 1,500 kilometers by 100 kilometers. The Geological Survey of Canada identified the resource in 1864, but nothing happened until 1954, when a rail line built by a partnership of American and Canadian private-sector companies opened up development. Other mines followed suit, and the ore was transported to Canadian and American steel mills until the 1980s, when production ebbed.

Since 2003, international companies have announced billions of dollars in mining projects in the Trough because high prices for steel and iron ore justified development. One project involves building an open-pit mine on Baffin Island in the Arctic Archipelago, where temperatures year-round average minus-30 degrees Celsius. Despite hostile conditions, Canada has the potential to become a major player in virtually all commodities but lacks the will, corporations and cash to make it happen. World production of iron ore in 2010 was 2.4 billion tonnes, according to the U.S. Geological Survey. China produced 900 million tonnes, Australia 420 million and Canada only 35 million.[21]

Canada lags in iron ore, but in little else. It is the world's third-largest producer of aluminum, ranks fifth in diamonds (and third in terms of their value) and second in uranium, is in the top five in molybdenum, nickel and salt, and in the top ten in gold and copper.[22] This is despite the fact that most of Canada has never been explored or visited by humans. All that would be needed to truly tap this wealth would be a Marshall Plan of sorts, or an infrastructure build out on an American, or Chinese, scale.

Instead, development has been restricted to those resource companies that can afford to build their own railroads, roads, ports, airstrips and power generation facilities. This investment, worthless after the mine stops producing, is only justifiable if deposits are gigantic and production can last for decades. Even then, costs have been so prohibitive that development is uneconomic because everything—from building materials to people, fuel and food—must be brought in by helicopter.

An example is the Howard's Pass lead-zinc formation in the Yukon, the world's largest such formation. Chinese mining interests have optioned the property, but they must spend at least $100 million simply to determine the viability of building a mine, mill, town, railroad, roads, power plant and airport to extract then export the ore over thirty years or so.[23]

A Marshall Plan for mining would yield another spin-off economic benefit because it would repatriate American and Canadian mining companies now forced to operate in dangerous or confiscatory jurisdictions around the world. Optimizing Canada's mining potential would also provide trade leverage over resource-challenged rivals in China, Japan, South Korea, Europe and elsewhere. For instance, countries buying resources could also be required to buy manufactured or value-added goods and services made in the merged U.S.–Canada, as Brazil and others have already begun to stipulate. This would mean deals to buy steel, and not just iron ore; pipes and transmission wires, not just copper; lumber, paper, furniture or building modules, not logs and pulp; and cars, trucks, planes, trains, financial services and machinery.

The Arctic could be developed responsibly, as Norway's Statoil has done with its extensive development in sensitive northern regions. This government-owned oil giant has explored and built—after extensive consultations with both local and national taxpayers and residents—gathering and liquefied natural gas facilities that export around the world. Engineering advances have dramatically reduced the environmental footprint attached to fossil fuel production in the Norwegian north, while simultaneously reducing costs and the risk of accidents.

Statoil is a model of state capitalism, and it has signed a memorandum of understanding with the U.S. National Oceanic and Atmospheric Administration—along with Shell and ConocoPhillips—to collaborate in the Arctic. The same sort of private-public partnership could, and should, include Canada's vast northern region, now dormant for decades due to a lack of political will.

They Could Have the World's Strongest Currency

A merger and monetary union would bolster living standards. The common currency would be backed by massive resources and enhanced economic prospects. Canada would avoid the "Dutch Disease," because commodity price inflation would not make manufacturing uncompetitive compared with the United States. Rather, its impact would be spread across the common currency area. A common currency would also eliminate the friction and costs to businesses that result from the fluctuating monetary values.

Between 1957 and 2010, the Canadian dollar has been worth as much as U.S.$1.07 and as little as 63 cents. This wreaks havoc on businesses. Besides, if the two currencies remain separate, the danger is that higher commodity prices will drive the Canadian dollar so high that the country's eastern region will completely deindustrialize. In my opinion, even if the two countries weren't to merge, they should still strongly consider merging currencies as soon as possible.

The creation of a common dollar would not result in the same fate that has befallen the euro. The problem with the euro has been that seventeen European Union countries have shared a common currency but not a common budget or central controls over spending. This has allowed irresponsible spending by Greece, Portugal and others and has undermined the euro's value. If the Eurozone members had merged their central banks and fiscal policies, there would not have been a crisis. The U.S. and Canada each have a central bank, but the two work in concert already and abide by similar policies.

Of course, currencies are only strong if their trade is positive and governments don't run up unmanageable debts. Control over government spending would be key. The track record of both countries is mixed, but the fact that the issue of debts and deficits remains prominent on both political agendas is a good sign that runaway expenditures are unlikely, merged or not. Besides, rating agencies keep governments in line and impose discipline.

Canada had driven itself into the debt ditch by 1995 and was downgraded on the credit scale. It recouped its AAA rating after a few years. The United States, downgraded in 2011, can also restore fiscal discipline and its credit reputation. But a merger would help fix the fiscal situations, because new revenues and jobs would be generated. Even if debts remained at current levels in absolute dollars, enhanced activity would reduce the debt in relative terms. This would translate into a stronger currency and lower interest rates than would otherwise be the case, reducing debt-servicing costs. In other words, an alliance could turn around these two countries' current economic situations more quickly than if there were no alliance.

Another benefit would be an opportunity to cut costs by eliminating duplication. If Canada and the U.S. were joined, there would be no need for two separate military forces and their administrative costs. Because of resource self-sufficiency and a secure northern border, there would also be less need for a military the size of America's.

Canadians spend 1.4 percent of GDP on average on military forces, the Americans 4.8 percent, by some calculations. If Canadian–U.S. military forces merged and total expenditures were reduced to 3 percent, still nearly double what others spend, the savings to taxpayers could be more than $300 billion a year, or nearly half what Washington spent on defense in 2011. There could also be savings by combining the other federal governmental bureaucracies.

The Best Synergy Would Be People

Before 1910, there were no restrictions on border crossing or employment, so millions of people traveled back and forth for jobs, to join the military or to pursue opportunities. Until the twentieth century, the two countries really operated as though they were one. The result was that some of the most successful industries, such as the telephone, the automobile and the oil industry in Alberta, were binational collaborations.

For instance, Alexander Graham Bell immigrated as a young man with his parents to Ontario from Scotland in 1870. He pursued a career as an elocutionist, and then began commuting regularly to Boston to teach deaf people. He also conducted research at home and at Boston University, where he found money and American financiers to support his efforts. In August 1876, he proved to the world that his telephone gadget worked. He was able to receive a vocal message transmitted to his Brantford, Ontario, home from an office several miles away. The sound traveled along a wire strung along farm fences.

Bell and his American partners obtained the first telephone patents in the British Empire, then the United States, and formed the

Bell Telephone Company. By 1894, Bell's original patent had expired and the market was opened up to six thousand new telephone carriers. But he pursued his experiments and invented the hydrofoil and several aeronautical innovations. He died in 1922, at the age of seventy-five, at his estate in Nova Scotia. Three countries claim him as one of their greatest men—Canada, the U.S. and Scotland—but he was based in Ontario and Nova Scotia for most of his life. The Bell story is not unique.

The Auto Industry

Another bilateral success has been the collaborative effort to build the automotive and petroleum sectors. These unique, and unappreciated, partnerships illustrate how well Americans and Canadians work together despite political obstructions. Without a border, the partnership would flourish even more.

The city of Detroit, on the U.S.–Canada border, has changed hands several times in the past three centuries, before and after war. In 1701, a French officer named Antoine de la Mothe Cadillac, along with fifty-one French-Canadians, settled there and called it Fort Pontchartrain du Détroit. Pontchartrain was a French aristocrat, and *détroit,* or "strait," referred to the river between lakes Huron and Erie. Years later, the British captured the settlement and shortened the name to Detroit. In the War of Independence, the town fell into American hands, then British, and back again in 1794.

This little border town would eventually become one of the world's foremost technological and industrial capitals. Its waterways connected iron ore mines in northern Michigan and Canada to foundries, steel mills, coal mines, labor and markets farther south.

Its proximity to raw materials made it the ideal crossroads for heavy industry. It also attracted talent and was the Silicon Valley of its day.

Eber Brock Ward came to Michigan with his parents, who were attracted to farming and the state's shipping industry. Records indicate that he was born in Ontario, but what's definitely known is that he became one of America's foremost industrialists. His career began when he joined his wealthy uncle in a shipbuilding and transport company. By 1855, he had become a ship's captain and decided to diversify by acquiring the rights to a steel-making process invented in Britain by Sir Henry Bessemer. The revolutionary process could produce steel for one-seventh the cost and in half the time. With this technology, Ward opened the Eureka Iron and Steel Company in Wyandotte, Michigan, downriver from Detroit.

The Bessemer process paved the way for the industrialization of Detroit. Ward's Eureka Iron made steel for the Union Army during the Civil War. He then profited from America's expansion westward by making potbelly stoves, barbed wire for homesteaders and miles of railroad tracks. During this time, agriculture, and the availability of land, attracted Europeans and Canadians to the region.

William Ford left Ireland for Montreal. He stayed briefly before reuniting with relatives in Michigan. He bought land and ran a successful farm where he raised his children. But his son, Henry, didn't like farming. He preferred to tinker with his father's agricultural machinery and eventually became one of the world's most famous men and the greatest automaker and industrialist in history.

Young Henry left home for a series of jobs as a mechanic, and eventually became an engineer at one of the region's many hotbeds of innovation, the Edison Illuminating Company, which became Westinghouse. While employed there, he briefly met the company's founder and inventor, Thomas Edison (whose parents also came from Canada to the U.S.). Years later, after Ford's and Edison's huge successes, the two would become lifelong friends.

In 1896, Ford founded the Ford Motor Company and tapped into an abundance of mechanics and engineers who were inventing new engines, brakes, gears and other technologies to replace horsepower. He had built his own horseless carriage prototype, but the market was small. They were expensive and were bought mostly as novelties by wealthy people. Ford changed all that.

He decided to make a car for a mass market and produced the reasonable and reliable Model T. He kept expanding his operation by cutting costs and prices. In 1913, he revolutionized manufacturing by adding a conveyor belt to the assembly line, enabling his workers to put together a car in ninety-three minutes. The price of the Model T tumbled from $850 in 1908 to $260 in 1924, and mass production had become a way of life.

In 1904, a Canadian named Gordon McGregor approached Ford. His family owned the Walkerville Wagon Company Limited in Windsor, Ontario, and he explained to his brothers: "There are men in Detroit who say every farmer will soon be using an automobile. I don't see why we can not build them here in the wagon factory."

They struck a deal that took Ford global. McGregor got the exclusive rights to make and market Fords in Canada and took advantage of the British Empire's tariff liberalization, which allowed manufacturers in one British jurisdiction to export throughout the rest of the empire. By 1927, Ford and Ford Canada had become the world's largest automobile manufacturer, with plants in South Africa, Australia and New Zealand and export markets throughout the British Empire.

At the same time, another entrepreneur surfaced by the name of William "Billy" Durant, a silver-tongued promoter from a French-Canadian family. He invented a different business model than

Ford's. He gave consumers a choice of cars and created a network of franchised dealers to sell and service them. He called his company General Motors. He, too, joined forces with a Canadian, Sam McLaughlin of Oshawa, Ontario, and they exported GM vehicles tariff-free throughout the British Empire. By the 1930s, the Canadian-made Buick became the royal family's car of choice.

Durant also became involved with Walter Percy Chrysler, whose family had been German pioneers for many generations in Chatham, Ontario. His father served in the Union Army and became a railroad engineer. Walter became a master mechanic. In 1911, he agreed to run the Buick factory for new proprietors of General Motors who had pushed Durant out briefly. When Durant made his comeback two years later, he paid Chrysler $10,000 a month, equivalent to $165,000 a month in 2010 dollars, plus stock options.

Three years later, Chrysler elected to strike out on his own and cashed in his options for $10 million. Within years, he bought control of the Maxwell Motor Company and turned it into the Chrysler Corporation. He also personally financed construction of the Chrysler Building in Manhattan, an art deco masterpiece topped off with eagles modeled after Plymouth hood ornaments.

These three companies became the economic cornerstones of both nations and converted their operations into war-armament machines when needed. After the Second World War, the two countries were the largest economies left standing. Industries worked overtime as governments improved and expanded infrastructure. Highway systems were built, crisscrossing the continent, and the St. Lawrence Seaway—the most expensive project of its kind in history—was completed after decades of discussion.

Growth was driven by demand for housing, cars and goods at home, by the influx of millions of Europeans escaping war-torn Europe, and by the Marshall Plan, or the rebuilding of western Europe. The population of the U.S. exploded from 132 million in 1940 to 152 million by 1950 and 180.6 million by 1960. Canada's grew from 11.38 million in 1940 to 13.7 million in 1950 and 17.87 million in 1960.

The U.S. was the world's biggest manufacturer of vehicles, while Canada was the second biggest, with half its output destined for export. But as the 1950s ended, Canada's car sales began sputtering. Its tariff-free export privileges throughout the Commonwealth began to disappear just as the sun began to set on the British Empire. Leaders panicked. If nothing changed, Canada would lose its manufacturing base and would run huge trade deficits as cars were imported. Detroit was also concerned about losses at its branch plants in Canada and the prospect of losing the Canadian market to smaller European imports. Canada undertook months of consultations and analysis and announced a revolutionary, and elegant, borderless manufacturing model that became known as the Auto Pact.

The deal was eventually signed in 1965 at President Lyndon Johnson's Texas ranch to little fanfare, but the impact was significant. Tariffs were eliminated on all vehicles, parts and raw materials, allowing Detroit to rationalize production into large-scale operations as though the border did not exist. In return, the Big Three guaranteed Canada its fair share of jobs and activities: if Canadians bought 12 percent of Detroit's vehicles, then 12 percent of the auto "pie" would remain in Ontario. The treaty became a template for trade arrangements and economic integration worldwide, including the European Union and the 1989 Canada–U.S. Free Trade Agreement.

The Big Three enjoyed a few decades of hegemony. Their management, shareholders and unionized workers benefited by easily passing along their costs—and inefficiencies—to consumers. But their market share began shrinking as their corporate complacency and inflexible business model provided openings for more aggressive and innovative carmakers from Japan, Korea and Germany. The Big Three remained profitable through most recessions, but in 2006 Ford was in trouble and restructured by laying off tens of thousands of workers, retooling, introducing new management practices and obtaining concessions from workers and retirees drawing pensions. This allowed the company to weather the 2008 financial catastrophe that drove General Motors and Chrysler into bankruptcy protection. Those companies were saved as a result of the collaboration of the United States, Canadian and Ontario governments. In other words, the most important single industry in both countries was a joint venture, sometimes requiring government intervention or help, forming a template for a comprehensive partnership.

Oil

Another example of American-Canadian economic achievement is the oil industry. Oil was first discovered in commercial quantities in Ontario and Ohio. Petroleum had been used as a fuel for centuries. Native peoples harvested oil "seeps" for use as canoe pitch or as salves. But finding the stuff underground in large enough quantities was a matter of happenstance and did not occur until the mid-nineteenth century. Up to then, wells were drilled, but to tap underground salt brine deposits. Sometimes these wells also produced small amounts of oil and natural gas as accidental by-products.

It was just such an "accident" that led to the discovery in southwestern Ontario, in 1858, of the first well to spew oil in large amounts. Word spread about the find. A year later, the first commercial well for the express purpose of extracting oil was drilled in Titusville,

Pennsylvania. It was dubbed the Drake well, after Edwin Drake, who led the drilling effort. The success of his well single-handedly sparked the oil boom.

At that time, petroleum's main commercial purpose was to be refined into kerosene, which was used to fuel lamps in place of whale oil. The market was huge, and drillers scoured the Appalachian Mountain region and the Ohio Valley to try to tap "seeps" and spent salt brine wells, where oil had also been found. A kerosene business developed throughout the Civil War and beyond. In 1870, a group of investors in Ohio formed Standard Oil. One of its backers was John D. Rockefeller, whose cunning and ambition enabled him to take over the oil business worldwide. By 1916, he was the world's first billionaire. By the time he died in 1937, he was worth $1.4 billion—an amount that, as a share of America's gross domestic product, would be equivalent to $192 billion today, according to *The New York Times.*

Rockefeller was ruthless and bought or drove competitors out of business. He was innovative and developed three hundred oil-based products, such as tar, paint, Vaseline and chewing gum. By 1900, Standard Oil was refining 90 percent of America's oil and 80 percent of the world's. Then, in 1904, *The History of the Standard Oil Company* by American journalist Ida Tarbell exposed his company's dirty tricks, price wars and unscrupulous activities and caused a public furor. New laws followed and legal action ensued. In 1911, the Supreme Court of the United States found Standard Oil in violation of the Sherman Antitrust Act and ordered it broken up into thirty-four independent companies.

After the Second World War, the Americans, through Imperial Oil (owned by Standard Oil of New Jersey, later known as Exxon), began to explore aggressively in Alberta, where the geological prospects seemed bright. But attempts yielded nothing until November

20, 1946. That day, an Imperial crew was drilling on a farm just south of Edmonton. The company had drilled 133 dry holes, or unsuccessful wells, and its failures were so legendary that the drilling rig manager, Vern Hunter, was nicknamed "Dry Hole."

But Hunter hit a gusher; the well, dubbed Leduc No. 1, spewed oil hundreds of feet into the air for weeks. It took so long to cap the well that a small lake of oil formed in the surrounding area, and photos of the Leduc plume of oil made headlines around the world. Like the Drake well of long ago, Leduc No. 1 ushered in western Canada's oil boom and an era of prosperity. The well had tapped a prolific geological formation that ran across much of western Canada called the Western Sedimentary Basin, and it caused a drilling frenzy in Alberta.

Leduc attracted more American money and curiosity. One visitor was Joseph Howard Pew, whose family built the Sun Oil Company and instituted the Pew Charitable Trusts. He was born in Pennsylvania in 1882 and took over the family business after graduating as an engineer from Massachusetts Institute of Technology. His interest in technology and the engineering side of the business attracted him to Alberta's gooey oil sands north of Edmonton, a petroleum-prolific region called Athabasca that spread across an area bigger than Rhode Island. He allocated funds to research the oil sands and helped convince the Alberta government to follow suit. The oil was difficult and expensive to produce. The tar-like sands had to be loaded onto trucks and conveyor belts, where upgraders, or giant ovens, "cooked" the tar until the sand and sediment fell to the bottom. Then the petroleum had to be further refined in order to produce light crude capable of becoming gasoline and other products.

By 1963, Pew was so convinced of the value of the oil sands that he rolled the dice and invested $250 million to build an oil sands plant, called the Great Canadian Oil Sands project. The plant was completed in September 1967 and is still in operation today. Even then, Pew understood the resource's strategic value to the United States. At the opening of the plant, he explained why: "No nation can long be secure in this atomic age unless it be amply supplied with petroleum . . . It is the considered opinion of our group that if the North American continent is to produce the oil to meet its requirements in the years ahead, oil from the Athabasca [oil sands] area must of necessity play an important role."

Sun Oil lost money for years as it wrestled with engineering, climatic, environmental and technological challenges. The Alberta government supported research by another group, led by Exxon and three other American oil giants, called the Syncrude consortium. From these two pilot plants has grown a giant industry, and plans are underway to at least double the oil sands' output. Along with oil production from other sources, Canada has become one of the world's ten biggest oil-producing countries, and with the oil sands the sky is the limit.

The oil sands reserves are second in size only to Saudi Arabia's, totaling 169.3 billion barrels by 2012.[24] Even if production were ramped up to ten million barrels a day, this deposit could provide oil for forty-six years. Joseph Pew was certainly prescient: in the twenty-first century, these deposits represent North America's ultimate energy trump card.

The stories of the oil sands, telephone, automobile and many other innovations and enterprises are bilateral stories. This is hardly surprising given the relationships, families, goodwill and friendship the two nations have built over more than two centuries.

Next Steps

Clearly, erasing the border would remove obstacles and generate great benefits to both countries. Americans would be lifted more quickly out of a moribund economy with diminishing opportunities, while Canadians would have access to the additional capital, manpower and technology needed to develop the North.

The politics would be challenging, however. In any deal, the "soft," or political and organizational, issues are the toughest to negotiate. The reason is obvious: those in charge of negotiations are more interested in protecting their own positions than in executing an amalgamation that may cost them their jobs. In American and Canadian politics, the added burden would be that both are hobbled by antiquated and unresponsive political systems that have become polarized when it comes to simple matters, never mind the questions that would be raised surrounding a deal as comprehensive as this.

The politics may be difficult, but so were those attached to the free trade agreement, the Auto Pact, building the St. Lawrence Seaway and negotiating hundreds more joint treaties. The way forward is for both countries to consider their options, select the most acceptable, and then launch preliminary negotiations. If the economics of a deal work, then the political planets will align.

CHAPTER FIVE

How a Merger Deal Might Be Structured

A speculator is a man who observes the future, and acts before it occurs.
—BERNARD BARUCH

MERGERS AND ACQUISITIONS COME IN ALL SHAPES AND sizes. They can be designed to protect an entity against aggression, an unfriendly takeover or both. Mergers arise to maximize profits by realizing synergies, economies of scale or cost reductions, or out of the need to increase talent, acquire resources or other assets, diversify, vertically integrate or become larger for security, research or competitive purposes. A more extensive U.S.-Canada partnership would fulfill all of these requirements and then some. Such a merger could be both defensive and offensive, and could be the biggest friendly transaction in history.

The largest deal to date was the $2 trillion merger, or reunification, of the German Democratic Republic, informally known as East Germany, with the Federal Republic of Germany, or West Germany, in 1990.[1] The transaction brought back together a country that had been partitioned after the Second World War. The western portion was controlled by the Allies and became a capitalist democracy; the east was controlled by the Soviet Union and became a communist dictatorship—one that compelled 3.5 million Germans to defect, so in 1961 the Soviets built the Berlin Wall to prevent others from doing the same. For two generations, the two nations remained divided, economically and psychologically.

In late 1989, East Germany and other socialist satellites were cast adrift after the fall of the Iron Curtain. Many, especially younger people, streamed into West German cities looking for work, and without a place to stay they slept in doorways and parks. East Germany was headed toward bankruptcy, with a population one-quarter of West Germany's and a moribund economy that fell, according to some estimates, to only 8 percent of West Germany's.[2] Some East Germans hung a banner on the Berlin border that underscored the desire for a merger. "I remember seeing it and realizing there was no choice but to unify, because it said, 'Bring the Deutsche Mark to East Germany or East Germans will go to the Deutsche Mark.' That certainly made the point that we had to move quickly," Dr. Kurt Biedenkopf, a Christian Democratic Union member of West Germany's Bundestag, told me in an interview in the spring of 1990.

In the months that followed, politicians from both countries negotiated the reunification, citizens of East and West Germany approved the merger via plebiscites, and the deal closed in October 1990. Five re-established East German states, or *länder,* that had been abolished in the 1950s joined West Germany in return for a generous currency swap, assumption of all debts, entitlement obligations, a pledge to modernize the eastern economy and a promise to clean up the environmental degradation caused by communist industries. In 2010, on the twentieth anniversary of reunification, estimates of the cost, spread over two decades, ranged upward from $2 trillion, depending upon what is included.

The world's biggest transaction was a tremendous achievement and was executed in less than a year. The transition from communism to capitalism, dictatorship to democracy and oppression to freedom was no less impressive. But for East Germans, readjustment took a toll. Most were retrained, and many lost their jobs for lengthy periods or had to relocate to West Germany or other parts of the European Union. Their incomes and growth continued to lag behind their western counterparts. But by 2012, Germany's economy was Europe's biggest, the fourth-biggest in the world[3] and the second-largest exporter after China.[4] From those frightening days of 1989–90, the country had developed into a prosperous, dynamic society.

The Germans united out of necessity. In 1992, the Russians were also in financial difficulty, and President Boris Yeltsin, in a bid to help pay down some of Russia's then $70 billion in foreign debt, was offering at a G7 meeting in Munich to sell oil fields, production plants and land to the United States or others. Foreign policy expert Walter Russell Mead suggested that the U.S. should take up the offer and buy all of Siberia for $1 trillion or $2 trillion.

President George H.W. Bush dismissed the idea of any purchases of Russian resources unless Moscow imposed major democratic and judicial reforms. As a result, joked Mead, Bush missed out on his chance to be memorialized on Mount Rushmore by undertaking a Louisiana Purchase–style takeover of Siberia.[5] It would have been the deal of the twentieth century because, using Western technologies, the value of commodities coming out of Siberia has tripled, if not quadrupled.

In 2010, Germany's reunification inspired a bold initiative by South Korea's government. That August 15, Koreans marked their sixty-fifth anniversary of liberation from Japan, and the Republic of Korea's president, Lee Myung-bak, chose that day to make an audacious proposal. He preemptively suggested that South Koreans levy a tax, and set aside the proceeds, to pay for the cost of reuniting and rebuilding its impoverished neighbor, North Korea. The cost of rebuilding the north was estimated to be about $1.5 trillion, or about one and a half times South Korea's annual GDP at the time.[6] "Reunification will definitely come,"

Mr. Lee said. "I believe that the time has come to start discussing realistic policies to prepare for that day, such as a reunification tax."

His announcement was all the more controversial because, just a few months earlier, in March, North Koreans had sunk a South Korean ship and killed forty-six sailors.[7] North Korea's dictator, Kim Jong-il, had also been terrifying all of his neighbors by developing nuclear weapons and threatening to use them. But he was aging and lacked a successor at the time. Concerns were that, after his death, there would be chaos or interference by China. So President Lee's announcement was both a signal to China to stay away as well as a message to the north's 24 million poor citizens that the South's 49 million would be willing to help them once their dictator died if they opted for democracy and capitalism.

The north reacted instantly: a spokesman called Lee's speech "an open declaration of war."[8] The next day, North Korea's Committee for the Peaceful Reunification of the Fatherland stated: "The unification tax put forward by a traitor derived from delusions of an emergency in the north. The south will pay dearly for the reckless remarks born of rebellious motives."[9]

The reunification initiative also rattled Japan, the U.S. and China. The concept intimidated some Japanese policy makers who suggested that reunification would vault the Koreas into greater economic and military importance in the region, outstripping Japan's. The union would create another bigger nuclear power and eventually lead to the withdrawal of American troops from South Korea. Chinese officials supported reunification, but only if accomplished by peaceful means. The U.S. supported unity but insisted that the merged entity would have to dismantle the north's nuclear capability before American troops would withdraw from South Korea.

Since then, the issue has been on the back burner, but relations have not improved with the ascension of Kim Jong-il's son, Kim Jong-un, in 2012. North Korea continues to struggle and South Korea to prosper, but there is no discussion of uniting the two nations or collecting a "reunification tax." But regime change is inevitable because of the extreme poverty of the north. As with Germany, a crisis might bring about détente, then discussions.

Likewise, a merger between Canada and the U.S. could take years, or could happen quickly, depending upon circumstances, public opinion and what type of deal was proposed. Would it be like Germany's, or would it be a targeted economic arrangement? Let's start with a look at a couple of mega-merger models, then explore some of the other possibilities for Canadians and Americans to consider that would realize synergies and enhance their partnership.

Option 1: Merger Model, a.k.a. Project Great Lakes

This first option takes an investment-banking approach. The deal would be complex. The U.S. had 313 million people in 2011, or roughly 90 percent of the population of the two countries' total of 347.4 million. Canada had 34.4 million, or roughly 10 percent. But Canada's resource wealth exceeded 10 percent of the total. So Canadians would be making an over-contribution in terms of resources.

I sat down with Craig Kelly, a chartered accountant based in Geneva, Switzerland, who is the chief financial officer for Oryx Petroleum, an international oil company with assets throughout Africa and the Middle East. He has had extensive merger-and-acquisition experience around the world at RBC Dominion Securities and Addax Petroleum, a leading independent international upstream company that was acquired by Sinopec in 2009 for close to $10 billion.

He and I devised a model to merge the U.S. and Canada based on standard industry practice, as though the two were companies. We code-named the deal Project Great Lakes: Canada would be referred to as "Muskoka" and the U.S. as "Adirondack." ("Muskoka" refers to the cottage-country playground of the wealthy in Ontario, "Adirondack" to its counterpart in upstate New York.) For evaluation purposes, we selected key metrics: the revenues of the two countries, or gross domestic product (GDP); land and total area, which also includes rights to resources 200 nautical miles offshore; debts; foreign reserves and gold assets; renewable resources such as water and farmland; and fossil fuel production and proven reserves. We added their totals and determined the percentage of assets and liabilities each country contributed toward the totals (see figure 1).

The chart on page 221 was based on 2010 figures taken from the *World Factbook,* an almanac of facts drawn from many sources and compiled by the U.S. intelligence agency. These figures are for demonstration purposes only, as is the year chosen, 2010. Any deal, commercial or sovereign, would evaluate more metrics from a variety of sources, including industry intelligence.

The light gray bars represent Muskoka's contribution in the various metrics, while the dark gray bars represent Adirondack's. The black vertical line through the bar chart is called an "equity line," which we set at 82 percent in an attempt to split the equity of the combined entity, or to divide the resources that each country brings to the merger, fairly or equitably. Setting the equity line at 82 percent is an attempt to divide the contributions fairly without regard to the relative importance, or weight, of any of the ten metrics. So it is a blunt instrument in terms of valuation, but nonetheless an interesting starting point. The reasoning behind each metric, and a breakdown of the percentage contributions follows on page 222.

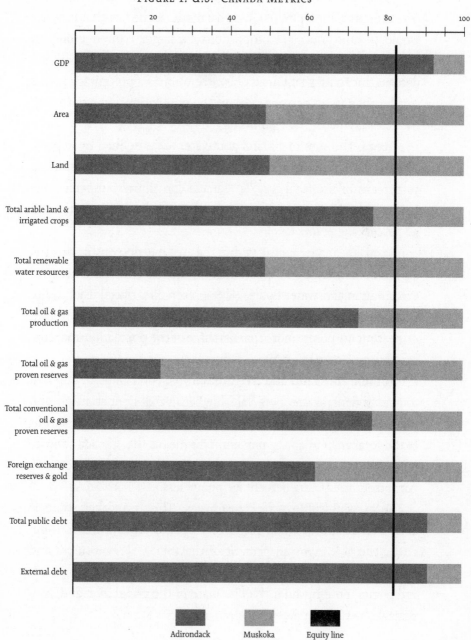

Figure 1: U.S.–Canada Metrics

Gross Domestic Product, or GDP. GDP is the size of a country's economy. Incorporated into this model is the fact that America would be contributing a proportionately larger economic output. The U.S.'s GDP represents 92 percent of the total and Canada's 8 percent, meaning that Canada's contribution is 2 percentage points smaller than its 10-percent share of the population and, conversely, the U.S.'s is 2 percentage points larger.

Area is the sum of all land and water areas defined by international boundaries, on- and offshore. Each country occupies roughly 50 percent of the total area. So Canada contributes 40 percentage points more than its share of the population and, conversely, the U.S. 40 percentage points less.

Land is a smaller metric within the area metric, constituting the land base defined by international boundaries and coastlines, and excluding inland water bodies (lakes, reservoirs, rivers). Each country occupies roughly 50 percent of the total, so Canada contributes 40 percentage points more than its share of the population and, conversely, the U.S. 40 percentage points less.

Total arable land and irrigated crops. Food lands, as opposed to land in general, are more valuable because of their strategic, and renewable, value in an overpopulated world. The U.S. has 78 percent of the total and Canada 22 percent. This means that Canada contributes 12 percentage points more than its share of the population and, conversely, the U.S. 12 percentage points less.

Total renewable water resources. This is another strategic asset that measures water resources that are replenished continuously. The U.S. owns 48 percent of the total water resources and Canada 52 percent. This means that Canada contributes 42 percentage points more in water than its share of the population and, conversely, the U.S. 42 percentage points less.

Total oil and gas production. Fossil fuels are the lifeblood of economies for the foreseeable future, and in this category Canada and the U.S. are blessed. U.S. production represented 77 percent of the combined total in 2010; Canadian production, 23 percent. This means Canada's energy contribution is 13 percentage points larger than its share of the population and, conversely, the U.S.'s is 13 percentage points smaller. This figure fluctuates annually based on consumption, price, economic growth, production levels and switching to ethanol and biofuels. In 2011, Canadian natural gas production dropped as more shale gas came onstream in the U.S. But oil sands output more than outpaced the increase in American shale oil.

Total oil and gas proven reserves. These figures are moving targets. Reserves are not the same as oil and gas discoveries. Discoveries are estimates, called "resources," which must be "proved up" through extensive drilling, analyses and audits before they can be added to balance sheets or official figures as reserves. The figures in this chart are proven reserves. They include conventional as well as unconventional sources (shale gas and shale oil as well as the oil sands). In 2010, Canadian reserves of oil and natural gas represented 74 percent of the total and U.S. reserves only 26 percent. This means that Canada contributes 64 percentage points more than its share of the population and, conversely, the U.S. contributes 64 percentage points less.

Since 2010, oil companies in the United States have discovered and set aside as reserves huge amounts of shale gas and shale oil, allowing reserve estimates to increase. But given the enormity of the Canadian oil sands deposits—169.3 billion barrels—a revision upward for the American percentage of reserves would be slight until reserves are proved. Some industry sources believe that shale oil deposits in the U.S. and Canada could be as significant as the oil sands reserves, but that's not yet known for certain. Besides, shale deposits of natural gas and oil exist in Canada too. Notably, much of the prolific Bakken formation, well known in North Dakota, also exists in Saskatchewan and Manitoba.

Total conventional oil and gas proven reserves. These figures exclude shale gas, shale oil and oil sands reserves. Here the figure is lower in absolute numbers. In 2010, the U.S. represented 79 percent of the total conventional proven reserves; Canada, 21 percent. This means that Canada contributes 11 percentage points more than its share of the population and, conversely, the U.S. 11 percentage points less.

Foreign exchange reserves and gold. This represents another fluctuating figure, but the published numbers for 2010 show that the U.S. had 70 percent of the total and Canada 30 percent. This means Canada's reserves and gold on hand represent a share 20 percentage points larger than its share of the population; the U.S., conversely, had 20 percentage points less.

Total public debt. This is one of many measures of government debt levels, and is defined as the cumulative total of all government borrowings less repayments that are denominated in a country's home currency. Public debt should not be confused with external debt, which reflects the foreign-currency liabilities of both the private and public sector and must be financed out of foreign-exchange earnings. In 2009, debts were proportionally similar. The U.S.'s debt represented 90 percent of the total and Canada 10 percent. Since then, the U.S.'s debt accumulation has outstripped Canada's, so that the Americans would contribute a disproportionate amount to the debt of a merged entity. By 2011, U.S. debt represented 93 percent of the combined total and Canada's debt 7 percent.

External debt. This is the total public and private debt owed to non-residents, repayable in internationally accepted currencies, goods or services. These figures are calculated on an exchange-rate basis—i.e., not in purchasing power parity (PPP) terms. In 2010, the U.S. represented 92 percent of the total and Canada 8 percent. Since 2009, private debt owed externally has declined, but public debt has increased.

DIVIDING THE PIE

Using the 82 percent "equity line," Canadians, or Muskoka shareholders, with 10 percent of the population, would be entitled to 18 percent of the equity of the new merged entity. Americans, or Adirondack shareholders, with 90 percent of the population, would be entitled to 82 percent.

Such asymmetrical mergers occur all the time in business. This transaction assumes that each person from Muskoka and Adirondack shares equally in the combined country's resources; however, Muskoka shareholders would be limited to 10 percent of the stock and Adirondack 90 percent based on population only. So the Canadians would have to get cash, or other assets and consideration, as compensation for contributing 18 percent of the assets, or 8 percent more than their 10 percent of the population.

Based on the 2010 figures, Kelly calculated that this Canadian over-contribution was worth roughly $16.943 trillion. That may seem astonishingly high, but Germany's reunification cost around $2 trillion, an obligation that was nearly double West Germany's 1989 GDP of $1.35 trillion.[10] The West German government also owed another $496 billion (1 trillion deutsche marks), or 47 percent of its GDP, and could not count on any help from East Germany, unlike in this arrangement.[11] That meant Germany's total public obligation was $2.496 trillion, or nearly twice the former West Germany's GDP. But this gigantic merger paid off because it was an investment, not an entitlement, as this would be. Also the investment, unlike West Germany merging with a dysfunctional East Germany, would be assumed and carried by a combined United States and Canada. By 2011, Germany's GDP was $3.114 trillion,[12] its public debt (including debts owed by lower levels of government and social security obligations) was down to 80.6 percent of GDP, its current account surplus was $204.3 billion, and its foreign reserves and gold totaled $238.9 billion.[13]

It is important to remember that a valuation of assets such as these is used only to start discussions. Another approach, such as evaluating all publicly owned assets like buildings, military bases, pencils, brooms or weapons, would be extremely difficult, if not impossible, to quantify. Besides, such assets would be irrelevant to merger discussions because they are not productive assets and would not contribute to the value of the transaction. In addition, evaluating private wealth in the two countries would also be irrelevant because a merger would not be about acquiring any private property but would be about compensation for "publicly owned" resources, opportunities, future jobs and other intangibles.

Negotiations would mostly boil down to horse-trading and focus on the relative and perceived value of national assets. The Americans would argue that they deserve more of the equity because they bring to the partnership the world's richest, most innovative economy, world-class universities and research facilities, and military protection. The Canadians would argue they deserve more because they bring to the partnership unprecedented opportunities in terms of resource or economic development, 34.4 million educated people, guaranteed resource self-sufficiency and ownership of Arctic shipping lanes.

So in this merger model, if the over-contributions of Canadians were distributed evenly (which they would not be; rather they would be distributed according to years of residency), *every Canadian would be entitled to a lump sum payment of $492,529.* The payout would be stretched over two or more decades and be equivalent to more than 100 percent of the combined GDP. This is simply what West Germany did.

Option 2: A Mining Merger Model

Canada has developed the world's most sophisticated mining "infrastructure," consisting of banks, lawyers, brokers, underwriters, investors, accountants, engineers and geological scientists who complete deals all around the world. By 2011, the TMX, or Toronto Stock Exchange, had become the world's seventh-biggest stock market in terms of equity raised, as well as the premier mining stock exchange in the world, and raised 80 percent of mining equity globally.[14]

Imagine Canada as an intermediate-sized mining company, with operations in a safe jurisdiction, that makes more profit than most and has reserves in the ground, the biggest land spread in the world to explore, promising geology and people who know how to develop mines under hostile conditions. Imagine the United States as a gigantic conglomerate with many diverse operating divisions (including mining and energy), a large revenue base, the biggest pool of risk capital in the world and a significant undeveloped land spread, albeit a smaller one than Canada's.

If these two "mining" entities merged, the Canadian mining shareholders would have to be compensated for contributing higher "profits," more land and upside potential.

PROFIT

"Profit" in this case refers to the fact that Canadian governments have a bigger cash flow, in the form of taxes and royalties, than their U.S. counterparts. In 2011, Canadian governments collected $17,933 per capita in taxes, or CAD$616.9 billion in total taxes and royalties, while American governments collected $14,811 per person, or USD$4.636 trillion.[15] So Canada's excess "profits" amounted to $3,122 per capita, or $107.396 billion in a year. In a business merger, this profit "stream" would be evaluated—for example, based on a multiple of ten, or $1.07 trillion.

LAND VALUE

Any land or other assets owned by individuals, corporations, foundations, charities or state, provincial or municipal governments would be exempt from the transaction because these would automatically be transferred if the two federal governments merged. The only lands included in this valuation would be those owned by the two federal governments. The U.S. federal government owns 2,995,370 square kilometers (1,156,519 square miles), or 31.1 percent of its country's landmass. The Canadian federal government owns 4,093,714 square kilometers (1,580,592 square miles)—41 percent of its territory. Canada would therefore contribute 1,098,344 square kilometers (424,073 square miles) more than the U.S.—an area nearly the size of South Africa.

So what would these vast lands be worth? There are three precedents in North America for large-scale land purchases between sovereign entities that offer a starting point for discussion. In 1803, the Louisiana Purchase cost $15 million for approximately 2,145,000 square kilometers (828,000 square miles). In 2011 dollars, that would make Canada's over-contribution of land worth $240.449 billion. In 1853, the Gadsden Purchase, when the U.S. bought part of Arizona and New Mexico from Mexico, cost $10 million. In 2011 dollars, that would make Canada's land worth $657.3 billion. In 1867, Alaska cost $7.2 million. In 2011 dollars, that would make Canada's over-contribution of land worth only $9.4 billion.[16]

Such estimates do not take into account the fact that Canada's lands are exponentially more valuable because their potential has been identified by geologists and government surveys and because modern scientific and engineering techniques can pinpoint and produce resources. These lands are also more valuable because of their geostrategic importance, as was the Gadsden Purchase, which provided land on which to build a transcontinental railroad that would link the Deep South to the Pacific Ocean without going through mountainous terrain. So taking that valuation, in today's dollars, of $657.3 billion, and multiplying it by a factor of ten, yields a value of $6.57 trillion for Canada's over-contribution of federal lands.

The Earn-Out Agreement

Mining deals always include an "earn-out" agreement to enable sellers to get a piece of the upside on raw land after a deal is closed. Investors don't know the value of future discoveries and royalties, so in essence these agreements allow both parties to divide profits beforehand. Such royalties can be enormous, and in this case a fund would be set up to receive, invest and distribute the proceeds to sellers or taxpayers. Such funds have been established in Alaska, Alberta and Norway to distribute royalty proceeds to residents.

Here's how an earn-out agreement for the U.S.–Canada merger would work based on precedents: Canadians would get half of all royalties paid to a new merged entity out of any energy and mining production on lands acquired from the Canadian federal government. (Provincial or state lands would remain the property of the provinces or states and would collect their own royalties to provide their government services.)

Royalty rates start low, until costs have been recovered; then they jump to 5 percent of gross revenues. To illustrate, an earn-out agreement would transfer half of all the future royalties paid by these operations, plus new ones, to a Canadian Heritage Trust Fund. The rest would go to the U.S.–Canada entity.

Canada's mineral and energy potential is similar to Siberia's or Alaska's, but has not been exploited. Opportunities have not been pursued because the owner, the Canadian federal government, is run not by businessmen or resource exploration companies, but by bureaucrats. The only oil production in Canada's North has been at Norman Wells in the Northwest Territories. In 1985, a twelve-inch pipeline, 869 kilometers long, was built with a capacity of up to 39,400 barrels per day, but oil companies have only shipped half of that amount since.[17] By contrast, in 2012 Russia, mostly Siberia, was producing an estimated 10.37 million barrels of oil daily[18] and Alaska's oil fields peaked at two million barrels daily in 1988. By 2012, production was declining, but they still produced 590,000 barrels a day.[19]

Canada's energy and mining resource potential in the Arctic is untapped. For instance, if any one of the three territories administered by the Canadian federal government (Northwest Territories, Yukon and Nunavut) contained an oil field the size of Alaska's, or an estimated 16 billion barrels,[20] the revenues would total $1.6 trillion at

$100 per barrel. A 5 percent royalty, stipulated in an earn-out agreement, would yield $80 billion at $100 a barrel. Half of that revenue would go into the Canadian Heritage Trust Fund and the other half to the U.S.-Canada partnership.

Other examples of royalty funds exist. By January 2013, the Alaska Permanent Fund had $44.2 billion in assets,[21] even after paying out annual dividends to every man, woman and child in Alaska since 1969. In 2008, for example, each Alaskan got $2,069 (including a one-time Alaska Resource Rebate of $1,200[22]) from the fund. By 2012, this had fallen, in step with oil production, to $878 per person.[23]

The Petroleum Fund of Norway, now called the Pension Fund of Norway, is one of the world's largest sovereign wealth funds, and by 2012 it had more than $613 billion in assets[24] on behalf of 4.88 million Norwegians. The fund finances the country's pensions and other entitlements in education, health care and social services that are among the most generous in the world. The fund also invests in businesses and stock markets, and by 2012 it owned roughly 1 percent of all the stock market equities in the world.[25]

By March 2012, the Alberta Heritage Trust Savings Fund had accumulated $16.2 billion in assets.[26] The fund is small, given the province's oil and natural gas wealth, because the provincial government has chosen to compensate residents through a generous tax system. There are no provincial sales taxes in Alberta, and Albertans pay lower provincial income taxes—a flat 10-percent tax compared to 15 percent in Saskatchewan on taxable incomes over $122,589 a year, 21 percent in Nova Scotia (on amounts over $150,000) or 24 percent in Quebec (on incomes over $80,200).[27]

To summarize, Canadians, in a mining-type transaction, would be entitled to $1.07 trillion for their additional "profit" stream (or higher tax collections); $6.57 trillion for their over-contribution of land and an earn-out agreement that would divert half of existing and future royalties into a fund for all Canadians.

ANOTHER MERGER COST:
TOPPING UP CANADIAN HEALTH-CARE BENEFITS

Another form of compensation that Option 2 would have to pay out to Canadians would be a subsidy to cover the difference between the costs of the Canadian health-care system and the American system. This would be equivalent to topping up "employee benefits," which companies must do after a merger if there are differences. U.S. health-care costs are dramatically higher than Canada's, so Canadians who chose to live, work or retire in the U.S. states would need to be subsidized.

Canadians could be issued fraud-proof health cards, valid anywhere in the fifty states, ten provinces or three territories. Americans would not be entitled to this benefit because if they lived, worked or retired in Canadian provinces, their health-care costs would be lower.

Roughly speaking, this health-care compensation could cost about $5 trillion, spread over forty years, if all Canadians moved to the United States. This figure, calculated for argument's sake only, is the difference between Canadian costs of $4,317 per capita and U.S. costs of $7,990 (or $3,673 per year), multiplied by 34.4 million Canadians over four decades. (Such a calculation would have to be adjusted based on how many Canadians used the U.S. system and on actual costs.)

But Option 2 would theoretically cost a total of $12.64 trillion—$1.07 trillion for Canada's higher tax or "profit" stream, $6.57 trillion for over-contribution of land and about $5 trillion for a health-care top-up—plus future inestimable amounts as part of an earn-out agreement.

232

Financing Merger Options 1 or 2

Option 1 totals $16.943 trillion. Despite this price tag, buying out Canadians wouldn't break the bank. The easiest way to finance this would be for the partnership to issue long-term bonds to Canadians as payment. In other words, Canadians would "take back a mortgage" to facilitate the deal. Some non-cash compensation could also be negotiated instead, such as lifetime free health care anywhere in the U.S. or Canada, free post-secondary education and tax credits.

Borrowing that amount of money from foreigners or commercial banks, or simply printing money to finance the transaction, could be ruinous. So Canadians would have to agree to accept debt in the form of long-term bonds or compensation in "kind." If the combined entity took on $16.943 trillion in debt to pay Canadians, it would be equivalent to 100 percent of the combined U.S. and Canadian GDP in 2011.[28] That would be added to their combined debt rate of 79 percent for a total of 179 percent,[29] roughly what West Germans undertook.

This is not desirable, but manageable. For instance, Japan retains high living standards even though its debt-to-GDP ratio hit 226 percent in 2011; at the same time, Greece hit the wall beginning in early 2010 after its debt hit 167 percent of its GDP (now 132 percent after debt forgiveness).[30] The difference between those two was that the wealthy Japanese population pays taxes and buys long-term Japanese bonds at low interest rates. Greeks dodge taxes and do not buy Greek bonds, either. Greece was left at the mercy of foreign bondholders and banks that, upon realizing the country was going bust, hiked interest rates so high they accelerated the bankruptcy they feared.

Arguably, this debt would be affordable. Looking at the simple math, a $16.943 trillion obligation could work this way: the $16.9 trillion could be paid in the form of twenty-year, government-backed bonds paying 1.7 percent (plus more if the rate of inflation exceeded 3 percent, up to a ceiling of 5 percent). The interest would cost $288 billion a year, but as much as 30 percent of this, or $86.4 billion, could be clawed back to governments in the form of sales and income taxes, bringing down the net cost of interest payments to $201.6 billion per year. These payments could be further offset by taxes and spending cuts: a dollar-a-gallon gasoline tax in the U.S. could raise $134 billion a year.[31] A merger of the U.S. and Canadian governments and militaries could result in spending cuts of 10 percent, but even if only 5 percent were cut, another $125 billion could be saved. Such taxes and cuts could total $259 billion a year, or more than the annual interest payments to Canadians.

Of course, interest payments would be one important issue, but paying the face value of bonds in twenty or twenty-five years would be another matter. This highlights an important distinction about this deal. These bonds would have collateral in the form of the vast resource assets of Canada. These assets could generate trillions in economic activity and could also be sold or leased to the private sector.

This is how Germany was able to simultaneously pay for reunification and build a powerful economy. The $2 trillion was an affordable investment, secured and wisely deployed, and not merely another government expenditure involving entitlements that do not generate accretive growth.

Option 2, or the mining deal, would cost $12.54 trillion, payable in $7.64 trillion worth of bonds and free health care worth about $4.9 trillion, plus the future proceeds from an earn-out agreement. That $12.54 trillion would be equivalent to 76 percent of the countries' combined GDP in 2011 of $16.475 trillion, and would be added to their debts in 2011 (of 80 percent of U.S. GDP and 69 percent of Canadian GDP, for a total blended debt-to-GDP ratio of roughly 79 percent.)[32] When added to the 76 percent of new obligations to merge and pay out to Canadians, the total debt-to-GDP ratio totals 155 percent. This would be less than Greece's 167 percent, Japan's 220 percent, Germany's 200 percent obligation in 1990 and less than Option 1's 179 percent.[33]

Here is how it would be financed:

- The free health-care total of $4.9 trillion would cost the merged entity $122.5 billion a year, based on U.S. per capita medical costs.
- The remaining $7.64 trillion could be paid in the form of twenty-year, government-backed bonds paying 1.7 percent (more if the rate of inflation exceeded 3 percent, up to a ceiling of 5 percent). The interest cost would be $129.8 billion a year, but as much as 30 percent of this, or $38.94 billion, could be clawed back to governments in the form of sales and income taxes for a net cost of $90.86 billion per year.
- The total carrying costs of this debt would therefore be $213.36 billion a year.
- These expenditures could be easily offset by taxes and spending cuts: a seventy-five-cent-a-gallon gasoline tax in the U.S. could raise $100.5 billion a year. A merger could result in spending cuts of 10 percent, but even just lopping 5 percent off federal government expenditures could save another $125 billion, for a total of $225.5 billion a year. Combined, these measures free up more than the payments to Canadians.

But Options 1 and 2 would also include another benefit for Canadians. Whether owed $16.934 trillion or $7.64 trillion in bonds plus health-care obligations, Canadians collectively would become the partnership's biggest creditor and the world's single largest creditor. This would entitle them to managerial rights and fiscal oversight, as is the case with any major creditor. So as a condition to any deal, Canadians would have to occupy important positions in a merger. They would have to hold the equivalent of the chair and a majority of seats on the board of governors of the Federal Reserve system; the majority of seats on the National Economic Council; and the positions of vice-president, Treasury secretary, budget director and director of the Congressional Budget Office. Once the bonds were paid off, these conditions could be relaxed, but Canadians would still have to hold at least 10 percent of the important jobs in the merged entity, or management of the combined economy.

How Would Canadians Distribute Their Windfall?

A side issue would be how Canadians would distribute such a windfall. In private-sector deals, proceeds from the sale of shares only go to "shareholders of record" as of the date the deal closed. In this case, it would mean that only those with Canadian citizenship, or who were legally residing in Canada as immigrants, would be entitled to the proceeds. Let's assume that total would be 34.4 million, plus a few million citizens living abroad.

My bias would be to pay out proceeds to the 34.4 million, and only to Canadian citizens living abroad who file and pay taxes in Canada. That may whittle the number down dramatically—Canadians who live offshore don't file taxes because, after all, that's partly why they don't live in Canada.

To be fair, not every man, woman and child in Canada could get the same payment. What follows is a formula for a fair payout based on years of residency. These years would not have to be concurrent.

For instance, a Canadian who lived thirty years in Canada, then left for seven years without filing or paying taxes, before returning for another ten years would be given credit for their forty years of residency.

The value of a unit of residency could be calculated by taking the median age of Canadians in 2011 as roughly forty years.[34] (This means there were as many Canadians older than forty years of age as there were younger than that.) To find the total number of units of residency spread across the entire population, the median age of forty is multiplied by the rounded-off population figure of 34.4 million, for a total of 1.37 billion units of residency.

Payout Under Option 1

Dividing 1.37 billion units of residency into the payout of $16.934 trillion establishes a value of $12,360 per unit of residency. A payout would be determined by multiplying that amount by the number of years of Canadian residency. Someone who had lived in Canada sixty-five years would be entitled to sixty-five times the annual residency unit value of $12,360, for a total of $803,400 in bonds. Here is a table of payouts:

Years	Payout
2	$24,720
10	$123,600
20	$247,200
30	$370,800
40	$494,400
50	$618,000
60	$741,600

Years	Payout
70	$865,200
80	$988,800
90	$1,112,400
100	$1,236,000

Canadian-born resident families would hit the jackpot. A family with two sixty-five-year-old grandparents, two forty-five-year-old parents with two forty-five-year-old spouses and four ten-year-old grandchildren would be entitled to 350 times the annual residency unit value, for a grand total of $4,326,000.

What would I be entitled to? I grew up in the U.S. and have lived in Canada for forty-seven years, so I would be entitled to $580,920. My husband, who immigrated at ten years of age, would get $753,960. My two Canadian-born children and two grandchildren would collectively get a total of $1,112,400.

The bonds could be sold, transferred or used as collateral after a certain "escrow" period of two or three years, in order to help dampen the inflationary aspect of such a huge payout. Canadians could pay off their personal debts, retire and relocate to a Sunbelt state permanently. Thousands, or millions, would.

As mentioned previously, after the first merger model, some Canadians could opt to be partially and gradually paid out through the tax system too. They could deduct their entitlement from taxes over a certain period of time, or receive a "negative income tax" payout annually if they paid no taxes. A wealthy Canadian entitled to a $500,000 payout under this deal could opt to use his or her payout to reduce taxes over time. A Canadian without income entitled to a $250,000 payout under this deal could get cash payments of $25,000 a year over ten years. They could opt for free health care.

PAYOUT UNDER OPTION 2

Dividing $7.64 trillion by 1.37 billion units of residency establishes a value of $5,576 per year of residency, not including the value of free health care anywhere for forty years. Someone who had lived in Canada sixty-five years would be entitled to a total of $362,440 in bonds plus free health care. On top of that would be annual payouts to Canadians of an unknown amount based on royalties from resource development on Canadian federal lands and offshore. Here is a table of payouts in terms of the bonds:

Years	Payout
2	$11,152
10	$55,760
20	$111,520
30	$167,280
40	$223,040
50	$278,800
60	$334,560
70	$390,320
80	$446,080
90	$501,840
100	$557,600

Canadian-born resident families with two sixty-five-year-old grandparents, two forty-five-year-old parents with two forty-five-year-old spouses and four ten-year-old grandchildren would be entitled to a collective total of $1,951,600, plus health care and future royalties.

I would be entitled to $262,072. My husband would get $340,136, and my two children and two grandchildren would collectively get a total of $501,840.

The bonds could be sold, transferred or used as collateral after a certain "escrow" period of two or three years, in order to help dampen the inflationary aspect of such a huge payout. Canadians could pay off debts, retire and relocate.

Option 2 consists of a cash payment plus health care and future royalties to be distributed from resource revenues. But in both options, the U.S.-Canada partnership could compensate Canadians through tax credits rather than by issuing bonds based on years of residency. A wealthy Canadian entitled to a big payout under this deal could gradually deduct his entitlement from his taxes over a few years. A Canadian with a small income entitled to a $250,000 payout under this deal could opt for cash payments of $50,000 a year over five years, plus interest in his declining balance of bonds.

Option 3: The World's Biggest Farm-In

All mergers are difficult to pull off, and this one would test the skills and steel of both nations, while also requiring a huge financing obligation. So this third option would be to create a joint venture, or special partnership, with the United States targeted at sharing in the development of Canada's resources. This option would not require a political merger, but could be consummated in the form of a treaty ratified and signed by both countries, along with a gigantic payment from the United States to Canada for participation in the joint venture.

A "farm-in" is oil-business slang for a business arrangement between an oil company and a landowner (usually a farmer or another oil company with exploration property). The company wants to farm in by drilling on the farmer's land in return for fees and an agreement to share the proceeds from any discoveries.

In that respect, Canada is the world's biggest farm-in. Some 89 percent of the country's lands and subsurface mineral rights— and 100 percent of its offshore—are publicly owned, or Crown lands. These lands are owned and/or managed by governments that lease them out, and never sell, to companies or individuals. Anyone can stake a claim, then apply for a lease. In other words, Canadian governments invite the world to farm in on the nation's endowment.

By contrast, the United States privatized most of its lands and is today a mixture of privately and publicly owned lands. This means that oil or mining companies interested in exploration over large territories must negotiate farm-ins with hundreds or even thousands of private landowners or governments. The Canadian situation is more orderly and simpler, which is why a large-scale farm-in—or right of first refusal to farm in—is possible.

Canada's lease terms vary based on whether the lands are to be used for mineral exploration, agricultural use, forestry, recreational use or tourism. For exploration, rules are strict, uniform and published annually by federal and provincial governments. They outline financial and environmental requirements and responsibilities that, if unmet, result in forfeiture of the leases. The lands then revert to the Crown and others can lease them. Governments also require minimum exploration and other expenditures to prevent entities from leasing and sitting on lands for years. But these are minimal, in practice, and companies or prospectors do sit on lands for years.

If discoveries are made, lessees must adhere to rules governing development. If production results, royalties must be paid to governments according to schedules outlined in the original leasing agreements. At any point along the way, leases can be, and often are, assigned or "farmed out" to others, but only after the consent of the government lessors.

Canada's ubiquitous and simplified land-ownership construct is also open to anyone. Much of the most valuable land is already staked, or leased, and has for years been awaiting better commodity prices, partners, infrastructure support or markets. But vast portions of provincial, and virtually all the federal, land has never been staked, let alone leased, and a gigantic farm-in arrangement with the United States—or others—is simply a bonanza for Canadians waiting to happen.

The country is undeveloped. In Canada in 2011, north of the sixtieth parallel, $662.1 million was spent on exploration in mining ($2.5 billion in the rest of the country)[35] and $120 million was invested by energy companies to acquire leases and explore over several years, resulting in production of only 10,900 barrels per day. Offshore drilling halted in the 1980s, and politicians have debated the issue of exploration there for years. By comparison, in 2011, Alaska (roughly one-third the size of Canada's North and with a fraction of its coastline) had $300 million spent by mining companies on exploration,[36] and several billion spent on oil and gas exploration, production and transportation. Estimates are that another $60 billion will be spent to improve oil production and find more oil in the region and offshore.

Option 3 would involve Canada offering the United States the right of second refusal on any future exploration permits or land leases, if Canadians had declined to do so. Americans could also have first rights to form partnerships with Canadians or any others who wanted to farm out their existing leases to raise cash for exploration or to build production facilities.

This option could also involve an offer by Canada to give American workers a chance at resource jobs that Canadians could not fill. This could be done by requiring resource companies or suppliers to recruit and advertise in Canada, and then, if unsuccessful, to do the same in the United States. Such rights are enormously valuable in commerce, and in this case a giant farm-in could yield trillions of dollars in economic activity, resource profits and wages for millions of Americans.

This deal would also give Americans a chance at picking up exploration leases now held by other foreigners. For instance, if a lease ends without renewal or is taken away from a lessee for failing to meet its obligations, the lease reverts to the Crown, or the federal or provincial governments. At that point, any Canadian would have the first right to pick up that lease, followed by any American. If a lessee wished to remain but needed money or technology or partners, then any Canadian and/or American would have the first right to participate in that lease or farm-in.

Granting the United States a farm-in deal would disrupt neither exploration activities nor labor markets. Arguably, these activities would accelerate dramatically. Americans who opted to work in Canada could do so on a project-contract basis, on a work permit with an extended stay, or as permanent immigrants, with their families, if they qualified. This would reverse the brain drain between the two countries.

The deal would not only be valuable, it would be virtually priceless, given the potential: this would be a farm-in involving participation rights and jobs in a concession the size of South America, with geological prospects as favorable as Alaska's or Russia's. Determining a value would be difficult and would involve a lump-sum-plus-royalty arrangement with Canadians. Perhaps the U.S. could assume the public debt of all fourteen Canadian governments (federal, plus ten provinces and three territories): roughly $1.2 trillion. In return, the Canadian governments would have to agree to reforms such as streamlining the country's land titles by resolving aboriginal land claims, speeding up approval processes, eliminating federal-provincial duplication and building infrastructure where it made planning sense. The elimination of government debt in Canada with such a payment would allow a dramatic decrease in the income, sales and other taxes paid by Canadians, thus reducing costs of living and the operating costs of doing business in Canada. It would stop the decline in manufacturing due to the high Canadian dollar and would provide funds to build needed infrastructure in the North, as well as to enhance its military capability.

Some provinces might not participate in such a transaction, or might opt to create their own farm-ins, but the right of second refusal for Canada as a whole would easily be worth $1.2 trillion, considering the benefit to Washington that access to opportunities, resources and jobs would bestow on its economy for decades. To illustrate, $1.2 trillion is equivalent to 7 percent of Canada's value as estimated in Option 1, or 75 percent of the value of another Alaska Prudhoe Bay discovery. Any proceeds would be shared by Canada and the United States in the form of income taxes paid by workers and corporations, as well as royalties from production.

As for the jobs, the benefits would be significant because Canada is forecast to face chronic manpower shortages in the future. In 2011, Canada allowed in 150,000 foreigners on work permits and 250,000 immigrants in total. If all these entries had been Americans, employed in highly paid resource jobs, this would have been a boon to the U.S. economy roughly equivalent to replacing all the jobs lost in the auto-manufacturing sector between 2000 and 2011. An agreement to hire demobilized military personnel under the Helmets to Hardhats transitioning program in the U.S. so they can work on Canada's infrastructure and resource projects could employ veterans, used to working in remote and difficult conditions, in highly paid jobs.

Canada will need 340,000 construction workers by 2020 and up to a million more foreign workers to fill positions in all provinces and sectors. This labor demand is in addition to the current annual influx of temporary workers and immigrants, according to the Conference Board of Canada.[37] If a merger or farm-in deal were negotiated, the additional exploration and infrastructure development that would result would lead to the creation of millions more jobs.

Such large-scale resource farm-ins, with huge price tags, happen around the world and are huge drivers of economic growth and living standards. In 2011, Russia approved a deal between one of its oil companies and BP for the exclusive rights to explore three Arctic offshore concessions the size of Michigan in return for a share of profits, royalties and 5 percent of BP's stock. (Based on a market capitalization value of $138.4 billion in early 2011, that 5 percent would have been worth nearly $7 billion, exclusive of profits and royalties.) The deal was not consummated following a disagreement. But in the high-stakes world of oil concessions, Chevron was negotiating to acquire rights to explore, with Russian partners, landmasses bigger than Texas.

In 2010, Iraq's new government initiated and signed no-bid deals with four of the world's largest private oil giants and oil-field servicing companies to produce and share in rehabilitating and producing oil from its gigantic oil fields. In 2012, Chevron signed an $800 million deal with Iraq's semi-autonomous region of Kurdistan. Immediately after its revolution in 2011, Libya began selling oil concessions to companies from friendly nations. Other African nations have been selling massive mining concessions to the Chinese for billions in cash

245

and loans, and giving them jobs, market access and infrastructure contracts. Nigeria also offered Gulf states a chance to lease tracts of farmland bigger than most emirates.

The value of large-scale access in Canada's North has already been established. In 1980, for instance, the Japan National Oil Corporation negotiated an interest-free, fifty-year loan of $1.2 billion to Dome Petroleum of Calgary in exchange for the rights to 25 percent of any oil produced from three out of four potential oil fields in the Beaufort Sea region of the Northwest Territories. The first $400 million was advanced for drilling in 1982, a program that yielded few results. Dome Petroleum eventually went out of business, but the point is that its cash-for-oil swap deal attached a value of $2.6 billion, in 2011 dollars, just to buy 25 percent of four offshore concessions without any proven reserves. It was represented as a loan, but it was a bold wildcat bet.

Sovereign-to-sovereign farm-in arrangements have never been done on this scale between Canada and the United States, and would immediately send China and others to the World Trade Organization to register official complaints. They would characterize the joint venture as discriminatory and contrary to liberalized trading precepts. But they would be incorrect. Selling rights for money amounts to a commercial arrangement by a resource-rich nation, and does not constitute a breach of trade laws. It would be a treaty.

An exclusive deal with the U.S. could not be characterized as a non-tariff barrier either. Countries reserve the right to sell resource concessions to anyone, and for as much territory as they wish. This deal would also not exclude others from participating in Canadian resource development. Foreigners with leases could renew them; they could lease lands Canadians and Americans were uninterested in; or they could lease land in partnership with Canadians.

The jobs-for-Americans component would not breach any

protocols, either, but would simply constitute a sensible and targeted form of immigration. Canada needs skilled and specialized resource workers, and as shown in chapter 4, the U.S. needs to create millions of jobs to eliminate its jobs gap. Such a deal would help generate jobs, both directly and indirectly, for Americans if resource activity and economic development in Canada exploded, as I suspect would happen.

The best way to realize all the synergies would be to extend this farm-in deal to a full merger, as in Options 1 or 2. But that may never happen, or may take years to come about. In the meantime, a farm-in rights agreement would provide an immediate benefit to both nations, build on their splendid business partnership and develop Canada in a responsible way with a trusted partner.

Option 4: A Farm-In with Other Countries

If the Americans were unwilling to merge economically or to undertake a farm-in arrangement of this size, China would leap at the $1.2 trillion farm-in deal. It would allow China access to Canada's resources and to employ millions of Chinese workers, as Beijing has been doing in developing resource-rich countries around the world. But China is not an acceptable partner, as its shoddy and unsafe work around the world and track record in Canada demonstrate. So is this a viable option? No.

But Canada could offer smaller deals to the U.S. as well as other developed nations that hold the same values, respect for the law and workplace standards. For instance, the Americans might want to pay for the right of second refusal (after Canadians) in only one region, territory or province and not the entire country. A consortium of

Europeans, led by the Germans, French or British, might want to farm in to another region. A group from Asia, comprising Japan, Singapore and South Korea, might agree collectively to buy leasing rights and labor-access rights in large areas.

In short, the development of Canada's hinterland could be sliced and diced. European Union countries, or their largest mining and oil corporations, could buy the rights to explore unleased portions of Nunavut or the Northwest Territories with Canadian partners for a ten-year period, subject to certain conditions being met by either side. South Koreans might be interested in the rights to all the natural gas in the Mackenzie Delta, from existing owners, in return for a Korean commitment to buy the gas production after they have built pipelines, liquefied natural gas plants and port facilities for export purposes.

American technology companies might be interested in buying the rights to farm in on regions where there is the potential to find rare earths, which are in scarce supply and are essential to the manufacture of hybrid cars, computer screens, fuel cells, fiber-optic equipment, nuclear reactors, televisions, lasers, alloys, refractive glass, magnets, batteries and X-ray machines.

U.S. utilities or big power users, like Google, might be interested in becoming partners to develop more of Canada's hydroelectric or offshore wind, solar or tidal energy prospects. And, most lucratively, the world's biggest oil and mining companies might spend hundreds of billions of dollars to acquire large concessions to explore in Canada's North, both onshore and offshore. Major multinationals and nation-states would welcome the opportunity to become partners with Canadian governments across vast tracts of land. Each deal would require sizable upfront payments to Canadian governments in exchange for exclusive privileges.

Option 5: Carve-Outs

In the business world, a "carve-out" involves a parent company selling a minority stake (usually 20 percent or less) in a subsidiary to raise cash. This is also known as a partial spin-off. Unlike the farm-in, which would not change Canada's open-door system of leasing, carve-outs would require an overhaul of the process. Instead of inviting in the world to lease lands—whether on a first-come, first-served basis or by giving Americans or others the right of second refusal after Canadians, as in Options 3 and 4—a new system would have to be created. In essence, a series of carve-outs would turn Canada's passive system, run by bureaucrats, into an active system run by a series of private-public partnerships.

Existing leases, if abrogated or ended, would not be renewed. Those lands and all others available for leasing would be placed into the care of a series of government-owned corporations that would be run by management teams, consisting of financial, geological and engineering experts. Canada and participating provinces would have to prepare their hinterland for exploration and development by "clearing title" of land claims and streamlining processes. These government-owned corporations with private-sector expertise could finance their corporate and exploration efforts by selling between 20 and 49 percent of their organizations to interested parties, private-sector corporations or sovereign wealth funds. (Limiting ownership to 49 percent would allow Canada's governments to retain control over operations.)

Colombia did this in 2012, abandoning a first-come, first served leasing system like Canada's. The reason was to spur investment and development. Mining investment by foreigners in Colombia had risen ninefold in the decade ending 2011,[38] following a drop in drug-trafficking violence. But a backlog of exploration licenses held by individuals or small mining firms clogged the system and prevented consolidations then development. In August 2012, Bogotá replaced its claim-staking system with one designed to auction land in large blocks. This replaced small players with limited capital with big, well-financed multinationals more capable of bringing discoveries quickly into production.

Another technique would be one similar to Nigeria's. There, and in other countries in Africa and the Middle East, governments negotiate concession deals with oil, mining or agriculture companies. These foreign private-sector partners must operate through Nigerian companies that are controlled by its government.

Such public-private partnerships would bring about growth, unlike the current system. Their management teams would be incentivized to find resources and develop them with partners. These carve-outs would remain under Canadian control: the public, or government, would put up the land and build infrastructure, wherever sensible and profitable, while the private sector would put up the capital and technology for exploration. If discoveries were made, or a major development advisable, the management—government and private investors—might spin these prospects off into another company and find a partner with the interest, money and expertise to build a mine or develop an oil deposit. At the end of such a process, the government and original private-sector partners would retain ownership of the underlying lease and earn royalties. The new operating corporations would farm in to the lease in return for their efforts at bringing development to fruition and would also share operating profits.

Option 5, like Options 3 or 4, would transform the role of Canadian governments/landlords from a passive one to an active one with private-sector partners. The regulatory role would remain intact, but would be divided by the theoretical "Chinese wall" to avoid conflicts. Canadian governments would continue to issue permits, grant environmental approvals and supervise all activities. The United States could be sold rights—for a large fee—to joint ventures within these public-private partnerships, but others might be interested in participating as well. Oil and mining corporations, privately owned or state-owned enterprises, and sovereign wealth funds would invest tens of billions in these carve-outs, eager for the opportunity to have access to resources in a safe jurisdiction such as Canada.

Conclusion

Canada's gigantic real estate holdings will be developed, hopefully, by and for the benefit of Canadians. But that is not a given. The world covets Canada's Arctic and hinterland and is ready to pounce. And Canada does not have the trillions in capital needed to develop itself, nor does it have the military forces to defend itself.

This chapter described two approaches to merge the U.S. and Canada, as well as others involving unique development initiatives. Other models may exist, and there may even be an appropriate partnership fit with Australia and New Zealand. All three former British colonies are politically compatible, but a merger would not yield the economic synergies of a U.S.–Canada partnership. This is because the Australian, New Zealand and Canadian economies are not sufficiently diversified. All three are overly dependent upon volatile commodity prices, and all have defense, labor and capital shortcomings.

Merging with the Americans is a preferred option for security, logistical, demographic, diversification, synergistic and innovation reasons. Canada and the U.S. offer what the other lacks, and the two share the same values, for the most part. But politics remains the biggest challenge and, realistically, a full-fledged merger is unlikely to happen soon despite the urgent need to address the challenges each country faces. Their political systems are somewhat dysfunctional and need repair, but their constitutional constraints render reform virtually impossible. One caveat to that pessimism is that public opinion has never been sought on this topic, and is always a wild card. Besides, as the Germans discovered, crises can arise that impose a sudden change of mind and result in a draconian shift in policy.

In fact, it's a damning indictment that these two countries have not already moved toward a partial or full merger since their free-trade deal in 1989. But it is hardly surprising. Neither nation has anything resembling a viable, long-term strategic plan, except to do more of the same. And that is why I have written this book.

CHAPTER SIX

Merger Politics

Cultures eat strategy for breakfast.
—PETER DRUCKER

A MERGER MAKES BUSINESS SENSE. BUT STILL, MANY CORPO-
rate consolidations fail, not over compensation or money
issues—payments are always negotiable—but when fights
erupt as to who will occupy the corner offices, will have the keys,
the titles and, ultimately, who will run the place. Another obstacle
can be a clash between two corporate cultures. If political infighting
takes over, an otherwise worthy union of compatible corporations
can be derailed. And, naturally, any transaction of this size between
two established nations would be daunting.

But conditions exist that could be conducive to a deal. Polls have
demonstrated increasing similarities between the populations in
terms of policies as well as a shared anxiety about the future. A 2012
poll showed that 26 percent of Canadians were pessimistic about the
economy in the coming year, and 54 percent said they were no better off than one year ago. A total of 63 percent expressed concern
about negative impacts from the U.S. "fiscal cliff" or deficit and debt
situation.[1]

Americans, for their part, have been concerned and demoral-
ized for additional reasons: the 9/11 attacks, expensive wars in Iraq
and Afghanistan, the real estate collapse and the financial meltdown in 2008. These setbacks have undermined confidence in the

system itself. In 2012, a *USA Today*/Gallup poll noted that only half of Americans believe in the so-called American Dream, or the opportunity for any hardworking, poor individual to be successful.[2] Another, in 2011 by GlobeScan, found that only 59 percent of Americans agreed "strongly" or "somewhat" that the free market was the best system for the world, down from 80 percent in 2002.[3]

American thought leaders have forecast that economic woes will contribute to a more dangerous world. Zbigniew Brzezinski, President Jimmy Carter's former national security advisor, wrote in his 2011 book *Strategic Vision* that America's economic decline would force reductions in military strength, thus making the world more dangerous.[4] In 2012, Ian Bremmer, an academic and foreign policy expert, waded in with *Every Nation for Itself: Winners and Losers in a G-Zero World* and concurred that the decline of Western influence was underway and that others would be unable to fill the void.[5] Even historian Robert Kagan, in his *The World America Made,* dismissed the "myth of American decline" but added that future economic constraints would create a disastrous geopolitical vacuum.[6]

But such fears often motivate and propel transformative policy shifts. In 1990, the Germans barreled ahead with reunification as the Iron Curtain's disappearance frightened and destabilized the continent. After the Second World War, Belgium, the Netherlands and Luxembourg formed a customs union for protection that would eventually become the basis for the European Union. In 1985, the report that the country's prospects were so dire convinced Canada's newly elected Prime Minister Brian Mulroney and his cabinet that free trade with the United States was its only option. In every case, fear led smaller nations to propose dramatic partnerships to bigger ones.

Canada's Royal Commission recommended free trade in 1985, but also indicated that Canada would have to make the first move, not the U.S. This was because Washington could not approach Canada for free trade without appearing to be an aggressor, even though free trade had been a stated objective going back many decades. "Since the mid-1970s, U.S. trade law has contained a provision authorizing the President to explore bilateral free trade with Canada," said the Royal Commission in its final report. "The United States has clearly indicated that any overtures toward free trade would, of necessity, have to come from Canada. Canadians have the largest interests at stake, but the Americans, we believe, would welcome a first approach from Canada."[7]

A merger proposal would have to evolve out of a similar process. A definitive study would be needed to determine Canada's future challenges and solutions, including various types of mergers with the United States. The research would have to be global, and would have to include public hearings and be conducted by credible, representative Canadians. Academics, think tanks and corporations should do studies, and cost-benefit analyses, on integration from a monetary union to a customs union, then ultimately to a political union. No such work has been seriously undertaken, despite obvious benefits to both countries.

However, this was the Royal Commission's approach in the 1980s, and it was designed to bypass the country's normal policy-making elite, with its anti-American biases. This elite, nicknamed the Laurentian Consensus, has been an informal alliance of prominent Liberals and left-leaning Conservatives who have inhabited the St. Lawrence watershed and dominated Canada's politics, civil service and media for generations. Its preoccupation has been Quebec, the United States and the creation of a welfare state.

By circumventing the cabal and the government's traditional policy makers, Macdonald's Royal Commission was able to recommend free trade even though it was a shocking and revo-lutionary initiative. Of course, if free trade shocked, a public rec-ommendation to merge with the Americans would generate an elevated reaction. The topic would invoke criticisms from Canada's phalanx of anti-American public intellectuals, academics, politi-cians and media pundits. Those in the clutches of the Laurentian Consensus would man the barricades to repel the attack on the concepts that have governed Canada, which are, according to Canadian humorist, and Giller Prize recipient for fiction, Will Ferguson, about "keeping the Americans out, keeping the French in and trying to get the Natives to somehow disappear."[8]

A Merger Is Becoming More Possible

America is a big country that thinks like a superpower. Canada is a big country that thinks small. Americans staged a daring revo-lution in 1776 and established a nation-state based on organizing principles, a constitution and a Bill of Rights. The country became a melting pot of people and regions, but Americans evolved into a defined nationality.

Britain gave Canada partial independence in 1867, then full autonomy in 1931, and the country has struggled ever since to stay happily intact. Its three founding groups—aboriginals, the French and the British—have not become a cohesive nationality. Instead, there are over 630 First Nations, many of whose members are dual U.S. citizens, who view their tribes as individual nation-states. The "French fact," or presence of this unique culture, has also been a national challenge. On November 26, 2006, despite two failed attempts by Quebec to secede, Canada's Parliament was pressured into passing a motion that "this House recognize that the Quebecois form a nation within a united Canada."

One interesting survey in 2009 revealed the differing degrees of allegiance within each country. Americans and Canadians were polled by a think tank, the International Association for the Study of Canada, with the support of Leger Marketing and the Association of American Geographers, on their levels of "attachment" to the federal governments, to states or provinces and to cities or towns.[9] Some 76 percent of Americans said they were attached to the United States, 50 percent to their states and 45 percent to a city or town. The responses were also broken down by the ethnic groups of the respondents: 78 percent of Caucasians felt attached to the nation, as did 72 percent of Hispanics and 70 percent of African-Americans. The Canadian poll was quite different. Only 60 percent of Canadians said they were attached to Canada, 55 percent to their provinces and 45 percent to a city or town. When the Canadian results were broken down by the primary language of the respondents, 73 percent of English-speakers felt attached to their nation, versus just 25 percent of French-Canadians and 60 percent of allophones, or persons whose first language is neither English nor French.

Both polls showed that immigrants and large minorities, like the French in Canada, lagged behind the majorities in attachment levels. French separatists have made their feelings known, but Grand Chief Mike Delisle of the Mohawk on Kahnawake Reservation spoke for many First Nations when he said in a 2010 interview with me: "We're not Canadian citizens. If I had to choose, I would be American in a minute. Our people go into the U.S. military forces, not the Canadian forces. We have lots of family down there and connections because of our traditional lands. But the concept of dual citizenship developed out of the Jay Treaty [in 1794]. We are Mohawk citizens only. We are not assimilated or acculturated and don't want to be." This may signal that such groups may be more amenable toward a merger—or, put another way, less likely to oppose one. Large minority groups and immigrants represent a significant factor in any debate, notably in Canada. By 2012, immigrants represented 20 percent of Canada's population and French-Canadians represented roughly 21.5 percent. In the U.S., Hispanics represented 16 percent, African-Americans 12.9 percent, and immigrants 13 percent, the majority of whom are also Hispanic.

RESPECT AND TRUST INCREASE

In general, Canadians and Americans like and trust one another, and appear willing to increase economic integration. Research also shows that so-called "anti-Americanism" fluctuates in reaction to Washington's policies or U.S. media opinion. By contrast, Americans steadfastly admire Canada because most know few details about the country or its occasional criticism of the U.S., but know only that it is a friendly neighbor. This attitudinal asymmetry was articulated in the 1940s by a British-born historian who worked in Canada and the U.S., John Bartlet Brebner, who said "Americans are benevolently ignorant about Canada, while Canadians are malevolently well informed about the United States."

Canadians are more invested in the United States because they are connected to their southern neighbor, both personally and professionally. For instance, in a 2010 poll, 55 percent of Canadians said they had occasionally visited the U.S., compared with 38 percent of Americans who had occasionally visited Canada. Only 4 percent of Canadians said they had never been to the U.S., while

32 percent of Americans had never been to Canada. In terms of economic interdependency, the same poll showed that only 2 percent of Americans said their incomes were "very dependent" on free trade, while 17 percent of Canadians said theirs were. In Canada, 33 percent thought their incomes were "somewhat dependent" on free trade, while 24 percent of Americans did. And while 28 percent of Canadians thought their incomes were "not dependent" on relations with the U.S., nearly three times as many Americans, or 73 percent, felt they had no dependency at all.[10]

As a result, Canadians are preoccupied with the U.S. and take their cues from its media, said Carleton University professor and historian Norman Hillmer. For instance, when so-called anti-Americanism reached a peak in the late 1960s during the Vietnam War escalation, "this 'anti-American' sentiment was inspired by criticisms in the American media of their own government's policies . . . And while we [Canadians] are paradoxical, and at times hypocritical, it does not make us anti-American," said Hillmer.[11]

In other words, if the U.S. media is highly critical of its own country, issues or president, then Canadians will likely be, too. If the U.S. praises Canada, favorability toward Americans increases. In 1999 and 2000, when President Bill Clinton, a Democrat, was popular, 71 percent of Canadians had a "favorable" opinion of the country. Then "favorability" rates began steadily falling, after the Iraq invasion and after conservative commentator Pat Buchanan labeled Canada as "Soviet Canuckistan" and accused the country of being a haven for Arab terrorists. By 2007, President Bush's unpopularity had resulted in a drop in favorability rates by Canadians to 55 percent. Then U.S. popularity among Canadians rose significantly to 68 percent after Obama won the presidency.[12] In 2012, this "Obama effect" remained during his re-election campaign, and a poll by Angus Reid Public Opinion showed that 72 percent of Canadians would vote for Mr. Obama, versus 10 percent for his Republican opponent.[13]

Another example of Canadian sensitivity to American media and public opinion was demonstrated in two polls by Ipsos Reid in 2005 and 2006, commissioned by the Canadian Institute at the Woodrow Wilson International Center for Scholars in Washington. From one year to the next, there was a sizable increase in favorable attitudes between the two populations, with 90 percent of Americans saying they viewed Canada as a friend and ally and 85 percent of Canadians sharing that view, up from 82 percent and 73 percent the year before, respectively. These results mirrored a major change in the relationship. In 2005, Canadians were still being criticized in the U.S. for not participating in the Iraq invasion, occupation and rebuilding. By 2006, Canada had committed to providing 2,500 combat troops in Afghanistan and was widely praised for that in the U.S.

Over the years, Americans have remained more constant in their support for Canada. A Gallup poll in 2012 recorded that 96 percent of Americans rated Canada as their favorite country. This is not a new phenomenon. In September 1939, a Gallup poll in the United States asked, "If Canada is actually invaded by any European power, do you think the United States should use its army and navy to aid Canada?" Some 63 percent of respondents said yes and 22 percent said no, compared to only 5 percent support for declaring war on Germany and sending American soldiers and sailors abroad to fight.

In 1986, 1990 and 1994, a series of Gallup polls taken for the Chicago Council on Foreign Relations found that 90 to 96 percent of American policy elites thought that the U.S. had a vital interest in Canada, as did 70 to 78 percent of the American public. Recent polls registered similar results, according to Gallup research.

POLLS SHOW TOLERANCE FOR MORE POLITICAL
AND ECONOMIC INTEGRATION

In August 2011, a survey by Ipsos revealed that 70 percent of Canadians agreed with greater integration with the U.S. by supporting the Beyond the Border perimeter security plan to blend customs, immigration, security and law enforcement efforts. They agreed the initiative was "necessary and prudent." Surprisingly, women respondents were more "hawkish" than Canadian men, in terms of supporting such American-style methods as increasing antiterrorism vigilance in both countries, the use of armed forces overseas by Canada and enhanced collaboration in these matters with the United States.[14]

The security perimeter represents another step toward European-style integration between the two countries, although this has been downplayed politically. Even if not fully understood, this level of polling support by Canadians signals an acceptance of more integration.

Few polls about an outright merger exist. In 1949, a poll found 21 percent of Canadians were willing to join the U.S. By 1964, this had jumped to 49 percent, said Hillmer. But the momentum likely ended that year as the civil rights movement led to violence and the Vietnam War escalated. Anti-Americanism peaked, due in part to the influx into Canada of disgruntled U.S. draft dodgers and deserters. As Hillmer has stated, Canadians also took their cues from the U.S. media and American expatriates living in Canada.

Arguably, the 1988 free-trade election in Canada was a "poll," or election-based plebiscite, on economic integration with the United States. At its outset, polls showed Canadians were divided 50–50 on the issue, but ad hominem attacks against the unpopular proponent, Prime Minister Brian Mulroney, and inaccurate propaganda against the proposal (all health care would disappear, along with all pensions) whittled down the final vote in favor of free trade to 43 percent. It was not a majority, but translated into 169 seats out of 295 in the House of Commons—a landslide by Canadian political standards, and a result that showed an appetite among nearly half of voters for both integration and risk-taking.

The next publicized poll by Leger Marketing was in September 2002, on the anniversary of 9/11, and it was based on a loaded question: Canadians and Americans were asked if they supported Canada becoming the fifty-first state. Despite that pejorative diminution of Canada's importance, and amid fears of more terrorist attacks, 20 percent of Canadians said they would be in favor, while 38 percent of Americans thought it was a good idea.[15]

Then, in 2007, the World Values Survey Association, a research network of thousands of social scientists, measured American, Canadian and Mexican responses to political union. It also compared survey results in 1990 and 2005 to measure whether values and attitudes were converging. The responses from the two northernmost nations were revealing. The most pointed question was "Would you favor or oppose having Canada and the United States form one country if it meant: a) you would enjoy a higher standard of living; b) you would lose your cultural identity; c) environmental issues could be dealt with more effectively; d) Canada would form twelve new states; e) slightly lower taxes but fewer government services; and f) a better quality of life."

About 77 percent of Americans and 41 percent of Canadians said they would opt for political union if it meant a better quality of life; about 66 percent of Americans and 41 percent of Canadians would support it if it would improve the environment; about 59 percent of Americans and 27 percent of Canadians would opt for a merger if it meant a higher standard of living; about 37 percent of Americans and only 11 percent of Canadians would opt for a merger if it meant twelve new states; about 34 percent of Americans and 17 percent of Canadians would opt for political union if it meant slightly lower taxes but fewer government services; and only 10 percent of Americans and 5 percent of Canadians said they would opt for a merger if it meant losing their respective cultural identities.

Some responses had shifted dramatically between 1990 and 2005. Initially, 43 percent of Americans said they would form one country with Canada even if their cultural identity were at risk, but by 2005 that had shrunk to 10 percent. (The equivalent Canadian responses went from only 11 percent to 5 percent during that time.) There was also slightly decreased support on both sides for political union in the context of all the other scenarios.

Declines were likely affected by cataclysms between those two years—9/11, the ensuing military interventions, tightening of the border and an admission by the Bush Administration that intelligence reports that weapons of mass destruction existed in Iraq were wrong. These events likely reduced interest in integration by Canadians, less inclined to sidle up to a bellicose U.S. whose decision-making had been flawed. As for Americans, these crises made them fearful of any outsiders.

The survey's authors concluded "concerns for national cultural identity underpin both the Canadian and Mexican publics' opposition to the idea of a continental political union. A comparison of how publics react to the higher standard of living and cultural identity scenarios once more graphically illustrates the fundamental dilemmas between the trade-offs of achieving economic gains and the threat posed to collective values that political union implies."

The World Values Survey also posed a second merger question:

"All things considered, do you think we should do away with the border between the United States and Canada and/or Mexico?" In the 2005 result, 22 percent of Canadians favored abolishing the border with the U.S., and 42 percent of Americans did. (Only 18 percent of Americans were in favor of abolishing their border with Mexico, compared with 51 percent of Mexicans.) Removing borders requires trust, and the level of trust among Canadians toward Americans rose between 1990 and 2005, from 55 percent to 63 percent. American attitudes had not been measured in 1990, but in 2005, some 64 percent of Americans polled trusted Canadians.

A more recent study, in 2010, by two political science professors at the University of Western Ontario for the Woodrow Wilson International Center for Scholars measured similar support levels for a merger. Entitled "Moving Closer or Drifting Apart: Assessing the State of Public Opinion on the U.S.–Canada Relationship," the survey showed that 18 percent of Canadians believed that political union was a good idea, 41 percent were neutral and 41 percent thought it was a bad idea. Of Americans polled, 42 percent believed it was a good idea, 46 percent were neutral and only 12 percent thought it was a bad idea.

These pollsters also divided respondents into those familiar and unfamiliar with the other country, based on personal or professional connections. Familiarity led to greater support for further integration. For example, Canadian support increased from 18 percent to 23 percent, while American support went from 42 percent to 48 percent. This confirmed that familiarity breeds greater trust, respect and support for a merger of some form.

Similar results were found by Gallup's pollster Tim Gravelle, who suggested that geographic analysis of all polling shows that favorability rates among Americans and Canadians toward one another increase in proportion to their proximity to the border. The Values Survey authors took this further and concluded that, as with the Europeans, free trade has ushered in an era of increased integration and a gradual convergence in terms of values, deriving from steadily increasing interactions.

There is one example in Canada where familiarity with Americans led to a political movement to integrate with and possibly join the United States. Newfoundland, with Labrador, is bigger than Nova Scotia, New Brunswick and Prince Edward Island combined. The territory remained a dominion, or self-governing colony, of Britain's until the Depression in the 1930s, when it went bankrupt and the British had to assume its debts and take control, forming a commission with locals to govern.

The Second World War brought prosperity to Newfoundland after the Americans were invited to set up military bases. Their soldiers became popular with the locals because "the Yanks' jaunty manner and easy social ways [made] an often stark contrast to the Canadian servicemen who at this time began to coin the epithet 'Newfie,'" wrote historian Karl McNeil Earle in the *American Review of Canadian Studies*. This had political repercussions and, wrote Earle, "in 1948 there was a short-lived but lively movement for economic union with the United States."[16]

After the war, Britain asked Newfoundland to decide by referendum whether to join Canada, remain under British rule or become an independent dominion. The first voting result was 44.5 percent for the coalition in favor of independence (and eventually U.S. free trade), 41.1 percent to join Canada and 14.3 percent to remain under British rule. A second referendum was held a month later because a simple majority had not been reached. The British, somewhat unnerved by polling support to join the United States, controlled the process and dropped British rule from the ballot. The final tally was 52.3 percent in favor of joining Canada and 47.7 percent in favor of independence and U.S. free trade.

Newfoundland demonstrated how socioeconomic factors can trump tradition and politics. Clearly, those opposed to joining Canada were not voting in favor of becoming the fifty-first state, but if they had won, their strategy would have been to sign a free-trade agreement with the Americans and then eventually seek statehood.

What Kind of Merger Would Work?

About 48 percent of Americans support a merger with Canada, but Canadian support lags at around 20 percent, with another 40 percent "neutral" or undecided. But in certain scenarios, Canadian support doubled—specifically, if a merger delivered a better quality of life or improvements to the environment. It also increased to 27 percent if a merger meant a higher standard of living. Among Americans, support jumped to 77 percent for a merger delivering a better quality of life, to 66 percent if it would improve the environment and to 59 percent if it improved living standards.

Americans are more interested in living standards than Canadians, suggested the World Values Survey authors, because proportionately more Canadians are "post-materialistic," or less preoccupied with the fulfillment of material needs such as security, sustenance and shelter. By 2007, their estimates were that 28 percent of Canadians and 18 percent of Americans were "post-materialistic."

These social scientists ascribed this post-materialism to the younger generations living in advanced industrial societies since the Second World War having enjoyed unprecedented prosperity, a social safety net and protection from enemies. The result: a "growing share of the public [who] no longer gave top priority to the quest for economic and physical security. Instead, there was growing concern for the quality of life."

"This shift in basic value priorities," the World Values Survey concluded, "has far-reaching implications; they seem to be linked with generational changes in prevailing motivations to work, in religious outlook, sexual norms, and political goals. There was also evidence of a gradual erosion of traditional nationalism and ethnocentrism, giving rise to an increasingly cosmopolitan sense of identity. Further, these orientations shaped support for economic and political integration among all three populations." The percentage of post-materialist persons in both countries was virtually identical, at around 28 percent of the population, until 9/11. Americans made safety and security a top priority after the attacks, while Canadians did not have to.

These findings indicate that two value propositions in any merger arrangement would have to be available. More Canadians place quality of life above quantity of material goods because they live in a relatively coddled country guarded by the superpower to their south. They might support a deal if health care and the environment were protected and they could move to a warmer climate with lower taxes and living costs. They also would want to be shielded from America's proclivity toward jingoism, from some of its more excessive demands on its residents, such as the possibility of a return to military conscription, and from its fractious politics. As Canadian historian Jack Granatstein wrote, "Canadians are Americans who clearly don't want to be U.S. citizens."

But Canadians are increasingly living under uncertain economic conditions and have become a "takeover target" among the world's rivalrous developing nations. And Americans live in a competitive economy that is also a terrorist target, and are more frightened of losing their possessions or of being attacked militarily. They both might support a merger that would secure economic growth and jobs, and also secure the borders, no matter the price.

The Politics of Regionalism in a Merger

The late Paul Cellucci, the former U.S. ambassador to Canada and governor of Massachusetts, believed a merger of values had already taken place, but that regional variances persisted. "The differences between people in the U.S. and Canada are not significant on one level. Both have free and open democratic societies, both support free trade with one another and both are prosperous. But I believe there are more differences within the countries than between the countries. For instance, people from Quebec and Alberta are as different as are people from Massachusetts and Mississippi," he told me in an interview in 2010.

In politics, regions matter more than other factors. For instance, Latinos in Texas vote differently than Latinos in California. Religious people living in the Deep South tend to be more socially conservative than their northern counterparts. In Canada, immigrants in Alberta vote Conservative, while in Ontario or Quebec they have traditionally voted Liberal (or Conservative since 2006). Blue-collar workers vote Conservative in Alberta, but their votes are divided among more left-wing parties in Ontario and Quebec or British Columbia.

These voting anomalies exist because people adapt and adhere to their local or regional political and social subcultures. The most dramatic illustration is the breakdown of voting between Democrats and Republicans in the five presidential elections between 1992 and

2008 into two super-regions. Twenty-one "blue" states, along with the District of Columbia, voted for the Democratic candidate at least four out of five times, while twenty-two "red" states consistently voted for a Republican. The remaining seven states were Nevada, West Virginia, Ohio, Arkansas, Florida, Colorado and Missouri; these are called swing, or "purple," states because neither party has enough support that they can count on winning them. In the 2012 election, four of the seven "purple" states—Nevada, Florida, Colorado and Ohio—voted Democrat.[17]

This means that, electorally, there are two Americas, one bedrock red and another blue. Election of the president of the United States is, in essence, tipped in one direction or another by voters in the seven purple states. These battleground states are where candidates concentrate their campaign appearances, fundraising efforts, advertising budgets, platform initiatives and recruitment efforts for vice-presidential nominees.

In 2004, Jeff Minter, a British computer game designer with a sense of humor, noticed this consistent red/blue trend. So he posted on the Internet a cheeky version of the U.S.–Canada map that went viral. He redrew the border to create two new nations: Canada was joined with the Democratic or blue states of New England, the Mid-Atlantic, the West coast, Illinois, Michigan, Minnesota and Wisconsin. He labeled this region the "United States of Canada." The rest—the Republican, or red, states—included the South and the Great Plains. He labeled this region "Jesus Land" because of a proclivity among its populaces toward social conservatism and religiosity. In effect, he illustrated the country's two distinct super-regions.

The twenty-two steadfastly blue-voting jurisdictions are also, like Canada, liberal on a range of policies. For example, same-sex marriages are legal in Connecticut, Iowa, Maine, Maryland, Massachusetts,

New Hampshire, New York, Vermont, Washington and the District of Columbia;[18] seventeen of the twenty-two have banned, restricted or imposed a moratorium on capital punishment;[19] eighteen have legalized, decriminalized or liberalized the use of marijuana for medical reasons, and in 2012, voters in Washington, Oregon and Colorado supported ballot measures to legalize marijuana for recreational use, making them the first jurisdictions in Canada or the United States to do so;[20] and two of the twenty-two, Washington and Oregon, were the first governments in the western hemisphere to legalize assisted suicide.[21]

Polls confirm that there is no longer a gaping divide nationally in terms of certain contentious social issues. Even in the divisive area of universal health care, a poll published in 2011 by the U.S.–based Opinion Research Corporation suggested that 40 percent of Americans believe Canada has a better system.[22] Other polls have shown similar results. Support for the legalization of marijuana is 66 percent in Canada and 58 percent in the United States. Support for gay marriage is 59 percent in Canada and 53 percent in the United States. And for capital punishment in cases of murder, 66 percent of Canadians are in favor, compared with 64 percent in the United States, even though Canada hasn't had capital punishment in decades, while capital punishment exists in most states.

Polls also showed mutual support for increased energy production and for pipelines through the U.S. to transport oil. In the spring of 2012, 65 percent of Canadians agreed it was "possible to increase oil and gas production while protecting the environment at the same time." In terms of the oil sands specifically, 57 percent of Canadians agreed that the overall benefits outweighed the negatives.[23] In the U.S., 57 percent of Americans supported building the Keystone XL pipeline to transport oil sands production to American refineries, despite concerns about risk of a spill, according to Gallup polling in March 2012.[24]

In September 2010, the Pew Research Center poll found that 50 percent of Americans favored gun controls over gun rights, while 46 percent chose rights over controls.[25] In 2010, a Canadian poll found 66 percent favored restrictions, in the form of a gun registry, to control gun ownership.[26] (Despite concerns in the two countries that controls were needed, Canada's gun registry system was scrapped in 2011 and gun controls in the U.S. were limited to only a few jurisdictions, such as New York City.)

A more comprehensive poll in 2012 registered a shift among Americans toward Canadian and European-style attitudes. The nonpartisan, nonprofit, ecumenical Public Religion Research Institute found that 67 percent of respondents favored raising the minimum wage dramatically and increasing taxes on wealthy Americans; nearly 80 percent believed the gap between rich and poor had grown in twenty years; and 60 percent felt society would be better off if the distribution of wealth were more equal. Two-thirds said the government should do more to narrow the income gap.[27]

Polls show that the "United States of Canada" represents a virtual, cohesive super-region, and if a merger occurred, the balance of power would tip toward the Democrats or "blue" states and liberal policies. Put another way, if Canadians became partners with Americans, there might never be another Republican in the White House.

The Outlier Regions:
Quebec and the Deep South in a Merger

American journalist Joel Garreau redrew the map of North America in 1981 in his book *The Nine Nations of North America.* His breakthrough idea ignored North America's borders and defined nine unique socioeconomic and cultural regions. These included: New England and Canada's Atlantic provinces; the industrialized regions of both countries, centered around Detroit; the Deep South; the Great Plains and the Prairie provinces of Canada; the rural U.S. Midwest; Miami and Puerto Rico; "Mexamerica" on both sides of the border; the Pacific Northwest and British Columbia; the Arctic regions and far west; and, lastly and on its own, Quebec.

Thirty years later, the nine nations no longer exist, given dramatic demographic shifts. For example, the ten largest cities in the U.S. in 1970 were New York, Chicago, Los Angeles, Philadelphia, Detroit, Houston, Baltimore, Dallas, Washington and Cleveland. Four decades later, the ten largest were New York, Los Angeles, Chicago, Houston, Phoenix, Philadelphia, San Antonio, San Diego, Dallas and San Jose. Deindustrialization, Mexican immigration and relocation by retirees changed the landscape.

There have been shifts in Canada too. Between 1960 and 2010, the four western provinces grew from 25 percent of the Canadian population to 29 percent, and Quebec declined from 30 percent to 20 percent. In 1970, Canada's five largest urban areas were Montreal, Toronto, Ottawa, Vancouver and Calgary. By 2009, the ranking had changed to Toronto first, by a significant margin, then Montreal, Vancouver, Calgary and Ottawa.

Of Garreau's "nine nations," and excluding Mexico, there arguably remain only three: the liberal "United States of Canada," the states that seceded in 1860 and comprise the so-called Deep South and, finally, Quebec.

The Deep South and Quebec are poles apart policy-wise, but are relatively homogeneous and culturally distinct compared with other regions. Not coincidentally, the two have aspired to leave their federal governments—one did briefly and one did not—and both have since learned to be disproportionately successful politically. Their residents vote strategically, usually as blocs. Quebec's voters were the cornerstone of the ruling Liberal Party for decades, but have supported separatist parties at the federal and provincial levels since 1976.

In the United States, the Deep South (Texas, Louisiana, Arkansas, Missouri, Alabama, Georgia, Florida, South Carolina, Tennessee, North Carolina, Virginia and West Virginia) had been loyal to the Democrats (nicknamed Dixiecrats) until the civil rights movement gained steam in the 1960s and alienated them. In 1968, southerners threw their support partially behind a breakaway party launched by segregationist Alabama Governor George Wallace. He carried five states, but Republican Richard Nixon won handily. Even so, Nixon engineered the Republicans' "southern strategy" and wooed the Deep South by promising to champion states' rights, among other pledges.

A disproportionate number of prime ministers and presidents have come from these two regions, as well as veteran legislators. As a result, the influence of Quebec, and its aggressive policy of protecting its French-speaking citizens, their language and culture—known as "francization"—have pulled Canada to the left in terms of policy, toward bilingualism, French-style statism, social democracy and pacifism. Referendums on independence from Canada failed by a 60–40 margin in 1980 and by a single percentage point in 1995. The aspiration has remained alive and, in 2012, Quebec separatists won election again. The Parti Québécois perpetuates the threat of separatism to extract special privileges and treatment, but its leaders are committed to leaving Canada someday. In March 2012, polling support for independence hit 45 percent.

In the U.S., the "southernization" factor has pulled the Republican Party and the United States to the right, or toward social conservatism, religious fundamentalism and support for the military or patriotism. And, like Quebec, the threat of secession continues more than a century after the U.S. Civil War. Immediately following the 2012 re-election of President Obama, hundreds of thousands of signatures were gathered on petitions in the Deep South asking state legislatures to begin the process of seceding from the country. But Texas Governor Rick Perry, an Obama rival, dismissed these initiatives out of hand, saying his state would never entertain secession again.

The power of these voting blocs in elections is well documented. In 2011, Prime Minister Harper won the election with 39.42 percent of the nation's popular vote, but obtained 48 percent of the popular vote outside Quebec. In 2012, President Obama won 51.02 percent of the national popular vote and made inroads in the Deep South, specifically in swing states such as Virginia and Florida, where minorities and urban migration had changed the electorate. But in the rest of the Deep South, he lost by mostly large margins, including nearly 16 percent in Texas and 27 percent in West Virginia.

Both of these outliers may oppose any merger if they believe their political clout would be diluted. On the other hand, Quebec separatists might overwhelmingly opt for a merger, as they did in 1988 with free trade, if only to get out from under English-Canadians. They would likely use negotiations to try to gain advantages or more autonomy for Quebec and the French language and culture. Likewise, a merger may appeal to some English-Canadians, if only to get out from under Quebec separatism by reducing its importance within a larger political entity.

The South may also support a merger because the addition of 34.4 million Canadians would result in an economic boom in their region. A major migration of Canadians would leave for America's warmer climates and lower living costs, and Canada's two million or so snowbirds would stay permanently in Florida, Arizona, California and other Sunbelt destinations if affordable health care was available.

The Political Parties in a Merger

Canada has five parties in its federal Parliament at any given time. The last time a single party obtained at least 50.1 percent of the popular vote was in 1957, when the Conservatives under John Diefenbaker got 53.7 percent. Brian Mulroney's Conservatives polled 50.03 percent in 1984, while the Liberals led by Louis St. Laurent received 50.08 percent in 1949. Since 2000, neither of the two dominant parties (Conservatives and Liberals) has garnered more than 39 percent of the popular vote. By contrast, only two parties dominate the U.S. system, with occasional—and marginal—third party candidacies. The result is that most successful candidates for president attract half of the ballots cast.

The differing systems intrigued American sociologist and political scientist Seymour Lipset. Sociologically, he observed a basic difference in orientation and political sensibility. "Americans do not know, but Canadians cannot forget, that two nations, not one, came out of the American Revolution. The United States is the country of the revolution and Canada is the country of the counter-revolution," he wrote in *Continental Divide.*

The counterrevolutionaries—a coalition of United Empire Loyalists from the U.S., aboriginals, the English and the French—feared being overrun by the rowdy and violent Americans. They supported the British, who promised to protect their lands, treaties, entitlements and Roman Catholic or Anglican religion from the aggressive, radicalized Protestant Americans.

Lipset also described how the two nations' political architecture diverged. Not surprisingly, Canada's three national parties were offshoots of Britain's three parties: the Tories (loyal to the Crown), Labour (socialists) and Liberals (anti-monarchy and privilege). But America's two national parties were branches of the same radical British party, the Liberal Party, or Whigs.

"[T]he new world [was left] to the Whigs and Nonconformists and to those constructive, less logical, more popular and liberating thinkers who became Radicals in England, and Jeffersonians and then Democrats in America," he wrote in 1997. "All Americans are, from the English point of view, Liberals of one sort or another . . . The liberalism of the eighteenth century was essentially the rebellion . . . against the monarchical and aristocratic state, against hereditary privilege, against restrictions on bargains. Its spirit was essentially anarchistic— the antithesis of Socialism. It was anti-State."

Canadians are not anti-state, but they are not socialists either. The Americans threw the tea in the harbor and told government to get out of their lives. The British North Americans obeyed their monarch and clerics and paid taxes to the Crown. Centuries later, Canadians rarely balk at tax increases (wealthy ones have the option of moving, paying a one-time departure tax and living tax-free somewhere); they enjoy government paternalism and are content with, or oblivious to, the fact that 89 percent of their country's landmass, much of their economy and many of their corporations are controlled or regulated by governments. They tolerate this, contrary to Americans, who have privatized most of their landmass and still complain about any and all taxation.

Canadian governments own the health care and education systems (universities are government-owned), most electrical utilities and power distributors, liquor monopolies, gaming monopolies and auto insurance monopolies. In Quebec, the province imposes severe language restrictions on public education, signage, advertising and the workplace. Everything, from television programming, to the number and content of radio stations, to banking practices, is regulated.

Another differentiator is the monarchy—technically, the king or queen is Canada's head of state. Polling, however, has shown that Canadians can be as fickle toward the royals as they are when polled about the U.S. For instance, Canadian "support" peaked at 52 percent immediately after the wedding of the popular Prince William, but had fallen to 18 percent after Lady Diana's death. A 2010 poll showed that a majority of Canadians wanted to get out from under their parliamentary monarchy system of government toward something resembling an American republic.

All of these political strains and parties would play a role, but independent voters must back any type of merger if it is to succeed. They are as important as parties. In 1952, for instance, only 22 percent of Americans were self-declared independents. By 2011, this constituency had risen to 30 percent.[28] It's not unusual for citizens to vote Democrat at the federal level, then Republican at the state level. In Canada, voting also veers wildly from Conservative to Liberal, NDP, Green and Separatist. These voters are driven not by ideology, but by issues, policies or candidates.

Support for a partnership would have to cross party lines in both countries. Democrats, who opposed free trade, might welcome the addition of 34.4 million liberal-minded Canadians. Republicans, who supported free trade, would not welcome another 34.4 million Democrats, but might support a merger that would enhance business, trade, economic growth, security and control over Arctic shipping and that would lock up all the energy and raw materials needed in future. Canadians, politically fragmented, would weigh whether the economic benefits and security of a merger outweighed the benefits of nation-state autonomy.

Templates for a Political Merger

Support would depend on the structure of a deal. How much Canadians would get as compensation is dealt with in chapter 5. But would a merger be total or partial? Would it be strictly economic or a combination of economic and political union, and if the latter, to what degree? Would it be done in stages? Would it look like Germany, the European Union, the Swiss Federation or a hybrid?

THE GERMAN MODEL

Germany's reunification was, like the Germans themselves, efficient and straightforward. Plebiscites were held in both East and West Germany and passed handily. The next issue was the mechanics. Each country had a constitution, so a merger required the writing of a new one. Constitutional experts advised that this could take years, so politicians opted to use the accession clause in West Germany's constitution. This allowed East Germany's *länders,* or states, to join immediately if their federal government and individual parliaments approved. Eleven months after the Berlin Wall was breached, the *länders* joined and the East German federal government simply disappeared. Its assets and bureaucracy were subsumed into the new, enlarged Federal Republic of Germany.

A full-fledged U.S.–Canada political and economic merger process could be similar. The writing of a new U.S.–Canada constitution would be onerous and likely impossible given the amendment thresholds required by each country's constitutions. In Canada, a national referendum would be held and in the U.S., the president and Congress would have to approve the start of talks. The U.S. Constitution has no provision for national referendums.

If a deal were approved, and a German approach undertaken, then the ten provinces and three territories could request accession from Congress as thirteen new U.S. states. Part of their admission to the union would have to involve special privileges for the provinces, which have more constitutional powers and privileges than U.S. states. If this were not possible, then compensation or dispensation of some sort would have to be negotiated.

One mechanism to accommodate this asymmetry—two distinct subnational structures—would be to give provinces the right to join as commonwealths, not states. Puerto Rico and the Northern Mariana Islands in the Pacific Ocean have this status. (Puerto Rico voted in the 2012 election to seek statehood.) Each has a republican form of government, and the president of the United States is their head of state. Their residents are U.S. citizens but cannot vote or serve in the military unless they live in the fifty states. They must adhere to U.S. federal laws and pay federal taxes. They cannot become independent or full-fledged states without the permission of Congress. Puerto Rico has two official languages, English and Spanish. The United States has no official language. Clearly, commonwealth status might be more attractive to a province like Quebec.

One challenge would be to reconcile and coordinate three legal systems: English Canada's, Quebec's and the United States'. In Germany, for instance, abortion was ruled unconstitutional in West Germany, but was legalized in East Germany. The compromise, after some debate, was that abortion would remain unconstitutional, but women could obtain the procedure within the former East Germany without being prosecuted.

In the U.S. and Canada, however, there already exists a mix of legal systems, state by state and province by province, that have coexisted smoothly for decades because of extradition agreements and treaties. Crimes and punishments vary and could continue to do so, as is the case in the European Union.

A German-style merger would also mean Canada's thirteen provinces and territories would join as states or commonwealths, but its Canadian federal government would disappear and its assets and bureaucracy would be subsumed into the newly merged entity or become employees of the Arctic region and its newly minted states of Yukon, Northwest Territories and Nunavut, where economic development would be accelerated.

In addition, Canadians would get a premium to exchange their dollars for U.S. dollars, as well as enormous compensation, in the form of entitlements and bonds, for their over-contribution of assets. This would turn Canadians collectively into the new country's largest creditors, or holders of government bond debt, which would entitle them to elect representatives who would have control, and oversight, over all the new country's budgetary, taxation and monetary institutions. Such control by fiscally conservative Canadian custodians might be welcomed by some Americans, if only to break Congressional gridlock and overspending habits.

THE EUROPEAN UNION MODEL

The European Union has taken a gradualist approach to unification because of the sensitivities within each nation about protecting their sovereignty and culture. The result is that Europe has spent sixty years creating a single economic zone as well as a fourth layer of government that sits on top of twenty-seven nation-states. The EU's efforts have been discredited since 2010 because of the sovereign debt and euro crises, but this was due to one mistake that could be easily avoided by the U.S. and Canada in their pursuit of a merger.

Europe's officials assumed, after becoming a customs union and single economy, that the next logical step was a monetary union. They were correct, but their execution was flawed. They created the euro, but did not impose fiscal and debt oversight or controls over those members that joined. The result has been catastrophic because several Eurozone members, such as Greece, were fiscally irresponsible and refused to comply to the point where they have had to be financially bailed out by the responsible members.

The EU single market, on the other hand, has been a model that has erased borders to allow the free movement of people, goods, capital and services. This has worked because its twenty-seven members have standardized their policies on trade, agriculture, fisheries and regional development, then established institutions to supervise and improve these common areas. At the same time, they retain control over their own national law enforcement, taxation, foreign, fiscal, environment, jurisprudence, defense and social policies, while, at the same time, collaborating in the areas of law enforcement, antiterrorism and national defense. For instance, a tax evader, terrorist or deadbeat dad living in one EU country where laws have not been broken will be investigated, arrested and extradited to another EU country to stand trial.

The U.S. and Canada could easily create a single economy, a monetary union and a political union step by step with compensation to Canadians for their over-contribution of assets. A fourth level of government could be formed, governed 50–50 by the two countries, which would be responsible for common areas of interest.

Representatives could be elected or appointed by Washington and Ottawa, and their responsibility would be to supervise and coordinate regional development. An adaptation of the EU model could work well in part because the two national and sixty-three subnational governments would remain intact. The template is less efficient than Germany's because of the cost and complexity of creating another bureaucracy, but may be politically palatable.

THE SWISS MODEL

Another possibility, no matter what type of deal was approved, would be to create a fourth layer of government based on the Swiss model, not the European Union's. The Swiss created their unique governance system following a civil war and in order to unite four linguistic groups into a cohesive federation. The Swiss do not have a president or prime minister; rather, their federal legislators choose seven people from slates of distinguished candidates proposed by major parties as members of the Federal Council of the Swiss Confederation. The oldest of the seven serves as president, and the position rotates annually in order of seniority. The result is that no individual is the Swiss head of state; the entire Federal Council is in charge.

Politically, the Swiss seven-member structure is both inclusive and decisive. Members of the Federal Council are drawn from all political parties and regions. Its structure prevents gridlock because meetings are held in private and, in case of a 3–3 split, the seventh member breaks the tie. The Swiss people are also actively involved in governance through regular referendums held to approve or reject federal and/or cantonal initiatives. The result is a successful and pleasant nation-state. The American and Canadian founding fathers rejected such a system, or governing via referendums, known as direct democracy, in favor of indirect democracy through elected representatives, to avoid the "tyranny of the mob."

That is another discussion, but the Swiss Federal Council may be an optimal binational structure should the two nations form a fourth layer of government atop their two existing federal ones. There would be the governments of the United States and Canada, plus a Federal Council, elected by Congress and Parliament from a roster of blue-ribbon nominees. Even better would be the creation of a Swiss-style state to replace the U.S. and Canadian federal governments. This would involve merging Congress and Parliament, then forming two legislative branches with a Federal Council as the executive branch.

Mexico Would Not Be a Merger Candidate at This Stage

Some Canadians may argue that a merger would be more acceptable if Mexico were involved in order to help counterbalance the influence of the United States. But Mexico's involvement as a partner in the North American Free Trade Agreement since 1994 has, in some ways, prevented the United States and Canada from moving dramatically beyond their initial, two-way free-trade agreement to a borderless customs union or monetary union as countries in Europe, Africa and the Caribbean have done.

The North American Free Trade Agreement grew out of the Canada–U.S. Free Trade Agreement and is not a trilateral deal but three bilateral trade agreements involving the three countries. In hindsight, Mexico's membership, in 1994, was premature and inappropriate because the country was a developing nation with weak political, judicial, police and military institutions, rife with systemic corruption. Nearly twenty years later, its per capita incomes are still one-third those of its two NAFTA trade partners.

Further integration with Mexico, aimed at erasing borders, is simply impossible, and perhaps will be for decades. And its participation in NAFTA has impeded any attempts to harmonize and standardize customs and other processes. In 2010, the United States and Canada realized, finally, they could only deepen their trade relationship bilaterally. But years have been lost in terms of taking the next steps because of Mexico's situation and a series of calamities.

The day Mexico joined NAFTA, on New Year's Day in 1994, an armed insurrection led by a leftist revolutionary group that opposed globalization took place in a southern region called Chiapas. The Mexican army pushed the group back into the jungle, but from their hiding places they mounted a clever media campaign to highlight the plight of the indigenous Mayans and others throughout the country who felt left out of the country's equation.

The uprising gave Mexico, and NAFTA, a black eye, and the armed struggle frightened away investment and cost the country billions. Then, on March 23, 1994, the country reeled when an assassin stepped up to a platform in Tijuana during the Mexican presidential election and murdered Luis Colosio, a popular front-runner. A man was arrested at the scene of the crime and was later convicted. He claimed to have acted alone, but few believed that story.

A new candidate was chosen in a hurry, and on December 4, 1994, Ernesto Zedillo was inaugurated as president. Two days later, the Mexican peso collapsed in value. Zedillo was faced with a currency crisis because the previous regime had secretly used all the country's foreign reserves and credit lines to artificially prop up the peso during the tumultuous year.

Within hours, U.S. President Bill Clinton orchestrated a

bailout involving loans and guarantees consisting of $20 billion from Washington; $17.7 billion from the International Monetary Fund; $10 billion from the Bank for International Settlements; and $1 billion from the Bank of Canada. Mexico eventually recovered, as did the peso, and the nation paid back all debts within a handful of years.

Around this time, Mexico's drug cartels began taking over the cocaine and heroin trade from the Colombian cartels. They succeeded and have turned Mexico into a major staging ground for narcotics smuggling into the United States. Their existence has become a corrosive and corrupting influence in the country. Military forces have had to replace police in many regions, and violence has become widespread. "By January 2012, the Mexican government reported that 47,515 people had been killed in drug-related violence since President Felipe Calderón began a military assault on criminal cartels soon after taking office in late 2006," said *The New York Times.*

The casualties included innocent bystanders, tourists, clergy, journalists, police and mayors. This drug war, plus poverty, has contributed to the constant flood of illegal immigrants into the United States, an influx that has provoked some states to pass draconian legislation to catch illegal immigrants, and led to the rise of vigilante groups taking it upon themselves to patrol the U.S. border. The United States has stationed thousands of troops along its southern border and built a fortified wall in high-traffic regions. The country has become enmeshed in a debilitating debate about immigration, illegal aliens and whether to support their dependents, and prosecution of the expensive war on drugs.

While the Mexican immigration and drug crisis is bilateral, its mud has splattered across NAFTA and made talks aimed at opening up the Canada–U.S. border difficult. American nativists such as

Phyllis Schlafly, Jerome Corsi or former CNN anchor Lou Dobbs have characterized NAFTA as a conspiracy between Canada and Mexico to destroy America and create a "socialist mega-state."

These and other controversies underscore that if Mexico had not joined the U.S. and Canada in a trade agreement, the two mature economies would have been well down the path toward a customs union, a monetary union or even a political union. Fortunately, they realized in 2010 that they must tend their bilateral relationship through a "security perimeter" arrangement, leaving Mexico aside. But the damage has already been done. The influx of illegal Mexican immigrants and drugs has damaged NAFTA's image in the minds of many Americans. The only way a merger can succeed in the United States is if the partnership is two-way with Canada.

America and Canada at the Crossroads

The overriding value proposition for a merger would be that Canadians and Americans could benefit more, with minimal cultural friction, if they became one entity. Both live in pluralist societies that are melting pots, which means that the assimilation skills required to create a new, larger entity already exist; both would cash in on resources in Canada that might otherwise remain undeveloped or become seized by interlopers; and both would gain access to one another's countries.

The arguments against a merger would be that the status quo is working and that cultures must be protected. Clearly, culture matters, but money matters more, as a 2012 poll in Scotland demonstrated. In 2014, the Scots will hold a referendum on whether to become independent or remain part of the United Kingdom. The debate has been emotional and is rooted in the desire of fiercely nationalistic Scots to get out from under the English.

A number of polls in early 2012 registered support for independence at between 44 and 51 percent. But *The Economist* found a poll that asked the "money" question and "found that just 21% of Scots would favor independence if it would leave them £500 ($795) a year worse off, and only 24% would vote to stay in the union even if they would be less well off sticking with Britain. Almost everyone else would vote for independence if it brought in roughly enough money to buy a new iPad and against it if not."[29]

The debate has focused on quantifying the impact of Scottish independence, and both sides have provided contradictory conclusions. Scottish nationalists have argued that independence would allow Scots to innovate, self-actualize as a nation and become more prosperous. But others have argued that a small nation without resources or access to a larger market would struggle to prosper, thus impairing future prospects. Prominent Scot historian Niall Ferguson, in a BBC interview I attended at the World Economic Forum in Davos in 2012, said he supported independence as a young man twenty years ago, but the opportunity had passed because "the [North Sea] oil is running out."

Whatever the outcome, Scotland's debate reveals how globalization and mass migration have reshaped attitudes, not only among those of the Scottish diaspora such as Ferguson, who lives in the United States, but among those left behind at home. People, even though ethnically and historically linked to their homeland, have little allegiance or attachment to that homeland if benefits, opportunities or safety disappear. Citizenship is political consumerism, and people (and corporations) reside where it makes the most sense or cents.

As Kenichi Ohmae posited in *End of the Nation State: The Rise of*

Regional Economies, maps are "cartographic illusions" and the citizen-consumer will increasingly refuse to be a vassal or taxable asset without his or her consent. For example, the French actor Gerard Depardieu left France in 2012 because of the socialist government's punitive 75 percent income tax, combined with insults toward him and wealth creation, and in early 2013 he accepted Russian citizenship from President Vladimir Putin, along with 13 percent income taxes. He became the world's highest-profile jurisdiction shopper, and Putin became the first leader from a developed country to entice a taxpayer with free citizenship. Some 214 million people don't live where they were born, and a poll in 2012 said another 640 million would leave home if they could, for a total of one in seven people globally. In this case, attachments are tenuous, and if the economic benefits of the Merger of the Century are proven to be substantial for Americans and Canadians, the transaction will happen. If not, it won't.

The same enmeshing trajectory has been traced in Australia and New Zealand since their free-trade deal in 1983. By 2010, integration had proceeded so dramatically that 41 percent of New Zealanders polled wanted to debate the possibility, while 25 percent supported joining Australia immediately as its seventh state. In 1901, New Zealand had been offered statehood and declined, but the Australian constitution still contains a provision inviting New Zealand in by a simple majority in Parliament.

The 25 percent in favor said a merger would boost the economy, jobs and living standards; that because New Zealand was too small to be independent and/or could not survive on its own, it would benefit from being part of a bigger state; that the two countries were basically the same country; that travel would be easier; and that the countries would experience greater success in international sporting events. Opponents said that New Zealand would lose its identity and culture;

that New Zealand deserved to be independent and is fine on its own; that Australia was not trustworthy; and that New Zealand would become a subsidiary if it joined Australia.[30]

Sir Don McKinnon, former secretary-general of the Commonwealth and former deputy prime minister of New Zealand, created a stir when he said a merger was "probably inevitable" and would likely occur within a generation as economic links between the two continued to grow. "We've got nearly half a million New Zealanders living in Australia anyway," he said. "By the time the next generation comes around, technology and the movement of people everywhere, New Zealanders won't want to be in the situation of paying taxes in both countries and all the time going through immigration and customs. They'll want to try to eliminate all those things."[31]

New Zealand Prime Minister John Key responded: "It's not going to happen and I don't think we should waste any time even thinking about it. The reality is what will make New Zealand a successful country are the same things that would make it a successful state of Australia."[32] But, as Sir Don McKinnon said, the issue won't go away. It won't there, and it won't in North America, either.

The same debate needs to occur in the United States and Canada. The conversation would be difficult, divisive and emotional. National narratives would collide. But a conversation would be healthy, if only to force policy makers, politicians and people on both sides of the border to take inventory, examine all options and come up with a better alternative than the Merger of the Century, if one exists. Critics cannot simply dismiss this idea. Merger or not, these countries must reinvent themselves. Inertia and procrastination are not options because of roiling events globally. As Shakespeare warned in *Henry VI, Part I*, "delays have dangerous ends."

CHAPTER SEVEN

If There Is No Merger Soon

We are relying on the U.S., and as a Canadian nationalist, I believe that defense is something you really have to pay for. If you are defended by somebody else, you are not really sovereign.

—JACK GRANATSTEIN

C ANADA HAS BECOME NEARLY AS DEPENDENT ON THE UNITED
States as it has historically been on Britain. The significance
of this idea, which many Canadians have not acknowledged,
recasts the proposition of a merger. It is not a new, shocking idea but
merely the logical result of integration and interdependency between
the two that have been underway for a long time.

Dependency has been by consent on the part of Canadians, but
the danger is that drifting into deeper integration, without compensation for resources or retention of control, constitutes, in stock
market terms, what's called a creeping takeover. Such transactions
involve investors who slowly acquire shares in a target company
until they obtain control. This is illegal in stock markets in developed
countries because creeping takeovers allow buyers to avoid paying a
premium to shareholders for control. The only defense against such
maneuvers is to recruit the assistance of a white knight, an acceptable partner who is willing to pay a premium for control. In the case
of Canada, the white knight would be the United States, but the
Americans have been doing most of the creeping.

Perhaps this glacial drift from sovereignty will be the chosen
path of Canadians and Americans—a tacit, unacknowledged coast-
ing into one another's arms. After all, this creeping takeover has

been ongoing with the complicity of Canadians and their leaders. In a sense, Canadians have been "voting" for a merger, whether they realized it or not, by selling their companies, assets and talent to Americans. They have spent trillions buying American products and services while exporting themselves as immigrants, travelers, students, investors, spouses and retirees.

By 2010, American corporations owned 10.34 percent of all Canadian business assets, including nearly half of its manufacturing and oil sectors; had captured 13 percent, or one dollar, out of every $7.60 in business revenues;[1] had 38.6 percent of all retail sales;[2] had bought 73.7 percent of Canada's exports;[3] and executed the majority of trades involving Canada's 4,800 publicly listed stocks on their own domestic exchanges.[4] As mentioned before, foreigners of all kinds owned 19.7 percent of business assets and 28.9 percent of business revenues.[5]

Canada's export of talent to the U.S. represents another symptom of this slow-motion alliance. One in ten Canadians lives full or part time in the U.S., and works there on temporary work permits, illegally or as independent contractors. The state of Florida estimates that spending and investment by Canadian tourists and retirees alone represents 8 percent of all real estate sales and employs 5.4 percent of all Floridians annually.[6] In 2008, I estimated that, based on $150,000-a-year salaries, the Canadian diaspora in the United States had an economic output of $165 billion, bigger than Manitoba and Saskatchewan's $130.6 billion in 2011.[7] That does not count the income generated by another 1.7 million Canadians who, according to Statistics Canada, live in countries other than the United States.[8]

The combination of a brain drain, immigrants who obtain citizenship then leave within a few years and low birth rates makes Canada one of the oldest countries in the world, as demographer

David Foot has pointed out.[9] The United States is a relatively young nation, demographically. This makes them complementary in addition to the reality that these two countries are more economically integrated than any other countries, including any two nations in the European Union.

Despite the need, a full-fledged coalition might still be rejected or prove to be politically impossible. If so, there are other options: Canadians and Americans can continue with the status quo or, alternatively, Canadians can dilute American ownership and dependency through aggressive and independent economic development. This is a "northern tiger" option, which will be explored in more detail later. But it would still entail massive amounts of capital.

The Status Quo Option for Canada

This is a very attractive choice for many Canadians, because the existing relationship has been beneficial. The two countries have prospered together, developed together and defended themselves together. Canada's business model has essentially developed high living standards by inviting Americans and others to invest in order to find resources or make products that can be exported back to them. Americans also protect the continent without asking Canadians to help defray some of their costs incurred in patrolling the Arctic and coastlines. Better yet, Canadians can retire or vacation in America's warmer climes. Even better, the Americans don't bully Canada, say status quo proponents, so there would be no compelling reason to speed up or deepen integration, much less to merge.

This view, however, is as questionable as its underlying assumptions: that Canada can prosper in future as currently constituted;

that manufacturing will remain despite Canada's low productivity and high dollar; that the economy can prosper if it becomes mostly dependent on volatile commodity prices; that Canada can count on U.S. investment and imports indefinitely; that protectionism won't arise in the U.S.; that the United States will protect Canada and its Arctic forever without charge; that Canada can compete directly against the U.S. for exports and talent; and that Canada can develop its hinterland or can reverse its damaging brain drain.

The biggest misconception about maintaining the status quo is the belief that the status quo can be maintained. The world becomes more treacherous. China, Russia, India and dozens more countries need North America's economic market share and living standards. Canada continues to lose people and remains one of the top ten countries sending immigrants to the U.S., at a pace of nearly 500,000 educated people every decade, or the population of Quebec City or Tucson, Arizona.

The Status Quo Option for the United States

The United States remains the world's foremost superpower. Its economy has been the world's most innovative and productive. Americans enjoy high living standards and they value enterprise, hard work and competition. They are proud and believe their country is superior. But after the catastrophe of 2008, a majority of Americans have a more nuanced view of their nation, and should. Triumphalism—the proposition that the United States is the greatest country in the world—is still trotted out in electoral stump speeches, but its inaccuracy makes many Americans uncomfortable and, outside their country, makes them appear boastful and foolish.

Americans, like Canadians, believe that their countries and their relationship are fine as is. The two have become one another's biggest customers, investors and suppliers. Canada has been a favored investment destination and is a compatible neighbor. Canada is not troublesome, as Mexico is, and has become dependent, economically and militarily. The partnership is not broken and doesn't need fixing, the argument goes, so the status quo is fine.

These views, however, are as questionable as their underlying assumptions: that Canada will remain loyal and tethered to the U.S. given the planned encroachment by China, Russia and others; that the United States can prosper in future as currently constituted; that manufacturing will remain despite international competition; that the U.S. can eliminate the jobs gap mentioned in chapter 4; that it can always produce or secure resources at affordable prices; that it can afford its military; that it can afford the world's costliest, for-profit, health-care system; that it can compete against China Inc. and other forms of state capitalism; that it can bootstrap its poor; and that it can stanch income disparity and innovate.

Domestically, Americans may be unhappy or worried about these issues, but their national conversation does not include reinventing themselves, questioning imbedded attitudes or debating about how the role of their state should change in light of state capitalism. The American narrative is that the 2008 financial catastrophe, the ongoing wars in the Middle East and the enormous debt load will eventually be remedied by a combination of fiscal discipline, free-market principles and American exceptionalism, or the belief that America is superior.

But China, Russia, India and dozens more countries covet America's market share and living standards. In relative terms, the United States is losing ground economically. The U.S. has been

damaged by the 2008 financial crisis, and the country's debts, inde-
cisiveness, political gridlock and neglect of its education and infrastructure, along with global events, have made it difficult to reduce
unemployment. Maintaining the status quo would deprive both
countries of possible synergies and opportunities.

The United States Must Foster Smarter Governments, Merger or Not

So-called rugged individualism, and reaching the American Dream,
would have been impossible without law and order. Free enterprise
exists only where there is government to impose rules, ensure safety
and supervise or create common goods such as education, roads and
power. In weak or failed states, business can only operate in gang-
ster-fashion without police or courts or permission from government officials in the form of licenses, zoning variances or contracts.
In failed states, there is corruption and no investment in science or
new technologies for the common good.

In the United States, the role of government has been powerful
and necessary to advance society from the elimination of slavery and
other injustices to the education of the masses. It has also sponsored
transformative research such as splitting the atom, inventing electronics, devising the Internet, cataloging the genome and exploring
outer space. If left to commercial interests, none of these investments would have been undertaken, because none would have paid
off. But if measured in terms of benefits to the country, and mankind, the rewards have been immeasurable.

Even so, government involvement of any kind is anathema to
some Americans and movements. They would shrink the size of the

federal government, slash taxes, eliminate entitlements and dismantle the central bank. Ron Paul, the libertarian Republican presidential candidate in 2012, articulated the role of the state: "The proper
role for government in America is to provide national defense, a
court system for civil disputes, a criminal justice system for acts of
force and fraud, and little else."

The same sentiment is not found elsewhere. Canadians, Europeans and Asians have largely cast their governments in starring
roles in their economies and societies. This has been done out of
necessity or, sometimes, as a temporary or emergency measure. For
instance, Canada could only build its transcontinental railroad in
the late 1800s with loans backed by Britain. Its government then
generated economic activity along the route through subsidies and
land giveaways. Canada also created hundreds of Crown corporations to do what the private sector couldn't or wouldn't do, such as
building infrastructure, creating a national airline, building a telecommunications network, conducting high-tech research, creating an aerospace industry and developing the oil sands. Some state
enterprises remain publicly owned, such as most of the country's
power utilities, but many, including Air Canada and Petro-Canada,
were privatized once they became viable and able to withstand
foreign competition. (The United States, it should also be remem-
bered, colonized its west by declaring war against its Indians to
take their land, by subsidizing private-sector interests to build
transcontinental railways with financial help and land grants, and
then by giving away land to settlers.)

Now an economic war is being waged internationally by a new
generation of state-owned enterprises and sovereign wealth funds.
And they are launching ruthless strategies and handing out entitlements to their national champions in order to generate economic

growth. They are not constrained by bottom lines, shareholders or domestic competition. Their firepower is formidable, their time horizon for strategic purposes or evaluation is long—not focused on the next quarter—and their government's backing gives them financial and diplomatic leverage around the world.

China Inc. is the world's biggest state capitalist and runs an empire that includes thousands of enterprises owned and managed by federal, state and local governments. Russia's model involves oligarchs who control large swaths of its economy, but only at the pleasure of the Kremlin. Singapore's Economic Development Board of technocrats, scientists, industrialists and investors has backed winners, defined niches, formulated policies and generated the highest living standards in the world.

Most countries, democratic or not, have had to build their economies with the help of state-owned or state-controlled corporations. Some, like Luxembourg, Singapore and Norway, generate higher per capita living standards than does the United States. Others with comparable incomes include Switzerland, Germany, Canada, Australia, New Zealand, the Netherlands, Austria, Sweden, Belgium, Ireland and Finland. Asia's "tigers" and others—Japan, India, South Korea, Turkey and Brazil—have used state capitalism to build strong economies.

In Singapore, private-sector executives run government agencies and are paid salaries and bonuses commensurate with those paid to executives shouldering similar responsibilities in the business world. Canada also uses private-sector talent to run its state-owned Crown corporations. Both nations built their economies with government involvement, as did Norway and Germany, where "mixed" economies have been guided by a partnership also involving the state, trade labor unions and capitalists.

Americans have not done this and relied more on their private sector, but this has also been propped up, bailed out or aided during wars, depressions, recessions or other emergencies. Governments have had to take on the private sector, namely the robber barons, when they monopolized the economy and abused society. Like Canada and others, the U.S. has created government agencies to lend mortgage funds, build essential infrastructure or divest assets. But times have changed, and new public-private partnerships and government strategies are required to counteract state capitalism's growing assault.

Combining Canada and the United States would constitute a form of super-state capitalism, because their consolidation would require government collaboration, continental planning, new institutions and the rationalization of sectors to realize synergies. This could result in a new and improved nation-state, better able to supplement and partner with the private sector.

In a *Financial Times* article in 2012 called "The Right Must Learn to Love the State Again," American political scientist Francis Fukuyama made the point that government reform, not abolition, was needed. He also asserted that U.S. history demonstrated the wisdom of this course, contrary to some revisionist version about the wisdom of a *laissez-faire* past.

"Distrust of state authority has of course been a key component of American exceptionalism, both on the right and the left," he wrote. "The contemporary right has taken this, however, to an absurd extreme, seeking to turn the clock back not just to the point before the New Deal, but before the progressive era at the turn of the 20th century. The Republican party has lost sight of the difference between limited government and weak government, reflected in its agenda of cutting money for enforcement capacity of regulators and the IRS, its aversion to taxes of any sort and its failure to see that threats to liberty can come from powerful actors besides the state."

As mentioned earlier, Fukuyama pointed out that Alexander Hamilton's belief in a centralized state led to a national economy and prosperity and that Theodore Roosevelt took on gigantic business interests more powerful than the state itself by busting the trusts, bringing the robber barons to heel and creating antitrust laws to level the business playing field. More recently, during the Depression, his cousin Franklin Roosevelt bridled Wall Street and banks, founded the Securities Exchange Commission and created government programs to reduce unemployment. In 2008, Wall Street and banks again destroyed the country's financial system, and massive federal government intervention saved the country from bankruptcy, he wrote.[10]

The Northern Tiger Option for Canada

Sir Wilfrid Laurier, prime minister of Canada between 1896 and 1911, envisioned Canada as a powerful rival to the United States. By 1885, a Canadian transcontinental railroad had been completed, linking the country's East with its empty western hinterland. The railroad was key to colonizing the West, as it was in the United States, where the completion of America's first transcontinental railroad in 1869, followed by two others, had created a booming national economy. But a series of mishaps and historical catastrophes destroyed Laurier's dream.

Laurier launched an ambitious scheme to populate the West with a recruitment campaign called the "Last Best West." The program, using commissioned agents, recruited millions of northern and eastern Europeans and Americans. In 1891, the population of the country was 4.83 million, and by 1911 it had increased by nearly 50 percent, to 7.2 million. Immigrant farmers, whether Europeans fleeing strife in their homelands or Americans hunting for more acreage, were enticed with free or cheap farmland along Canada's newly minted railroad.

Laurier's "Last Best West" campaign, the accession of two new provinces, Alberta and Saskatchewan, and plans to build another, more northerly, transcontinental railroad pointed the country toward the goal of becoming more than simply a string of small ex-colonies along the U.S. border. In 1904, Laurier even boasted, "The nineteenth century was the century of the United States. I think we can claim that it is Canada that shall fill the twentieth century."

But the U.S. had a head start. By 1890 its population had already reached more than 62 million, compared to Canada's 4.83 million in 1891. This, in turn, led to industrialization and mass production in its cities, and by 1911 the U.S. population had also increased by nearly 50 percent, to over 92 million.

Laurier, the first francophone leader of Canada, devised policies to catch up to the giant to the south. He wanted a decentralized political system, a second railroad to open up northerly portions of the country, more autonomy from Britain, and trade reciprocity, or free trade, with the Americans. Unfortunately, his dream was crushed in 1911 when Canadians voted him out of office, rejecting free trade and another railroad.

Then Britain's control over Canada's foreign policy cost the country dearly. On August 4, 1914, Britain declared war on Germany, and Canada was dragged automatically into the war, along with other former colonies. French-Canadians opposed this, fighting conscription into the military and thus widening the rift between English and French that persists to this day. The war ruined the Canadian economy, and employment did not return to pre-war levels for a decade. Then the Depression, a Prairie drought and the Second World War dragged Canada down and drove the country into the arms of the Americans. The two world wars bankrupted Britain and "forced" Canada to borrow from Wall Street to finance its war effort.

After 1946, the U.S. and Canada embarked on a busy, unprecedented economic growth spurt. They were intact after the war and invested heavily in building infrastructure at home and financing, then benefiting from, the Marshall Plan and reconstruction abroad. These initiatives, along with simultaneous postwar baby booms, kept their economies prospering for decades.

The 1960s, however, brought social and political unrest and economic turbulence. Washington became preoccupied with the Cold War, Vietnam and the civil rights struggle, and Ottawa became preoccupied with terrorists and the Quiet Revolution in Quebec. The Americans dealt with challenges at home and abroad, but Canada faced a nation-breaking struggle with Quebec separatism. Focus turned inward. In 1968, Pierre Elliott Trudeau was elected as a bilingual change agent to repair French–English relations, and his motto was to create a "just society," not necessarily a prosperous one. In a speech in 1980, he said, "Canada will be a strong country when Canadians of all provinces feel at home in all parts of the country, and when they feel that all Canada belongs to them."

Two generations, and two defeated referendums later, Quebec remained alienated, as the "attachment" polls (a descriptive coined in a poll in chapter 6 describing loyalty to political jurisdictions) illustrated. Another poll in June 2012 demonstrated 38 percent support for secession, and provincial voters elected another separatist government (and 49 percent of Canadians outside Quebec said they did not care if Quebec left).[11] Nearly half of Quebecers said they would support independence from Canada if the flaws they perceived remained unaddressed. This referred to Quebec's refusal to agree and ratify constitutional changes after the constitution was repatriated from Britain in 1982.

Such "flaws" are upsetting to French nationalists but have been irrelevant, or unknown, to most Canadians. To them, the debate is tedious and has weakened the confederation. Canadians have become, like children in an unhappy home, anxious and preoccupied about whether a damaging divorce will happen. And this war of attrition has been the intention of the separatists all along. "We will eventually leave," former Quebec Premier Jacques Parizeau, of the separatist Parti Québécois, told me in 1988, "because we are always going to be a pain in the neck."

The Quebec issue has dominated the Canadian national conversation. This is why a "northern tiger" strategy must include policies to unite the country. Since these are emotionally laden, the subject is avoided and some have suggested that Canada can become strong and powerful merely by implementing a mass immigration strategy in the hopes that this will accelerate economic growth (and avoid dealing with the unity conflict). But mass migration is irrational because it puts the cart before the horse. Immigration does not generate economic activity; it's the other way around.

The latest incarnation of this demographic panacea was published in May 2012 by *The Globe and Mail,* in a series called "Our Time to Lead: The Immigrant Answer," which presented the case that "Canada needs a flood of immigrants." It concluded: "Between now and 2021, a million jobs are expected to go unfilled across Canada. Ottawa is making reforms to the immigration system but isn't going far enough. We need to radically boost immigration numbers [from 250,000 to at least 400,000 or more annually]. With the right people,

Canada can be an innovative world power. Without them, we'll drain away our potential."[12]

Opening the taps to immigration certainly worked in the "Last Best West," but the cost and circumstances were different. Back then, there was no costly welfare state to support those unable to succeed, and besides, immigrants were handed immediate wealth and opportunities in the form of free land and existing export markets via a subsidized railroad.

More to the point, Canada has had the highest per capita immigration rate among developed nations since 1986, but it has not built a "northern tiger." That year, an ad hoc yearly target of 250,000 was established. Entry requirements were lowered to meet the annual quota and about 6.25 million people flooded into the country, usually lacking language, education, skills or professional credentials. By 2012, about 1.7 million of these new arrivals had moved elsewhere, and many others had become marginalized.

Immigrant incomes were only 60 percent of the Canadian average, and their unemployment rates were double on average and up to five times higher for those with university degrees. By contrast, before 1986 immigrants quickly reached average incomes because they were only admitted if they had bona fide credentials, a job and proficiency in English or French, said Jason Kenney, Canada's minister of citizenship, immigration and multiculturalism. In 2011, he began instituting reforms to revamp immigration policies to attract only those with English or French, skills or pre-arranged jobs.

However, even if reforms attract millions, the problem of Canada's brain drain won't abate. The estimated 2.7 million Canadian citizens, or 8 percent of the population of Canada, permanently living abroad is five times as high as the proportion of Americans living outside the United States. Of these 2.7 million, 1.1 million had been born in Canada and 82 percent of them had left for the U.S. The rest who left were immigrants who returned home, such as the estimated 300,000 educated Chinese-Canadians who live in Hong Kong.

Adopting a Tiger Mentality

Becoming a "northern tiger" might prove to be a far more challenging endeavor than joining forces with the Americans. Canada would have to support rapid economic and resource development policies. It would have to learn how to become an exporting nation like the Americans, Germans, Japanese, Koreans and Chinese have become. Instead, Canada exports 1,250 products, but twenty-six of these products represent 50 percent of the total, and these are products or services transferred between U.S. parent companies and their Canadian branch plants.

Such "exports" are known as "intra-firm trade," or related party or non–arm's length transactions. Canada, along with Poland and Sweden, has the highest proportion of such intra-firm trade because all three have small domestic economies unable to scale sufficiently to mount global export initiatives. But Canada has more related party trade than any other country in the world: about 51.2 percent of Canadian exports to the U.S. are in this category and 42 percent of U.S. exports to Canada are. These include computers, electronics, vehicles and parts, and chemicals. So Canada is not a nation of exporters, carving out new markets in the traditional sense, but is successful at hosting foreign investors who employ Canadians and export goods, commodities and services back to themselves.

Clearly, foreign investment and free trade has yielded huge benefits, including, according to an OECD report, the fact that countries, like the U.S. and Canada, with interlocking supply and distribution chains suffered less during the 2008–09 financial and trade crisis than did those without enmeshed trading relationships. However, a "northern tiger" cannot be built simply by attracting more branch plant operations to build things or extract resources, because the Americans, Germans, Japanese, Koreans and Chinese are no longer required to build branch plants to get inside tariff barriers. They can simply export tariff-free from their domestic plants or use supply chains in cheap labor countries to export around the world.

A 2010 study by Statistics Canada called "Plant Death and Exchange Rate" concluded the obvious—that a high dollar, tariff reductions and branch plants have contributed to greater job loss than if the economy had been built and owned domestically. "When a domestic-controlled plant and a foreign-controlled plant have similar efficiency levels in terms of productivity, employment, and age, changes in tariffs and real exchange rates have a greater impact on the exit probability of the foreign-controlled plant . . . One possible explanation is that a multinational has a greater capability, and thus a higher likelihood, to shift its production to another country whenever the domestic Canadian environment changes to its disadvantage. Another possible explanation is that multinationals are more sensitive to changes in profitability."

Obviously, a "northern tiger" approach must optimize capital formation through lower taxes, then dramatically reward and enable resource extraction and the export sector. This could slow the brain drain to the United States and attract productive immigrants. But Canada, like other resource-rich economies, must diversify into services and manufacturing, no matter what, to build a sustainable economy as the United States did. This is because capital-intensive and foreign-owned resource industries do not spawn generations of entrepreneurs; they give jobs to worker bees, then leave after the ore body, oil field or low currency benefit disappears.

Edward Glaeser, a professor of economics at Harvard University, wrote in 2012 that countries like Canada and Australia cannot be as resilient or sustainable as the United States in the long run because the nature of their wealth does not depend on a culture of enterprise: "A recent paper I co-wrote . . . examined the long-run impact of mining across the U.S. Fifty years ago, the economist Benjamin Chinitz noted that New York City appeared even then to be more resilient than Pittsburgh. He argued that New York's garment industry, with its small setup costs, had engendered a culture of entrepreneurship that spilled over into new industries. Pittsburgh, because of its coal mines, had the huge U.S. Steel Corp., which trained company men with neither the ability nor the inclination to start some new venture. A body of literature now documents the connection between economic success and measures of local entrepreneurship, such as the share of employment in startups and an abundance of smaller companies."[13]

Canada's other impediment to enterprise has been its relatively small market and its big, stolid banks. These institutions have been protected from direct American competition in return for being heavily regulated to remain solvent. The Canadian banking model has provided stability but has also shut out small startups and entrepreneurs, fostering concentration of power domestically. Not surprisingly, for most of its economic history, Canada's big banks have preferred to finance big foreign multinational operations in Canada, big real estate developers, big shopping malls and big retailers. Until the 1980s, the country was a form of "financial feudalism," but since then free trade with the U.S. and others has introduced competition, requirements to be more productive and new opportunities. Even so, banking laws inhibit risk capital and the country lacks a vibrant venture capital and angel investment infrastructure, as exists in the United States.

Generating enterprise in a nation like Canada would be a tall order. Canada's workforce consists of struggling immigrants, branch plant employees, unionized workers and a swollen public sector. Mort Zuckerman noted the difference between the two. He is one of the most successful members of Canada's diaspora in the United States, the 188th-richest American in the world, a billionaire real estate and media tycoon who immigrated from Canada in the 1960s. What attracted him, and half his graduating class from McGill University, he said, was the variety and vibrancy of the United States economy and its "can-do-spirit."

In an interview with *U.S. News & World Report,* a publication he personally owns, he told a reporter that "the United States is still the global leader in the volume of manufactured goods; it is still the world's technological leader and the largest market for information technology; it is still the world's most innovative economy and home to 80 percent of the world's top universities; it is still the magnet it was for my fellow Canadian students and the top destination for foreign scholars, drawing many of the world's best and brightest to our universities and labs."[14]

Likewise, Jeff Skoll, America's 139th-richest man, left Canada in 1993 to earn an MBA at Stanford University. His family left Montreal for Toronto in the late seventies after the first separatist election. After becoming an electrical engineer, and working in Canada, he then headed to the United States for business graduate school. He made his fortune founding eBay, and is a philanthropist and producer of social documentaries such as *A Matter of Inconvenience, Waiting for Superman* and *Fast Food Nation.* "Growing up in a middle-class family in Canada, I really didn't know much about philanthropy, running a company, or starting companies," he said in an interview with *The Huffington Post* in 2012. "But I did always have the uber goal of trying to find these big issues and make a difference . . . I've always avoided politics. In Canada growing up we never talked politics. In America, it's a much different thing. But maybe that's the next frontier—to really engage politically—because that ultimately is where the power is held."[15]

A "northern tiger" strategy must emulate the American model. First, Canada must become a cohesive nation-state, then it must develop its natural advantages, such as resources, and create a robust enterprise culture along the way. Possible methods to grow the economy, apart from an outright merger, are described in chapter 5: vending Canada's federal Crown lands into a partnership with the Americans in return for compensation and future royalties; a gigantic farm-in with Americans; or carve-outs, which would consist of public-private partnerships with Americans or others to manage development.

Then, paradoxically, the "northern tiger" would be better off adopting the U.S. dollar to grow more quickly. A single currency would level the playing field. The indirect service and manufacturing jobs that would result from massive northern development could locate inside Canada, close to activities, rather than in the lower-cost United States. Also, a shared currency would eliminate the danger of basing the Canadian economy mostly on commodities, with accompanying volatility, or of further succumbing to the "Dutch Disease" and hyperinflation as development accelerated.

Obviously, a restructuring of the Canadian state, and state of mind—whether a merger or "northern tiger" approach—is required no matter what happens. Canada needs to change or it will drift, deindustrialize and deteriorate. Put simply, Canada has no choice but to choose. Either it embarks on reforms to nation-build, or, alternatively, it pursues a merger with the wealthy and enterprising Americans, who will build the nation.

Canada Must Be Governed Like Australia, Merger or Not

Australia and Canada, former British colonies, both inherited Britain's institutions, a massive resource base and populations of disenfranchised and abused aboriginals. But the similarities end there. Canada has had to deal with tensions and disputes between its English- and French-speaking citizens, which Australia has not had to do.

Proximity to the U.S. allowed Canada to outperform Australia until the 1990s. That is when Australia began to pull away in terms of growth after streamlining approval procedures for resource development, liberalizing its economy, reforming agricultural policies, recruiting only skilled immigrants and opening up its hinterland to development by resolving aboriginal land claims. This has allowed Australia to capitalize more dramatically on the commodity super-cycle since 2000 than has Canada, mired with an inefficient and ensnarled resource development system.

Harnessing its potential, Australia is aggressively catching up. According to Credit Suisse's Global Trends analysis, in 2011 the United States represented 25 percent of the world's $231 trillion in assets, Canada 2.8 percent and Australia 2.7 percent. Australia's share of wealth was nearly identical to Canada's, despite a population—22.485 million—roughly two-thirds that of Canada. "Australia has experienced robust growth since the turn of the century [2000], with wealth per adult quadrupling over the past decade . . . The proportion of those with wealth above USD $100,000 is the highest of any country—eight times the world average. With 1,861,000 people in the global top 1 percent, Australia accounts for 4.1 percent of the members of that wealthy group, despite having just 0.4 percent of the world's adult population."[16]

In 2012, the International Monetary Fund forecast that Australia's GDP would grow to $50,175 per capita by 2017, Canada's to $47,322 and the Americans' to $59,708, figures that were PPP-adjusted.

Canada has much to learn from Australia's reforms. One of the impediments to Canada has been the lack of political unity due to the fragmentation of its political system. Australia's reforms were easier to undertake because its states have always been part of the federal decision-making process through its elected senate. That chamber has seventy-two members, twelve from each of the six states irrespective of their population. This legislative body, like its American counterpart, counterbalances the House of Representatives, where representation is only by population.

By contrast, Canada's Senate is comprised of 105 members who are patronage appointees chosen piecemeal by the prime minister of the day. Canadian Senators can remain in office until age seventy-five and do very little if they choose. Most are somewhat productive, but all are partisans and mostly represent commercial or other vested interests. Throughout the country's history, attempts to reform the Senate have been blocked by heavily populated Quebec to prevent any dilution of, or counterbalance to, its influence in the House of Commons. This has impeded the creation of a more cohesive nation-state and allowed regions and language groups to be played off one another, or co-opted financially, by federal politicians. This Canadian realpolitik has failed to create a strong sense of nationality or a commitment to move forward together. It has divided the electorate and alienated residents of Newfoundland and the West. The country has become a collection of provincial "nation-states" with a coordinating body—the federal government—that irritates and co-opts, but rarely leads. More than two dozen attempts to reform the Senate have failed in decades past. But applying the American or Australian formula is the simplest solution: an equal representation of senators, elected at large, for each province and territory. The U.S. has two senators per state, and Australia six per state, irrespective of population. Another formula would be the same number of senators for each region: Ontario, Quebec, Atlantic Canada, Western Canada and the northern territories.

In the absence of this, Canada's governments operate like cats on a leash, often disagreeing but permanently tethered together. For instance, the Ontario and Quebec premiers internationally embarrassed Alberta's oil sands industry by excoriating it as environmentally unacceptable at the 2009 UN Copenhagen Conference on Climate Change. Then, in 2012, the leader of the official opposition, Thomas Mulcair, did the same. These attitudes widened the East–West divide and, if unaddressed, will unravel the nation-state more dramatically than if Quebec were to secede.

Western alienation has been a constant throughout the country's history, as has Quebec alienation. The difference is that the West has become fully viable as an independent entity. In 2010, Alberta's GDP was $70,826 per person, Quebec's was $40,394 and the national average was $47,322. By 2013, Alberta and Saskatchewan will match Quebec in size economically, and by 2030 the four provinces in the West will overtake the rest of the country in size and importance. This pre-eminence must be matched with king-size political influence and is not.

Another battle has pitted Quebec against its Atlantic Province neighbors over the issue of hydroelectricity. Quebec's energy strategy has been to build massive hydroelectric facilities to pro-vide cheap power for its industries and export power to the United States. The province's Crown corporation, Hydro Quebec, also undertook an anti-competitive strategy of bottling up power genera-tion in Newfoundland and Labrador by refusing to allow the power to be transferred through Quebec to U.S. markets. This was one of the conditions of a sweetheart, confiscatory sixty-five-year contract Quebec signed with Newfoundland and its power utility, which agreed to unfavorable terms because it was in financial trouble at the time. The "geographic stranglehold" had yielded a windfall to Quebec of $19 billion by 2010, according to an estimate by former Newfoundland Premier Danny Williams.[17]

In 2009, Quebec tried to monopolize the power grid in the East by negotiating a $3.2 billion takeover by Hydro Quebec of New Brunswick Power, because of its financial struggles. That deal, how-ever, was abandoned a year later due to political resistance.[18] Then, in 2012, the hydro wars broke out again when Prime Minister Stephen Harper unveiled a federal loan guarantee to facilitate construction of a new $6.2 billion Newfoundland and Labrador hydro project, along with three transmission lines to Nova Scotia to export power directly to the United States, bypassing Quebec. Quebec's National Assembly condemned the loan guarantee, one official called it "treasonous" on the part of Ottawa, and the province threatened legal action against its neighbors and the federal government.[19]

Clearly, the West and all parts of the country must gain full-fledged status and protection from predatory or rivalrous provinces by being a bigger part of the federal decision-making process. An elected Senate would do the trick, forcing compromise and consen-sus, but without that there remains little hope that Canada can forge a national identity and national development strategy.

Such tension regarding Quebec, Ontario and the rest has undermined the nation-state and reduced the federal government to behaving like a fiscal shock absorber through a system of transfers and generous social policies. The result is that Canada has the dubious distinction of being the most devolved, and least powerful, federal system in the developed world. According to a 2009 OECD study, its federal government controlled 35 percent of all government spending, compared with 55 percent in the U.S., 72 percent in Australia and an average of 70 percent worldwide.[20] Ottawa functions more like a European Union construct than like Washington, Canberra or Berlin.

Nation building has taken a backseat to adjudicating provincial or language squabbles. To make matters worse, there are also jurisdictional overlaps embedded in the constitution left behind by the British. The result is that the provinces have fought bitterly at times with the federal government, to the detriment of the country. Throughout the 1980s, development of a gigantic offshore oil field was held up because of a dispute between Ottawa and Newfoundland over its ownership and royalties. This followed a battle between Ottawa and Alberta over the federal government's right to tax Alberta's resources and exports.

The two levels of government overlap, causing duplication and expense. For instance, marriage is a federal matter, but divorce is a provincial one. The Criminal Code is federal, but the execution of laws is provincial. Natural resources, environment and land use are provincial matters, but the federal government can meddle every step of the way. The federal government is responsible for the welfare of aboriginal people, but most outstanding land claims have involved provincial Crown lands. This pits the two levels of government against one another because the federal government finances the legal battles the aboriginals wage against the provinces. This illogical bifurcation has prevented settlements, impeded economic development and alienated First Nations.

Canada Must Resolve Its Aboriginal Situation, Merger or Not

Australia's federal government created a process to resolve aboriginal claims. The search for a solution began in 1979, when an aboriginal named Paul Coe filed a class-action lawsuit claiming the entire country. His lawsuit was a watershed, and, even though unsuccessful, it led to a succession of High Court cases that forced major reforms by defining the rights of the country's original residents.

Then a definitive, landmark decision resulted from the efforts of an aboriginal named Eddie Mabo. His battle resulted in the High Court of Australia overturning, in 1992, the legal doctrine of *terra nullius* ("land belonging to nothing, no one") that was the basis for Britain's ownership claim over the entire continent. Because the land belonged to no one, the reasoning went, there was no need to sign treaties with aboriginal peoples. After the Mabo case established aboriginal claims, the Native Title Act was passed in 1993, and hundreds of land-use agreements since.

Canada, by contrast, is a clutch of treaties and land or rights claims whose legitimacies are complicated by courts and the lack of definitive legislation. Australia's laws have established a process to verify, evaluate and adjudicate claims. The National Native Title Tribunal hears claims to establish their validity and to rule on their merits by determining whether lands, rights and/or compensation should be awarded. This process has, in essence, enfranchised the

517,200 Australians of aboriginal extraction—representing 2.5 percent of the population—by giving them their day in court.

This has reaped benefits that have eluded First Nations in Canada, given its current tangled treaty predicament. This makes a difference when it comes to economic development. For instance, in 2002, laws enabled Michael Rann, premier of South Australia, to spearhead his state's resource development, reduce its high unemployment and reverse its population decline. South Australia had only four mines at the time, but a decade later, after streamlining regulations, negotiating with aboriginals and installing renewable energy sources, was generating 29 percent of its power through wind and had twenty-three mines in operation. Another forty mines were in various stages of development, including the world's largest uranium discovery, worth $1.4 trillion. "Activity also resulted in finding one of the world's biggest copper and gold finds. Our uranium mine will produce more than all of Canada's uranium mines put together," Rann told me in 2012. His government initiated training programs for aboriginals, other locals and prison inmates and was able to spread the wealth and other benefits.

In Canada, one of the biggest growth industries across the country's Crown lands has been armies of consultants, lawyers, civil servants and First Nations bands involved in land claims and litigation. About 3.4 percent of Canada's population is aboriginal—a total of 1,172,790 First Nations, Inuit or Métis in 2006[21]—and there are 1,300 claims across the country languishing in courts or negotiations because the country lacks a cogent, fast-track settlement mechanism.

The federal government controls, and owns, the Crown lands in the three territories of Yukon, Northwest Territories and Nunavut. Only Nunavut has a comprehensive agreement between its Inuit residents and the federal government, and legal settlements are incomplete in the other two territories. Hundreds more legal cases involve Crown lands owned by the provinces, municipalities and private interests. Some have dragged on for decades because neither level of government has been capable of reforming, supervising or expediting this process.

Instead of facilitating, the federal government has made the issue of aboriginal rights more complicated. In 1982, Canada repatriated its constitution from Britain and added Section 35, which guaranteed protection of aboriginal and treaty rights. Then, in 1995, the federal Parliament promised "an inherent right to aboriginal self-government." This was a major pledge that has not been defined by courts, but ever since, Canada's First Nations (roughly 700,000 of the 1.17 million aboriginal population) have added self-government to the list of claims for land, rights and compensation.

In 2008, the federal government announced the creation of the Specific Claims Tribunal to expedite claims. But the tribunal did not post its rules and procedures for three years, until 2011. And use of the Tribunal is optional, not mandatory. This has done little to clean up a backlog of decades, and most outstanding claims remain in limbo.

These claims fall into three main categories: claims that original treaties were abrogated, ignored or inadequate; claims that the federal government failed to protect aboriginal peoples from exploitation; and claims for lands where treaties never existed. Some date back hundreds of years. For instance, the eight thousand members of the Mohawk First Nations live on the 12,000-acre Kahnawake reserve in suburban Montreal. They are claiming 25,000 acres of nearby urban land—or billions of dollars in exchange. In an interview in 2011, Mohawk Grand Chief Mike Delisle explained his band's position: "They [governments] call it a land claim, we call it a land grievance. Here the issue is the *seigneurs* were granted [by France, three hundred years ago] the right to rent the [Mohawk] land and pay us. This revenue eroded. This is about loss of rents, loss of use, loss of economic opportunity, loss of lands. It's big."

In 2008, the members of the Whitefish Lake band in Ontario filed the largest land claim in Canadian history, against Canada's Attorney General for $550 billion. This amount represented roughly half the historical proceeds that have been derived from the gigantic nickel-producing area around Sudbury. The band claimed that in 1878 the Canadian justice department gave permission for them to sell timber rights to prospectors, who flipped them months later for fortunes because of nickel discoveries. The case rests on whether the federal government abrogated its responsibility to protect them from being exploited 130 years ago.

The American aboriginal track record is worse. Lands were expropriated or stolen, Native Americans killed or relocated onto reservations, and compensation has been miserly. They were granted U.S. citizenship in 1924, and in 1968 the Indian Civil Rights Act was passed. After the Second World War, in which 44,000 Native American men served in the armed forces, a federal government commission, which included tribal leaders, began adjudicating land claims and handing out compensation. But remaining Native Americans were given defined reservations, and the issues of claims and rights are not as significant, or as economically damaging, as they are in Canada.

"In Ontario many of the new claims involve land within municipal boundaries. Some bands are claiming the right to administer these lands. There have been just a few isolated [violent] incidents to date but they are a forewarning of events to come," wrote Timmins columnist Gregory Reynolds. "There was the jailing of seven Ontario native leaders for blocking efforts by two mining companies. There is the illegal occupancy of a housing subdivision in Caledonia with attendant violence and vandalism. There is a claim of the Whitefish Lake Band members to the bulk of the nickel bodies in Sudbury and area, accompanied by a $550 billion lawsuit . . . The Mining Association of Canada sees access to land as a problem requiring government action if the industry is to stay healthy."[22]

The province of British Columbia is mired in litigation involving most of its territory. In 1992, a treaty commission was created and, by 2011, sixty claims, covering two-thirds of the province, had been accepted as valid. One year later, only two had been settled.

In 2012, six Algonquin communities in western Quebec, after decades of negotiations on a number of claims, threatened to launch the biggest land dispute in Canadian history. They claim rights and ownership to a territory larger than France, spread across eastern Ontario and western Quebec and encompassing private urban lands, Mohawk territory, Cree lands and some of the world's most prolific gold-mining regions. This followed lawsuits by the eastern branch of the Algonquins in Ontario claiming rights to lands in two major cities and on Mohawk reserves.

A political and legal vacuum in Canada has led to battles and frightened away investment. It is not unusual for a mining company to suddenly be served with lawyers' letters from one or two bands claiming rights to land, years after millions have been invested in exploration or development. By contrast, Australia cleaned up resource development with a system that is transparent. Prospectors and exploration companies can examine all outstanding claims and settlements, thereby replacing uncertainty and chaos with security. But in Canada there is no "clear title" to vast portions of the country, due to government incompetence, which represents a major competitive disadvantage going forward, merger or not.

Canada Must Militarize, Merger or Not

A strong military is not a requirement for independence, but as Jack Granatstein has said, a country that mostly relies on another for its protection is not truly sovereign. Unless a merger happens, Canada must increase its military expenditures for a number of reasons. The United States will not, and cannot, defend Canada and the rest of the world at its own expense indefinitely. Eventually, Canada may be invoiced tens of billions of dollars annually by Washington for security costs, particularly if the relationship ebbs or sours. This means Canada must pay for, or replace, U.S. protection as the world becomes more desperate for its resources.

Australia and other nations, such as tiny Norway and Singapore, support proportionately larger military forces than Canada's to defend their resources and living standards. Norway, with huge offshore and Arctic reserves near Russia, has only five million people and is equivalent to 19 percent of Canada in economic size, but its military and reserves are 72 percent the size of Canada's. Singapore, close to aggressive China and with only five million people, has an armed force bigger than Canada's: 71,600 active personnel and 350,000 reservists.

Australia began boosting military spending in 2010, because of worries about China, to defend its sizeable offshore resources and on the assumption that the U.S. will eventually have to prune its armed forces around the world. In 2011, Australia's forces totaled 59,023 personnel and 43,016 reservists, or 88 percent of Canada's personnel, but its $24 billion defense budget was more than a billion dollars higher than Canada's $22.8 billion. By 2025, forecasts are the country will be spending $40 billion. If Canada were to match that proportionately, the Canadian defense budget would have to more than double from 2011 levels, to $50 billion by 2025.

Of course, the U.S. has been willing to patrol and defend Canada since the Second World War through the North American Aerospace Defense Command, or NORAD. Formed in 1958, this joint organization provides warning, air sovereignty and defense for the region out of its headquarters in Colorado Springs. But since the 1950s, Canada has chopped its armed forces budget dramatically, to 1.4 percent of GDP, about what most OECD countries spend. The U.S. spends more on defense than the next twelve highest-ranked countries combined—a group that excludes Canada—an amount equivalent to 4.8 percent of its GDP.

"The Americans are a superpower and we're not. They have global responsibilities and we've always been a colony. That shapes attitude. So does the fact that we have a Quebec and they don't, and Quebec has always been against military," said Granatstein in an interview he gave me in 2010. "That being said, we have been very laggardly in the twentieth century in terms of our military commitment relative to our size and status in the world."

Sovereignty is not only about having big armies and navies; it is also about defending the national interest through restrictive and nationalist policies. For instance, Washington talks about free trade, then embeds protectionism or "Buy America" policies into laws. They talk about open-door investment policies, then forbid investors from Dubai, China and elsewhere from buying strategic assets. Other countries subsidize national corporate champions, discriminate against outsiders and use sovereign wealth funds for political purposes. In trade, the Europeans subsidize agriculture. Asians block imports, then keep their currencies low to undercut competitors in export markets.

But Canada has been the boy scout of free trading nations. It is open to investment by countries that deny reciprocal access to their markets. The country has allowed too many foreigners to buy too many of its head offices and great multinational corporations for too many years. This is not the way a nation-state protects itself. Outright protectionism is not a smart tactic because it invites retaliation or complaints at the World Trade Organization. But controlling foreign investment, foreign ownership and resource development—and demanding reciprocal rights—is what Canada should do more effectively. It's what nations do.

Canada has intervened and blocked foreign takeovers from time to time, but has been lenient since the mid-1980s. In 2003, global giants began targeting established resource companies everywhere, so as to position themselves for coming shortages and commodity price increases. In Canada, within a handful of years, foreigners bought every one of its major steel companies; Inco, the world's largest nickel mine; Alcan, the world's largest primary producer of aluminum; many oil companies; many mining companies; and several high-tech outfits. All of Canada's strong financial sectors, its banks, brokers and insurers, would have been bought out by foreigners, with disastrous results, if aggregate ownership limits of 25 percent had not been legislated to protect them decades ago.

In 2008, the recession ended the takeovers for a while, but the superpowers have hovered, buying smaller corporations—or shares in them—and waiting for opportunities to acquire control, strategic assets and other corporations. Fortunately, the proposed buyouts of the world's largest potash company, in Saskatchewan, and the country's only stock exchange, in Toronto, rallied public opposition and the deals did not proceed. But this economic nationalism was reversed in 2012 when gigantic uninvited bids by CNOOC and Malaysia's Petronas to buy two major oil companies were approved. As stated before in this book, Canada's decision to allow these demonstrated that others can bully their way into its economy.

The United States, by contrast, protects its "national interest"—domestically and internationally—irrespective of free-market principles or private-property rights. For instance, after huge amounts of oil and gas were discovered in Alaska in 1968, Washington summoned interested parties, banged heads together and imposed a comprehensive revenue-sharing agreement within weeks. More recently, Washington pressured a Dubai group to back out of a deal to buy a company that managed major American seaports and forced the same Chinese group that took over a major oil company in Canada in 2012 to back off.

Australia fiercely defends its "national interest" too, and in 2012 it imposed draconian measures to control foreign takeovers and ownership. Any foreign entity must get approval to buy or invest in an existing or new business, real estate or resources. They must also get approval to buy Australian-owned assets abroad. Canberra also restricts foreign companies, state-owned enterprises or companies controlled by foreign governments or their agencies from investing in the country. They must even get approval from the government to buy property to house an executive or diplomat.[23]

Canada Must Develop the North, Merger or Not

On February 16, 1958, rookie Prime Minister John Diefenbaker outlined in a speech "a new vision, a new hope, a new soul" for Canada. He promised to open up the Canadian North to resource development and settlement for Canadians. He was a Prairie populist who was concerned about completely losing control to the Americans as the sun set on Britain's empire and its geopolitical influence.

"This national development policy will create a new sense of national purpose and national destiny. [Sir John A. Macdonald] opened the West. He saw Canada from East to West. I see a new Canada—a Canada of the North," he said. His party won the largest majority in the country's history.

In 1957, Canada's North was an undeveloped colony. First Nations and Inuit could not vote. Development was nonexistent. So was infrastructure or even full sovereign control. The previous federal government had delegated to a New Jersey company, Federal Electric, the power to hand out permits for travel in the North. This was a security measure because the company had built and operated sixty-three American military facilities (the DEW Line, or Distant Early Warning sites) across Canada as part of its Cold War effort to detect incoming Soviet bombers.

At that time, the Americans had more invested in Canada's North than Canadians did. These defense facilities were eventually removed at Canada's request. But the only sizable Canadian infrastructure investment in the North up to that point had been the port of Churchill, finished in 1929, a trading post on the Churchill River, named after the first Duke of Marlborough. The government had built an all-weather airport on Hudson's Bay, a 1,060-mile rail link from Winnipeg and a deep-sea port designed to ship Prairie wheat around the world. Western Canada's provinces insisted on the scheme because they were upset with the Canadian Pacific Railway's monopoly and needed an alternate route. The port was supposed to be the "Gateway to the Arctic," but has become a sleepy town more dependent on polar bear tourism and government subsidies than much else. In 1997, an American logistics company bought the railroad and port facilities from the Canadian government, and as the Keystone XL Pipeline from the oil sands stalled in 2012, talk turned to possibly shipping the bitumen via rail to Churchill, then by ship to Canadian, U.S. or European markets.

Diefenbaker undertook Northern development. His government approved voting rights for the First Nations and Inuit. His government passed the first Canadian Bill of Rights. The first female minister was appointed to his cabinet, and the first aboriginal to the Senate. He launched a national development plan that included "roads to resources" in the territories and western provinces and proposed to build gigantic infrastructure schemes such as railroads, power plants and dams to open up the hinterland and irrigate food lands.

His vision ended with his tenure in 1963, and the country's agenda was hijacked by a terrorist organization called the Front de libération du Québec, or FLQ. The group was a Marxist-Leninist, Quebec-nationalist paramilitary group that was active until 1970. It executed 160 violent incidents that killed eight, injured many and bombed the Montreal Stock Exchange in 1969. A year later, the group's actions culminated in two attacks, known as the October Crisis, that involved the kidnapping and detention of a British diplomat for weeks, and the abduction and murder of Quebec's deputy premier, Pierre Laporte. The separatist movement sprang out of those events and has traumatized, and monopolized, the federal political agenda since then.

The result was that the North, owned and managed by the federal government, remained neglected. Prime Minister Stephen Harper's spending initiatives, announced in 2007, were welcome, but schemes as ambitious as the Canadian Pacific Railway, St. Lawrence Seaway or Trans-Siberian Railway were needed. Development, fanning out from the remote settlements of Inuvik in the western Arctic and Iqaluit in the eastern Arctic, was needed. The logistics, and costs, would be formidable; for instance, Inuvik is as far from New York City as is Quito, Ecuador, and Iqaluit as far from New York as is Cancún, Mexico. But nation building is an expensive proposition and not for the politically faint of heart.

The potential, however, would be as enormous as the price tag. The region around Inuvik could become a miniature Norway, with offshore and onshore natural gas and oil fields. Norway gathers, processes and exports liquefied natural gas around the world from facilities above the Arctic Circle. There is also oil in the western Arctic, and major discoveries—subsequently abandoned—were made in the 1980s. Exploration could recommence out of nearby Tuktoyaktuk to prove up the promising quantities of oil that have already been found.

In the eastern Arctic, Iqaluit, the tiny capital of Nunavut, could become a hub for exploration in the oil-prone region between Canada and Greenland and a shipping and supply center for iron ore and other mining operations across the archipelago, as well as for the Northwest Passage.

But these territories will remain dormant without a Marshall Plan for the North to sensibly create infrastructure that would reduce the costs of operating there in order to encourage exploration and development. In the northern, inland three-quarters of Canada, equipment, fuel, people and housing must be mostly airlifted by helicopter. The costs of exploration are at least three times as high as on lands where road, rail or tidewater transportation exists. So are building, maintenance and energy costs.

Canada has one rail line to the Yukon, another to the oil sands region and only one piece of infrastructure that traverses the Arctic Circle, called the Dempster Highway. To compare, Alaska has twenty-five major seaports and Siberia has fifty seaports on the Arctic Ocean or in cities located on rivers deep within Siberia's interior to provide access to northern shipping lanes. At the dawn of the twenty-first century, Canada's North was a vast, undeveloped "nation" atop a narrow ribbon of development along the U.S. border that is dependent upon the U.S. economy.

This neglect has led many countries, including the United States, to challenge Canada's ownership of its Arctic coastal regions. For instance, in 1985 a U.S. icebreaker, the *Polar Sea*, traversed the waters through the Canadian Arctic Archipelago without first seeking permission from the Canadian government. When newspapers discovered this, a diplomatic flap followed. The Canadian government issued a declaration reaffirming Canadian rights to the waters. But the United States refused to recognize the Canadian claim for the so-called Northwest Passage. There is also an official land dispute between U.S. and Canada over a portion of the Beaufort Sea that could contain billions of barrels of oil.

In 1988, the two governments agreed to disagree. They signed the Canada–U.S. Arctic Cooperation Agreement, which resolved the practical issue without solving the sovereignty questions. In essence, the United States agreed to notify Canada when its ships would transit the region, and Canada would automatically grant its consent. But in 2005, it became apparent that U.S. nuclear submarines were traveling without permission through Canadian Arctic waters after the U.S. Navy released photos of the USS *Charlotte* at the North Pole. Another quarrel ensued, then worsened, after the U.S. ambassador to Canada stated that the Arctic waters were international. The Canadian government responded by proclaiming its intention to enforce its sovereignty there.

By 2030, the Northwest Passage may be open to shipping. In December 2012, Gazprom made history by completing the first delivery of liquefied natural gas from Norway to Japan along its Arctic route. But the deep waters between Canada's islands are most valuable as a shipping lane because they could accommodate supertankers that are too big to pass through the Panama Canal and must currently navigate around the tip of South America. This is why the

United States, the European Union, Russia, Japan and now China consider these waters an international strait, a designation that would entitle foreign vessels the right to "transit passage." Canada has been told it cannot close the passage.

In 2011, Chinese academics urged their government to officially dispute Canada's Arctic sovereignty. According to a policy paper published in 2011 by Professor David Wright, a research fellow at the Canadian Defense and Foreign Affairs Institute, "Li Zhenfu of Dalian Maritime University in Liaoning province, probably the single most strident and influential Chinese commentator on Arctic affairs today, seems distressed by the prospect of Canada controlling the Northwest Passage and, in the process, becoming any wealthier and more important geo-strategically than it already is."[24]

In 2012, China officially pressured Canada to help get Beijing a seat at the Arctic Five talks as an observer, giving it identical status to that enjoyed by the European Union, which abuts the region. Canada gave way. This is another example of Canada being placed in an untenable situation and struggle to get hegemony over its territory. The reality is that the Arctic will belong to whoever puts up the money to develop its resources and is capable of outmuscling all others. Therefore a U.S.–Canada merger solves the problem. Canada simply cannot hold onto its real estate indefinitely, given its relative weakness. But if Canada continues to undertake token development, the superpowers will fill the vacuum and the North will become a battleground or, alternatively, a de facto American protectorate because of its strategic importance to Washington. Until then, any incursions or threats from Russia or China would invite pushback or intervention by the U.S. military.

Canada Must Become More Like America, Merger or Not

The path toward staking a more robust nationhood on resources alone is fraught with pitfalls such as currency fluctuations, commodity price swings and the difficulties of dealing with aggressive investors such as China and others. In fact the road to resource wealth may be over for a few years, according to some commentators in 2012, who began to signal an end to both the commodity super-cycle and an end to China's rapid growth rates. Indications are that neither will abate dramatically, but as developed countries slow under their demographic and debt burdens, prices may resume a downward slide. This tenuousness underscores the necessity for any country like Canada to be diversified and not solely dependent on selling oil, metals, beef and other commodities. This represents another reason to merge with an industrialized America. America's manufacturing sector is, contrary to conventional opinion, as big as China's and considerably more competitive. "There's a huge productivity gap between China and the U.S.," said *New York Times* columnist and author Tom Friedman in an interview at the World Economic Forum, held in Tianjin, China, in fall 2012. "Both manufacture $1 trillion, but 100 million are employed doing this in China and only 10 million in the U.S."

In May 2012, Morgan Stanley linked China's slowdown with the end of the super-cycle. "China's growth is downshifting to a lower plane. I suspected we're headed now for two decades down as far as prices are concerned. This is the sunset of the big commodities super-cycle," said Ruchir Sharma, head of Morgan's global emerging markets equity team.

But history shows otherwise. Two centuries' worth of records reveal a pattern that involves two decades of price declines, most recently ending in 2003, followed by one or often two decades of price gains. In 2012, near the ten-year mark, copper prices began falling, perhaps a harbinger of the beginning of twenty more years of poor prices, Sharma surmised. If so, that would be dreadful news for Canada and any plans to develop resources or its North on a bigger scale.

But other experts, such as Canadian mining tycoon Pierre Lassonde, believe it's important to note that this may be similar to other exceptional periods of innovation, such as the decades-long economic expansion resulting from the invention of the railway, car and settlement of the American West. That super-cycle lasted forty years, and the massive expansion of emerging economies may result in the same duration of demand for commodities. "I believe we are in a super-cycle that began in 2003 and is just taking a pause right now," Lassonde told a conference of mining analysts in Toronto in 2012.

Joining the American economy would eliminate the cyclical risk for Canada, because the two economies would remain diversified even if Canada's commodity-based economy tripled or quadrupled in size. Without a merger, the bad news is that Canada, with its economy based on resources and branch plants, doesn't hold enough cards to guarantee a bright future on its own.

The Best Option

Canada can become a more significant economy, and more independent, if its people and politicians are willing to support actions, risks and sacrifices necessary to achieve greater independence through scale. This would, by the way, also benefit the United States indirectly because Canada would, presumably, buy more goods and services from Americans if it grew dramatically.

The catch-22, however, is that Canada cannot easily become bigger without financial support from the United States. Europeans will be preoccupied for years with their internal and expansion challenges, and China would be undesirable as a major partner. This means that any high-growth initiative would, ironically, result in more reliance, not less, on American capital, market access, manpower and corporate participation or ownership. Put another way, becoming a "northern tiger" may only be achievable through deeper integration, or a merger, with the existing "northern tiger" to the south.

Of course, Canadian conspiracy theorists believe that Washington has impeded Canada's progress toward economic independence for decades in order to slowly annex the country. If that were the intention, then American politicians and tacticians have been thoroughly inept for two centuries. Given its military and economic clout, annexation would have been simple. As comedian Jon Stewart once joked: "I was in Canada and this Canadian woman wouldn't leave me alone. 'What do Americans really think about Canada?' . . . and I was like, 'We don't.' As a matter of fact, until we run out of natural resources, you guys are pretty safe. But when that day comes . . . [*sound of knocking on a door*] 'Hey, Canada, um, we're out of wood, and—I don't know how to put this—get out.' We would do it too."[25]

In June 2012, two Canadian historians debated the proposition that "The U.S. has coveted Canada since the War of 1812." Professor Stephen Clarkson maintained that U.S. policies have been designed to prevent Canada from becoming a "core country" in order to restrict it to a branch plant role of economic "complementarity": "In 1947, when negotiations over a free trade agreement with Ottawa were again on the U.S. government's agenda, another [U.S. State Department] document pointed out it had always been its policy to integrate Canada fully within its economy."[26]

Professor Jack Granatstein disagreed. Americans became more dominant because Canada had no national plan and dithered for 130 years over free trade: "Canada has survived and prospered—we will continue to survive and prosper—because we are strong, but also because we share the North American continent with a great democracy of terrific energy, ambition, resources and wealth. We shout at and argue with the Americans, but today we live secure in the belief that democracies do not go to war with each other. This relationship is a model."[27]

The only invasions of Canada by Americans—at the outset of the American Revolution and the War of 1812—were responses to incursions and threats from the British, who used Canada as a staging ground for attacks, Granatstein added. In fact, he went on to say, all invasions and threats ended in 1846, when the U.S. and Britain signed the Oregon Treaty, which permanently established the border.

Even so, many Canadians will always continue to suspect America's intentions. This belief has cast an anti-American tinge across Canada's politics and policy-making that has been as damaging as has been Quebec separatism. In fact, anti-Americans and separatists are alike: both are haughty and resentful, but unwilling or unable to become truly independent or to otherwise change their situation. They wallow in complaints and inertia and represent a dangerous distraction that prevents the country from securing a sound place in the world.

Expat Americans, like me, resent slurs made against the United States in Canadian public and private life and regret that attitudes have occasionally translated into unhelpful policies. For instance, I suggested to Prime Minister Stephen Harper in 2011, after disappointment that the Keystone XL pipeline proposal had been postponed, that Canada should have recruited, and should in future recruit, Americans and U.S. veterans to fill job vacancies in the oil sands and elsewhere. I made a similar suggestion to a premier. Both leaders liked the idea, but nothing happened. Obviously, bureaucrats and policy makers figured that it was more politically correct to run off to China or to entice Irish plumbers to immigrate to Canada than to hang a recruitment shingle in Detroit or Cleveland to give America a helping hand.

Some Canadians may need to feel superior to Americans, a dangerous and foolish trait given their country's dependencies. In 2001, the Canadian Broadcasting Corporation aired a special called *Talking to Americans,* starring comedian Rick Mercer, that attracted 2.7 million viewers—making it, as the CBC boasts on its website, the most-watched Canadian comedy special in history.[28] I found the show offensive because it deployed a *Candid Camera* format to ambush Americans by asking dumb questions or asking them to repeat dumb statements. Many did so out of politeness, and they were ridiculed. For instance, university students and professors were asked to condemn and sign a petition to halt the Saskatchewan seal hunt as well as the Toronto polar bear hunt. Others were asked to condemn Canada's practice of euthanizing senior citizens by setting them adrift on northern ice floes. The show was a cheap shot, but it received plaudits and was nominated for a Gemini Award (the Canadian equivalent of an Emmy). Then the 9/11 attacks occurred and Mercer had the good sense to decline the nomination for the award.

My advice to Canadians is that, loathe America or love it, a merger is the best and only comprehensive solution we have, notwithstanding the political challenges it would present. This transaction would be the most audacious, and important, in the history of either nation. On the other hand, it would be less difficult than the amalgamations the Germans and Europeans have achieved, or what the plucky South Koreans envision, and the rewards would be far greater. The added benefit would be that the United States and Canada and their values would be protected for generations, and their combined talent pool would be harnessed to innovate and invent technologies that would enhance the quality of life for all.

But such an undertaking requires the foresight and the financial derring-do of a Thomas Jefferson, as well as the fortitude of those courageous Americans and Canadians who built railroads in the middle of nowhere and risked their lives by settling in desolate, dangerous spaces. If those traits have endured, then this merger will happen.

Conclusion

What if America Fails? And what happens to Canada if it does?
—COVER BLURB ON *THE WALRUS* MAGAZINE, NOVEMBER 2012

THE HEADLINE THAT APPEARS ON THE TITLE PAGE FOR THIS chapter would not appear in a U.S. periodical. Americans may worry about many things, but not about the neighbors and not about failure. Canadians, on the other hand, do—and should, because, deep down, as the *Walrus* teaser reveals, Canadians know they have a nice country, but they remain reliant on the United States. Canada, essentially, is a semi-autonomous jurisdiction buttressed, economically and militarily, by the United States.

Canadians, and their media, often behave like dependents. They ridicule their "masters" and exhibit the symptoms of dependency by harboring resentment and fretting about the U.S. a lot—what it thinks or says about Canada, or about anything; what it does or doesn't do. Interestingly, Quebec separatists have similar attitudes toward Canada: they resent its dominance and are hyper-vigilant about what it thinks or does. But such attitudes are not productive. They represent the mentality of colonialism—hardly surprising, given Canada's history.

Another symptom of dependency surfaced in 2012 when the Canadian federal government, in the aftermath of the Keystone Pipeline disappointment, immediately lunged into the arms of the Chinese superpower. Increasing trade with Asia represented a sensible economic diversification, but within months China had pulled off the biggest foreign takeover in the world in Canada, defied Canadian public opinion, acquired more ownership in the oil sands, negotiated a sweetheart trade deal and gained unprecedented entry to the North American market and the Arctic. Canada's leap within months into such a far-ranging intimacy with China was uncharacteristic and bore more resemblance to a rebound than a rational courtship. Besides the indecent haste, Canada could have undertaken a more reasonable approach by developing a multilateral Asian strategy and focusing on building ties with those countries that were democratic and offered to Canadian traders a respect for the rule of law. This rashness might have been pique or strategy, to gain approval of the Keystone Pipeline, but will instead land the country in the grasp of a ruthless superpower whose aggressiveness could damage the country's most important relationship.

Instead of colonial grumbling and resentment, I have always promoted economic nationalism in Canada, whether it's been my battles against the damaging separatists in 1995 or my efforts to fend off strategic acquisitions by foreigners. Now I have written a book that proposes to merge Canada with the United States. This may, to some, appear to be an about-face. But it is not. Americans are not foreigners; they are kin. Americans and Canadians are no longer distant cousins but siblings. They are not separate but entwined, their interests are aligned, their challenges similar and their people compatible.

A merger occurs daily with every cross-border business trip, courtship, marriage, conference, scholarship, corporate transfer, retirement or shopping excursion. Canada's psychological and economic dependency on the United States is substantive and entrenched. To disavow, ignore or be oblivious to this would be to pursue policies that could cast Canada adrift in a world of very mean streets. Americans, on the other hand, would simply move on, even if spurned, because that's what nation-states do. They look after themselves first and don't worry about the neighbors unless they fuss or become threatening.

This thought experiment poses the ultimate existential question to Canadians and, to a lesser extent, Americans. Both need to digest the question of a merger and make a commitment. Absent a merger, America will face increasing adversity and competition for resources. It will become unable to police the world at its current grand scale, at the expense of its society's well-being. Inevitably, Canada on its own won't make the G20 cut, will drift or will become increasingly partitioned by inappropriate countries such as China or Russia. It could become a resource battleground.

Combined, however, they would strengthen. The United States is the only nation with the capital, scientific prowess and motivation to fully develop Canada and its wilderness in a sustainable and responsible way. And Canada's resources and Arctic region, the world's future Panama and Suez canals, would bestow upon the United States unbelievable opportunities.

This is a wake-up call designed to prompt Canadians and Americans to have a conversation about future options. Canadians must take account. They own an untouched, wealthy wilderness, but their greatest asset, by far, is that the most powerful, innovative country in history really, really likes and respects them. These two realities—geography and goodwill—make Canada the envy of the world.

Even so, opposition would be fierce among Canada's elites, who would lose their exalted positions. China, Russia and OPEC members would attempt to intervene because a U.S.–Canada union would diminish their geopolitical importance and trade reach, and halt their incursions into the U.S. through Canada. Finally, Britain would agonize over the prospect, especially after centuries of keeping the two apart, and especially since Australia and New Zealand might consider joining the U.S.–Canada alliance, as they should. (Alternatively, Britain may find itself minus Scotland, out of the European Union and in need of new alliances. In 2014, the Scots will vote on independence from the United Kingdom, and by 2017 British Prime Minister David Cameron has promised a referendum on remaining part of the European Union. A Canada–U.S deal might attract newly independent Scotland and/or Britain.)

My guess is that if Canadians signaled they wanted to join forces, the Americans would smother them with whatever they requested: compensation; free medical care and other entitlements; half the future profits from resource development; and appropriate positions in the institutions that would be created to manage the future of these 347.4 million North Americans. I also imagine that a deal could catch the imagination of both publics and, if so, happen more quickly than politicians can imagine, as occurred in Germany. Perhaps this grand partnership would also eventually force Mexico to get its act together or face isolation.

At the very least, Canada must examine the benefits of a monetary union, then customs union, with the United States as a way of eliminating its high currency and inadequate workforce obstacles. This would require the creation of new binational institutions and payment by the U.S. of a significant premium to Canadians for their currency. For instance, the West Germans offered East Germans a one-for-one exchange rate for their nearly worthless East German marks in wages, pensions and some savings. In this case, the two dollars are roughly at par in value, so the Americans would have to offer sweeteners such as co-management of a combined central bank and a generous swap premium, for cash, investments and savings, of considerably more than one for one.

This book has explained why a merger should happen and suggested how this new nation-state could be structured. Opponents will demonize this as a sell-out, or an annexation of Canada by the United States. But they would be wrong. This transaction must deliver mutual benefits: Canadians must be paid for their assets and must occupy a special place setting at the board of directors' table, and Americans must appreciate the significance and benefit. Simply put, the Merger of the Century, or steps toward integration, could transform these countries and, by so doing, revamp the world at large. By joining Canada's endowment with America's industrial colossus to protect shared values, they would finally, and unequivocally, be the greatest country in the history of the world.

Acknowledgments

THIS IS A BOOK THAT HAS TAKEN THREE YEARS TO COMPLETE, but a lifetime to write. I immigrated to Canada from Chicago at nineteen years of age during the Vietnam War and left my family behind. But, like most expats and Canadians, I have intensely followed America's tumultuous politics, its social revolutions, foreign wars and cultural upheavals. As a journalist, I have worked and traveled in both countries, as well as in Mexico. In essence, North America has been my beat, and business, sociology and politics have been my passions.

It was in that spirit that I first articulated the thesis of this book. My editor, Jim Gifford, at HarperCollins; his publisher, David Kent; and my agent, Linda McKnight, were enthusiastic. Not coincidentally, all three have family in the United States, and David, like me, is a dual citizen.

This project has gone through many incarnations and has been shaped by the patient and perspicacious Jim Gifford. Alex Schultz was the first outside reader and provided important suggestions and encouragement. Shepherding the finished manuscript through its final, tedious stages involved heroic efforts by Lloyd Davis, Sue Sumeraj, Noelle Zitzer and Kelly Hope.

This project has been the culmination of all the articles and books I have written and interviews I have conducted over the years. It also stands on the shoulders of contributions, reportage and ideas gleaned from dozens of authors, journalists, academics and thought leaders, many of whom have been noted in these pages. Also key to this project were Craig Kelly, Jack Granatstein, Paul Cellucci and Donald Macdonald, who provided insights and valuable information.

Finally, thanks to my friends and colleagues who have put up graciously with my preoccupation, social absences and uncharacteristic secrecy concerning this project. And this book would not have been possible without the encouragement and support of my husband, John Beck, and my Canadian children, Eric and Julie. They have added value by providing constructive criticisms, sensitivity and advice. Polling among the four of us has been running 2–2 vis-à-vis a merger, which may be exactly how it all shakes out in the end. So thanks to all, and then some.

Notes

INTRODUCTION

1. J.L. Granatstein, *Yankee Go Home? Canadians and Anti-Americanism* (Toronto: HarperCollins, 1996).

2. Polly Vernon, "Graydon Carter: Literati? Glitterati? I'd rather have a quiet night with the missus," *The Observer*, October 25, 2009, http://www.guardian.co.uk/lifeandstyle/2009/oct/25/graydon-carter-editor-vanity-fair.

3. Vivian O'Donnell and Susan Wallace, "First Nations, Métis and Inuit Women," Statistics Canada, last modified February 24, 2012, http://www.statcan.gc.ca/pub/89-503-x/2010001/article/11442-eng.htm; and Alexia Cooper and Erica L. Smith, *Homicide Trends in the United States, 1980–2008,* U.S. Department of Justice, Bureau of Justice Statistics, November 2011, bjs.ojp.usdoj.gov/content/pub/pdf/htus8008.pdf.

4. "International Trade: Canadian Economy (NAICS 11–91)," Industry Canada, last modified November 24, 2011, http://www.ic.gc.ca/eic/site/cis-sic.nsf/eng/h_00029.html; and "Foreign control in the Canadian economy: 2009," Statistics Canada, *The Daily*, October 13, 2011, http://www.statcan.gc.ca/daily-quotidien/111013/dq111013b-eng.htm.

5. "FP500: Largest foreign-controlled companies," *Financial Post,* June 19, 2012, http://business.financialpost.com/2012/06/19/fp500-largest-foreign-controlled-companies/.

6. "Provincial Outlook," Royal Bank of Canada, December 2012, www.rbc.com/economics/market/pdf/provfcst.pdf.

7. "GDP per capita (US$)," The World Bank, http://data.worldbank.org/indicator/
NY.GDP.PCAP.CD.

8. "Update 2: U.S. household debt burden eases in Q2," Reuters, September
16, 2011, http://www.reuters.com/article/2011/09/16/usa-economy-wealth-
idUSS1E78F0XE20110916; and Tavia Grant, "Record high household debt in Canada
triggers alarm," *Globe and Mail,* December 13, 2011, last updated September 6, 2012,
http://www.theglobeandmail.com/globe-investor/personal-finance/household-
finances/record-high-household-debt-in-canada-triggers-alarm/article4181115.

9. "Energy use (kg of oil equivalent per capita) in Canada," Trading Economics, http://
www.tradingeconomics.com/canada/energy-use-kg-of-oil-equivalent-per-capita-wb-
data.html; and "Energy use (kg of oil equivalent per capita) in the United States,"
Trading Economics, http://www.tradingeconomics.com/united-states/energy-use-kg-
of-oil-equivalent-per-capita-wb-data.html.

10. "Homeownership Rates for the 75 Largest Metropolitan Statistical Areas: 2005
to 2011," U.S. Census Bureau, http://www.census.gov/housing/hvs/files/annua111/
ann11t_16.xls; and "Data source for Chart 14.1: Home ownership rates by age group, all
households," Statistics Canada, http://www.statcan.gc.ca/pub/11-402-x/2011000/chap/
fam/c-g/desc/desc01-eng.htm.

11. "Tax Burdens, 2010 definitive results (and changes to 2011)," OECD, Centre for Tax
Policy and Administration, http://www.oecd.org/ctp/taxpolicyanalysis/taxburdens-
2010definitiveresultsandchangesto2011.htm.

12. "Emerging vs. developed countries: Power shift," *The Economist,* August 4, 2011,
http://www.economist.com/blogs/dailychart/2011/08/emerging-vs-developed-
economies.

13. Simon Rogers, "Gun homicides and gun ownership listed by country," *The Guardian,*
July 22, 2012, http://www.guardian.co.uk/news/datablog/2012/jul/22/gun-homicides-
ownership-world-list.

14. "Petroleum and Other Liquids: U.S. Imports by Country of Origin," U.S. Energy
Information Administration, http://www.eia.gov/dnav/pet/pet_move_impcus_a2_
nus_epoo_imo_mbblpd_m.htm.

15. "Goods and Services Deficit Increases in October 2012," U.S. Census Bureau, http://
www.census.gov/indicator/www/ustrade.html.

16. Jon Clifton, "150 Million Adults Worldwide Would Migrate to the U.S.," Gallup, April 20, 2012, http://www.gallup.com/poll/153992/150-million-adults-worldwide-migrate.aspx; and "Facts & Figures," International Organization for Migration, http://www.iom.int/cms/en/sites/iom/home/about-migration/facts--figures-1.html.

17. "Poll shows NZ–Aust union worth considering," TVNZ One News, March 14, 2010, http://tvnz.co.nz/national-news/poll-shows-nz-aust-union-worth-considering-3414685.

18. Margaret MacMillan, *Paris 1919: Six Months That Changed the World* (New York: Random House, 2002).

19. Gordon T. Stewart, "Three Lessons for Mexico from Canadian–American Relations," *Revista Frontera Norte* 3, no. 6 (1991): 29–46, https://docs.google.com/viewer?a=v&q=cache:z2KbGAERNdsJ:www2.colef.mx/fronteranorte/articulos/FN6/2-f6_Lessons_for_Mexico_from_canadian-american.pdf+&hl=en&gl=ca&pid=bl&srcid=ADGEEShRGuCELj3vsKFTxFfefVZpOJMFomYbMEf__DqoL_5ipDZo7GDDHnuBJlwFho8gdgXQQHAc1BGr4Kesnh3t9Vs5goaDayJecp340efWo8bo65hBZN3wBbbWwOCyKWnKrtnpk3eo&sig=AHIEtbRt2RmLUECYOvICVRoSCkXQgu7SqQ.

20. Stanley Meisler, "Fear of U.S. May Weigh on Canadian Voters," *Los Angeles Times*, November 20, 1988, http://articles.latimes.com/1988-11-20/news/mn-461_1_free-trade-agreement.

21. "The State of the News Media 2012," Pew Research Center's Project for Excellence in Journalism, http://stateofthemedia.org/2012/newspapers-building-digital-revenues-proves-painfully-slow/newspapers-by-the-numbers.

22. Canadian Press, "Super Bowl lures record number of TV viewers in Canada, U.S.," *The Chronicle-Herald* (Halifax, N.S.), February 7, 2012, http://thechronicleherald.ca/artslife/60121-super-bowl-lures-record-number-tv-viewers-canada-us; and "4.6 million viewers watch 99th Grey Cup on TSN and RDS," TSN, November 28, 2011, http://www.tsn.ca/cfl/story/?id=381490.

23. "It'll cost you: Scottish independence would come at a high price," *The Economist*, April 14, 2012, http://www.economist.com/node/21552564.

24. "Canada," *World Factbook*, Central Intelligence Agency, https://www.cia.gov/library/publications/the-world-factbook/geos/ca.html.

25. Diane Francis, *Fighting for Canada* (Toronto: Key Porter, 1996).

26. *Breaking Point* (Toronto: CBC Television, 2005).

27. "Description of the AFN," Assembly of First Nations, http://www.afn.ca/index.php/en/about-afn/description-of-the-afn.

28. "Recruiting and Retention in the Canadian Forces," Department of National Defence and the Canadian Forces, last modified October 2, 2012, http://www.forces.gc.ca/site/news-nouvelles/news-nouvelles-eng.asp?id=3792.

29. "Canada's Navy at a Glance," Department of National Defence and the Canadian Forces, last modified August 14, 2012, http://www.navy.forces.gc.ca/cms/12/12_eng.asp.

30. "Status of the Navy as of November 21, 2012," United States Navy, http://www.navy.mil/navydata/nav_legacy.asp?id=146.

31. "Trade in Goods with Canada," U.S. Census Bureau, http://www.census.gov/foreign-trade/balance/c1220.html; and Derek Burleton and Diana Petramala, "Canada's Declining Reliance on the U.S.—Where to Grow from Here?," TD Economics, February 1, 2012, www.td.com/document/PDF/economics/special/dp0212_trade.pdf.

CHAPTER ONE: INTERNATIONAL THREATS

1. Jared Diamond, "What's Your Consumption Factor?," *The New York Times,* January 2, 2008, http://www.nytimes.com/2008/01/02/opinion/02diamond.html.

2. "Commodity Prices: The End of a Historic Boom," The World Bank, Global Economic Prospects 2009, http://web.worldbank.org/WBSITE/EXTERNAL/EXTDEC/EXTDECPROSPECTS/GEPEXT/EXTGEP2009/0,,contentMDK:22002357~pagePK:641676 89~piPK:64167673~theSitePK:5530498,00.html.

3. "Emerging vs. developed economies: Power shift," *The Economist,* August 4, 2011, http://www.economist.com/blogs/dailychart/2011/08/emerging-vs-developed-economies.

4. "Top 10 largest economies in 2020," Euromonitor International, July 7, 2010, http://blog.euromonitor.com/2010/07/special-report-top-10-largest-economies-in-2020.html.

5. Andy Stern, "China's Superior Economic Model," *The Wall Street Journal,* December 1, 2011, http://online.wsj.com/article/SB10001424052970204630904577056490023451980.html.

6. Jonathan Woetzel, Lenny Mendonca, Janamitra Devan et al., "Preparing for China's urban billion," McKinsey Global Institute, February 2009, http://www.mckinsey.com/insights/mgi/research/urbanization/preparing_for_urban_billion_in_china.

7. Joyce Appleby, *The Relentless Revolution: A History of Capitalism* (New York: Norton, 2010).

8. Agence France-Presse, "Bangladesh workers riot over soaring food prices," *Google News*, April 12, 2008, http://afp.google.com/article/ALeqM5g7DFz2n2qmBIx-UVdGeBwG_vGfpw.

9. Stefan Steinberg, "Financial speculators reap profits from global hunger," Centre for Research on Globalization, http://www.globalresearch.ca/financial-speculators-reap-profits-from-global-hunger/8794; and "The FAO Food Price Index fell further in November," Food and Agricultural Organization of the United Nations, June 12, 2012, http://www.fao.org/worldfoodsituation/wfs-home/foodpricesindex/en.

10. "Riots, instability spread as food prices skyrocket," CNN, April 14, 2008, http://edition.cnn.com/2008/WORLD/americas/04/14/world.food.crisis.

11. Wael Gamal, "Police shoot boy dead in troubled Nile Delta town," Reuters, April 8, 2008, http://www.aljazeera.com/news/middleeast/2008/12/2008121511544968722.html.

12. Kathie Klarreich, "Food Riots Lead to Haitian Meltdown," *Time*, April 14, 2008, http://www.time.com/time/world/article/0,8599,1730607,00.html.

13. "Anti-government rioting spreads in Cameroon," *The New York Times*, December 7, 2008, http://www.nytimes.com/2008/02/27/world/africa/27iht-27cameroon.10504780.html?_r=2.

14. Lutfi Sheriff Mohammed and Edmund Sanders, "Clashes kill 5 when shoppers riot in Mogadishu," *Los Angeles Times*, May 6, 2008, http://articles.latimes.com/2008/may/06/world/fg-somalia6.

15. Marla Dickerson, "Mexico is freezing prices on scores of food staples," *Los Angeles Times*, June 19, 2008, http://articles.latimes.com/2008/jun/19/business/fi-mexinflation19.

16. Nick Olle, "Brazil halts rice exports as world food prices climb," *ABC News*, April 25, 2008, http://www.abc.net.au/news/2008-04-25/brazil-halts-rice-exports-as-world-food-prices/2415634.

17. Ibrahim Saif, "The Food Price Crisis in the Arab Countries: Short Term Responses to a Lasting Challenge," Carnegie Endowment for International Peace, June 23, 2008, http://carnegieendowment.org/2008/06/23/food-price-crisis-in-arab-countries-short-term-responses-to-lasting-challenge/1gvl.

18. Sean O'Grady, "Russian wheat export ban threatens higher inflation and food riots," *The Independent,* August 6, 2010, http://www.independent.co.uk/news/business/news/russian-wheat-export-ban-threatens-higher-inflation-and-food-riots-2044769.html.

19. Evan Fraser and Andrew Rimas, "The Psychology of Food Riots," *Foreign Affairs,* January 30, 2011, http://www.foreignaffairs.com/articles/67338/evan-fraser-and-andrew-rimas/the-psychology-of-food-riots.

20. "Arable land (hectares per person)," The World Bank, http://data.worldbank.org/indicator/AG.LND.ARBL.HA.PC.

21. Aditya Chakrabortty, "Secret report: biofuel caused food crisis," *The Guardian,* July 3, 2008, http://www.guardian.co.uk/environment/2008/jul/03/biofuels.renewableenergy.

22. Larry Elliott and Heather Stewart, "Poor go hungry while rich fill their tanks," *The Guardian,* April 11, 2008, http://www.guardian.co.uk/business/2008/apr/11/worldbank.fooddrinks1.

23. Javier Blas, "Land leased to secure crops for South Korea," *Financial Times,* November 18, 2008, http://www.ft.com/intl/cms/s/0/98a81b9c-b59f-11dd-ab71-0000779fd18c.html.

24. "New World Bank Report Sees Growing Demand for Farmland," The World Bank, September 7, 2010, http://go.worldbank.org/XWESR02MT0.

25. Hiroko Nakata, "Fears growing over land grabs," *Japan Times,* December 18, 2010, http://www.japantimes.co.jp/text/nn20101218f2.html.

26. Song Jung-a, Christian Oliver and Tom Burgis, "Daewoo to cultivate Madagascar land for free," *Financial Times,* November 19, 2008, http://www.ft.com/intl/cms/s/0/6e894c6a-b65c-11dd-89dd-0000779fd18c.html.

27. *Ibid.*

28. Sungwoo Park, "Daewoo Logistics Says Farm Deal May Cost $6 Billion," Bloomberg, November 20, 2008, http://www.bloomberg.com/apps/news?pid=newsarchive&sid=a1anvJxPYq20&refer=africa.

29. "Editorial: Food security deal should not stand," *Financial Times*, November 19, 2008, http://www.ft.com/intl/cms/s/0/20cf7936-b670-11dd-89dd-0000779fd18c.html.

30. Tom Burgis and Javier Blas, "Madagascar cancels Seoul land plan," *Financial Times*, March 19, 2009, http://www.ft.com/intl/cms/s/0/97665f2e-1426-11de-9e32-0000779fd2ac.html#axzz#KMH79DqL.

31. "UN body fails to back 'land grabs' code of conduct," Reuters, October 15, 2010, http://af.reuters.com/article/idAFJOE69E0CM20101015.

32. "Family Farms Overview," National Institute of Food and Agriculture, last updated June 18, 2010, http://www.nifa.usda.gov/nea/ag_systems/in_focus/familyfarm_if_overview.html.

33. "The financial picture of farms in Canada," Statistics Canada, 2006 Census of Agriculture, last modified October 5, 2009, http://www.statcan.gc.ca/ca-ra2006/articles/finpicture-portrait-eng.htm.

34. "Economic and Policy Analysis: AFIDA (Agricultural Foreign Investment Disclosure Act)," U.S. Department of Agriculture, Farm Service Agency, last modified July 11, 2012, http://www.fsa.usda.gov/FSA/webapp?area=home&subject=ecpa&topic=afa.

35. "Losing Our Grip: How a Corporate Farmland Buy-up, Rising Farm Debt, and Agribusiness Financing of Inputs Threaten Family Farms and Food Sovereignty (or, 'Serfdom 2.0')," National Farmers Union, June 7, 2010, http://nfu.ca/press_releases/2010/06-07-losing_grip.pdf.

36. "Major Foreign Holders of Treasury Securities," U.S. Department of the Treasury, December 17, 2012, http://www.treasury.gov/resource-center/data-chart-center/tic/Documents/mfh.txt.

37. American Chamber of Commerce in Shanghai, *Viewpoint: Chinese FDI in the U.S.*, June 2010, http://www.amcham-shanghai.org/ftpuploadfiles/publications/viewpoint/vp_financial.pdf.

38. Wayne M. Morrison and Marc Labonte, "China's Holdings of U.S. Securities: Implications for the U.S. Economy," Congressional Research Service, December 6, 2012, http://www.fas.org/sgp/crs/row/RL34314.pdf; and James A. Dorn, "The Debt Threat: A Risk to U.S.–China Relations?," *Brown Journal of World Affairs* 14, no. 2 (Spring/Summer 2008): 151–64, http://www.cato.org/sites/cato.org/files/articles/dorn_bjwa_142.pdf.

39. "Gulf Says Amauligak May Be Commercial Discovery," Oilpatch History, June Warren-Nickle's Energy Group, September 25, 1984, http://www.nickles.com/history/article.aspx?id=8217.

40. "Gazprom successfully completes the world's first LNG shipment through the Northern Sea Route," Gazprom Marketing and Trading, December 6, 2012, http://www.gazprom-mt.com/WhatWeSay/News/Pages/Gazprom-successfully-completes-the-world's-first-LNG-shipment-through-the-Northern-Sea-Route.aspx.

41. Claudia Cattaneo, "Canada's natural gas dreams closer to reality after Petronas moves," Financial Post, June 28, 2012, http://business.financialpost.com/2012/06/28/canadas-natural-gas-dreams-closer-to-reality-after-petronas-moves.

42. Carol Christian, "53 charges for CNRL, contractors," Fort McMurray Today, April 22, 2009, http://www.fortmcmurraytoday.com/2009/04/22/53-charges-for-cnrl-contractors.

43. Diane Francis, "China must improve its construction record," Financial Post, March 31, 2012, http://opinion.financialpost.com/2012/03/31/china-must-improve-its-construction-record.

44. Ryan Cormier, "Guilty pleas in 2007 deaths of two Chinese workers in northern Alberta tank collapse," Edmonton Journal, October 1, 2002, http://www.edmontonjournal.com/opinion/blogs/Guilty+pleas+2007+deaths+Chinese+workers+northern+Alberta+tank+collapse/7326885/story.html.

45. Diane Francis, "We ignore risks of foreign buyouts and China trade deal at our own peril," Financial Post, November 23, 2012, http://opinion.financialpost.com/2012/11/23/we-ignore-risks-of-foreign-buyouts-and-china-trade-deal-at-our-own-peril.

46. Alex Shoumatoff, "Agony and Ivory," Vanity Fair, August 2011, http://www.vanityfair.com/culture/features/2011/08/elephants-201108.

47. "More than 100 elephants a day slaughtered by poachers," International Fund for Animal Welfare, October 20, 2009, http://www.ifaw.org/africa/node/17271.

48. "China loans Angola US$15b," Channel NewsAsia, March 6, 2011, http://www.channelnewsasia.com/stories/afp_asiapacific_business/view/1114670/1/.html.

49. Liz Alderman, "Looking for Investments, China Turns to Europe," The New York Times, November 1, 2010, http://www.nytimes.com/2010/11/02/business/global/02euro.html.

50. "Chinese company fired from Polish highway project," *Want China Times*, http://www.wantchinatimes.com/news-subclass-cnt.aspx?id=20110616000021&cid=1102.

51. "What we do," TAQA (Abu Dhabi National Energy Company), accessed January 9, 2013, http://www.taqaglobal.com/about-us/what-we-do.aspx?sc_lang=en.

52. Gregor Stuart Hunter, "Former Taqa chief's case thrown out by US judge," *The National* (United Arab Emirates), September 30, 2011, http://www.thenational.ae/business/energy/former-taqa-chiefs-case-thrown-out-by-us-judge.

53. Fiifi Arhin, "$75m Aboadze plant expansion cost 'inflated,'" *The New Statesman* (Ghana), July 29, 2011, http://www.thestatesmanonline.com/pages/news_detail.php?newsid=10463&section=1.

54. "U.A.E. closes airspace to MacKay, Natynczyk," *CBC News*, October 11, 2010, http://www.cbc.ca/news/canada/story/2010/10/11/military-dubai011.html.

55. "YBM Magnex used by mob to bilk investors," *CBC News*, June 8, 1999, http://www.cbc.ca/news/business/story/1999/06/08/ybmmagnex990608.html.

56. Kim Murphy, "Russian Capitalism Still Has Muscle Behind It," *Los Angeles Times,* June 26, 2005, http://articles.latimes.com/2005/jun/26/business/fi-russbiz26/2.

57. Michael Mainville, "Russians force out Canadian hotel staff," *Toronto Star,* August 18, 2004.

58. Clifford J. Levy, "An Investment Gets Trapped in Kremlin's Vise," *The New York Times*, July 24, 2008, http://www.nytimes.com/2008/07/24/world/europe/24kremlin.html.

59. "Concentrated fury: Blast from Browder," *The Economist,* May 16, 2011, http://www.economist.com/blogs/easternapproaches/2011/05/concentrated_fury.

60. Joe Nocera, "Turning the Tables on Russia," *The New York Times,* April 16, 2012, http://www.nytimes.com/2012/04/17/opinion/nocera-turning-the-tables-on-russia.html.

61. Stephanie Baker-Said, "Browder, Branded a Danger to Russia, Posts 2,549 Percent Return," Hermitage Capital Management, http://hermitagefund.com/newsandmedia/index.php?ELEMENT_ID=775.

62. Luke Harding, "'Harassed' head of BP venture exits Moscow," *The Guardian*, July 25, 2008, http://www.guardian.co.uk/business/2008/jul/25/bp.oil.

63. Terry Macalister, "BP hit by fresh troubles as pressure builds on chief executive Bob Dudley," *The Observer*, September 4, 2011, http://www.guardian.co.uk/business/2011/sep/04/bp-boss-dudley-fresh-troubles.

64. Nicolas Van Praet, "He's back—Russian billionaire Deripaska strikes partnership with Quebec miner," *Financial Post*, March 28, 2012, http://business.financialpost.com/2012/03/28/hes-back-russian-billionaire-deripaska-strikes-partnership-with-quebec-miner.

65. Claudia Cattaneo, "Russians follow Chinese into Canada's oil patch," *Financial Post*, April 16, 2012, http://business.financialpost.com/2012/04/16/russians-follow-chinese-into-canadas-oil-patch.

66. Meirion Jones and Susan Watts, "Wikileaks cables show race to carve up Arctic," *BBC Newsnight*, May 12, 2011, http://news.bbc.co.uk/2/hi/programmes/newsnight/9483790.stm.

67. Agence France-Presse, "Hilton owners were cheeky: Chavez," *Google News*, October 14, 2009, http://www.google.com/hostednews/afp/article/ALeqM5jc-YeSwTAuh-5vkdouPA7v2Eu4Ow.

68. "Expropriated Companies in Venezuela Get Little to No Compensation," *What's Next Venezuela?* (blog), July 16, 2010, https://www.whatsnextvenezuela.com/expropriation/expropriated-companies-in-venezuela-get-little-to-no-compensation.

69. "'A Blatant Extortion,'" *The Wall Street Journal*, May 13, 2009, http://online.wsj.com/article/SB124217032839812731.html.

70. Simon Romero and Clifford Krauss, "Ecuador Judge Orders Chevron to Pay $9 Billion," *The New York Times*, February 14, 2011, http://www.nytimes.com/2011/02/15/world/americas/15ecuador.html.

71. Joe Carroll, Rebecca Penty and Katia Dmitrieva, "Chevron's $19 Billion 'Distaster' Gets Hearing: Corporate Canada," *The Washington Post*, November 29, 2012, http://washpost.bloomberg.com/Story?docId=1376-ME7GSM6TTDY001-2350LVR19PR931ENTUMJHHFAV8.

72. Clare Ribando Seelke, Liana Sun Wyler and June S. Beittel, "Latin America and the Caribbean: Illicit Drug Trafficking and U.S. Counterdrug Programs," Congressional Research Service, http://fpc.state.gov/documents/organization/142364.pdf.

73. Jason Dean, Andrew Browne and Shai Oster, "China's 'State Capitalism' Sparks a Global Backlash," *The Wall Street Journal,* November 16, 2010, http://online.wsj.com/article/SB10001424052748703514904575602731006315198.html.

74. David Rachowitz, "[*Petroleum Intelligence Weekly* Ranks World's Top 50 Oil Companies—]Suncor Up, ConocoPhillips Down in *PIW*'s New Top 50 Oil Rankings," *Petroleum Insights* (blog), December 8 2011, http://petroleuminsights.blogspot.ca/2011/12/suncor-up-conocophillips-down-in-piws.html.

75. Jeff Rubin, *Why Your World Is About to Get a Whole Lot Smaller* (Toronto: Random House, 2009).

76. Barry Sergeant, "Top 100 Mining Companies: What a Difference a Year Makes," Mineweb, January 12, 2010, http://www.mineweb.com/mineweb/view/mineweb/en/page67?oid=95737&sn=Detail.

77. Peter Navarro, *The Coming China Wars: Where They Will Be Fought and How They Will Be Won* (Upper Saddle River, NJ: Financial Times Press, 2006).

78. Stephen D. King, *Losing Control: The Emerging Threats to Western Prosperity* (New Haven, CT: Yale University Press, 2010).

79. Edwin M. Truman, "Sovereign Wealth Funds: The Need for Greater Transparency and Accountability," Peterson Institute for International Economics, August 2007, http://www.iie.com/publications/pb/pb07-6.pdf.

80. "Sovereign Wealth Fund Rankings," Sovereign Wealth Fund Institute, last updated December 2012, http://www.swfinstitute.org/fund-rankings.

81. Kelvin Soh and Andrea Hopkins, "Scotiabank buys into Guangzhou Bank for C$719 million," Reuters, September 9, 2011, http://www.reuters.com/article/2011/09/09/us-scotiabank-idUSTRE7881NU20110909.

82. "Foreign control in the Canadian economy, 2010," Statistics Canada, *The Daily,* June 22, 2012, http://www.statcan.gc.ca/daily-quotidien/120622/dq120622b-eng.htm; and "Foreign ownership of U.S. companies jumps," Reuters, August 27, 2008, http://www.reuters.com/article/2008/08/27/us-companies-ownership-usa-idUSN2744743020080827.

CHAPTER TWO: BILATERAL THREATS

1. Ingrid Peritz, "Farmer stands up to Homeland Security," *The Globe and Mail,* May 21, 2010, http://www.theglobeandmail.com/news/national/farmer-stands-up-to-depart-ment-of-homeland-security/article1367625.

2. "Manuel Moroun and family," *Forbes,* http://www.forbes.com/profile/manuel-moroun.

3. U.S. Chamber of Commerce and Canadian Chamber of Commerce, *Finding the Balance: Reducing Border Costs While Strengthening Security,* U.S. Chamber of Commerce website, February 2008, http://www.uschamber.com/sites/default/files/reports/0802_finding_balance_report.pdf.

4. Patrick Grady, "How Much Were Canadian Exports Curtailed by the Post-9/11 Thickening of the U.S. Border?," Global Economics Ltd., May 30, 2008, global-economics.ca/border_post911.pdf.

5. Tom Walsh, "Chrysler boss Marchionne: We're in it together," *Detroit Free Press,* June 4, 2010, http://www.freep.com/article/20100604/COL06/6040387/Chrysler-boss-Marchionne-We-re-together.

6. Diane Francis, "Ottawa should regain some control over Quebec immigration," *Financial Post,* September 23, 1997.

7. "Remarks by Richard B. Fadden, Director, Canadian Security Intelligence Service, to the Canadian Association for Security and Intelligence Studies (CASIS) Annual International Conference," Canadian Security Intelligence Service, October 29, 2009, last modified November 27, 2011, http://www.csis-scrs.gc.ca/nwsrm/spchs/spch29102009-eng.asp.

8. "Testimony of Secretary Janet Napolitano Before the United States Senate Committee on the Judiciary, 'Department of Homeland Security Oversight,'" U.S. Department of Homeland Security, March 9, 2011, http://www.dhs.gov/ynews/testimony/testimony_1299683039975.shtm.

9. Dan Heath, "National Northern Border Counternarcotics Strategy released," *Press-Republican* (Plattsburgh, N.Y.), January 21, 2012, http://pressrepublican.com/0100_news/x370172404/National-Northern-Border-Counternarcotics-Strategy-released.

10. "Drug Situation in Canada—2006," Royal Canadian Mounted Police, last modified December 17, 2007, http://www.rcmp-grc.gc.ca/drugs-drogues/drg-2006-eng. htm#marihuana.

11. Stephen T. Easton, "Marijuana Growth in BC," Fraser Institute, June 17, 2004, http://www.fraserinstitute.org/research-news/news/display.aspx?id=11726.

12. Tina Hotton Mahony, "Homicide in Canada, 2010," Statistics Canada, last modified October 26, 2011, http://www.statcan.gc.ca/pub/85-002-x/2011001/article/11561-eng.htm.

13. "Petroleum and Other Liquids: U.S. Imports by Country of Origin," U.S. Energy Information Administration, December 28, 2012, http://www.eia.gov/dnav/pet/pet_ move_impcus_a2_nus_epoo_imo_mbblpd_m.htm; and "Canada's Energy Future: Energy Supply and Demand Projections to 2035—Energy Market Assessment," National Energy Board, November 2011, last modified October 31, 2012, http://www.neb-one.gc.ca/ clf-nsi/rnrgynfmtn/nrgyrprt/nrgyftr/2011/nrgsppldmndprjctn2035-eng.html.

14. "Petroleum and Other Liquids: U.S. Imports by Country of Origin," U.S. Energy Information Administration, December 28, 2012, http://www.eia.gov/dnav/pet/pet_ move_impcus_a2_nus_epoo_imo_mbblpd_m.htm.

15. "Economics and energy outlook," Imperial Oil, accessed January 9, 2013, http://www.imperialoil.ca/Canada-English/operations_sands_glance_outlook.aspx.

16. "Permit for Alberta Clipper Pipeline Issued," U.S. Department of State, Office of the Spokesman, August 20, 2009, http://www.state.gov/r/pa/prs/ps/2009/aug/128164.htm.

17. "North America leads shift in global energy balance, IEA says in latest World Energy Outlook," International Energy Agency, November 12, 2012, http://www.iea.org/ newsroomandevents/pressreleases/2012/november/name,33015,en.html.

18. Robert Redford, "Stand together against the tar-sands scourge," *The Globe and Mail*, November 21, 2011, http://www.theglobeandmail.com/commentary/stand-together-against-the-tar-sands-scourge/article4201189.

19. Bloomberg News, "Re-elected Obama has no reason to block Keystone XL pipeline," *Financial Post*, November 14, 2012, last updated January 4, 2013, http:// business.financialpost.com/2012/11/14/re-elected-obama-has-no-reason-to-block-keystone-xl-pipeline/

20. Nick Snow, "Judge dismisses Sierra Club's oil sands lawsuit," *Oil and Gas Journal*, August 3, 2011, http://www.ogj.com/articles/2011/08/judge-dismisses-sierra-clubs-oil-sands-lawsuit.html; and Canadian Press, "Chiquita joins companies avoiding fuel made from oilsands," Fresh Plaza, December 16, 2011, http://www.freshplaza.com/news_detail.asp?id=90640.

21. Diane Francis, "Cree Chief Won't Buy Separatist Line," *Financial Post*, June 25, 1994.

22. Diane Francis, "Separation would be 'totally unacceptable' to Quebec Mohawks," *Financial Post*, August 10, 1996.

23. Diane Francis, "Foreign interests attack oil sands," *Financial Post*, September 23, 2011, http://opinion.financialpost.com/2011/09/23/foreign-interests-attack-oil-sands.

24. Shawn McCarthy, "'Ethical oil' ad sparks war of words between Ottawa, Saudis," *The Globe and Mail*, September 20, 2011, last updated September 6, 2012, http://www.theglobeandmail.com/news/politics/ethical-oil-ad-sparks-war-of-words-between-ottawa-saudis/article2173999.

25. *Ibid.*

26. Tom Parry, "CSIS warns business leaders of Chinese cyber-spies," *CBC News*, September 21, 2012, http://www.cbc.ca/news/politics/story/2012/09/21/pol-parry-csis-nexen-warnings.html.

27. Greg Weston, "Hackers infiltrate Calgary-based technology firm," *CBC News*, September 28, 2012, http://www.cbc.ca/news/canada/story/2012/09/28/cyber-attacks-canada-infrastructure.html.

28. Reuters, "Report points finger at China as Calgary-based oilpatch software firm recovers from hacker attack," *Calgary Herald*, October 28, 2012, http://www.calgaryherald.com/business/Report+points+finger+China+Calgary+based+oilpatch+software+firm+recovers+from+hacker+attack/7313957/story.html.

29. Nathan Vanderkippe and Shawn McCarthy, "Without Keystone XL, oil sands face choke point," *The Globe and Mail*, June 8, 2011, last updated June 13, 2011, http://www.theglobeandmail.com/report-on-business/industry-news/energy-and-resources/without-keystone-xl-oil-sands-face-choke-point/article2052562.

CHAPTER THREE: WHY A MERGER MAKES SENSE

1. Peter Burrows, "Apple vs. Google," *Bloomberg Businessweek,* January 14, 2010, http://www.businessweek.com/magazine/content/10_04/b4164028483414.htm.

2. Larry Page, "Supercharging Android: Google to Acquire Motorola Mobility," Google official blog, August 15, 2011, http://googleblog.blogspot.ca/2011/08/supercharging-android-google-to-acquire.html.

3. Valentina Pasquali and Tina Aridas, "Total Debt in Selected Countries Around the World," *Global Finance,* accessed January 9, 2013, http://www.gfmag.com/tools/global-database/economic-data/11855-total-debt-to-gdp.html.

4. "United States," *World Factbook,* Central Intelligence Agency, https://www.cia.gov/library/publications/the-world-factbook/geos/us.html.

5. Pasquali and Aridas, "Total Debt."

6. "Canada," *World Factbook,* Central Intelligence Agency, https://www.cia.gov/library/publications/the-world-factbook/geos/ca.html.

7. "United States," *World Factbook*; "Canada," *World Factbook*; "China," *World Factbook,* Central Intelligence Agency, https://www.cia.gov/library/publications/the-world-factbook/geos/ch.html; and "Hong Kong," *World Factbook,* Central Intelligence Agency, https://www.cia.gov/library/publications/the-world-factbook/geos/hk.html.

8. "Table 1. U.S. International Transactions," U.S. Bureau of Economic Analysis, http://www.bea.gov/international/xls/table1.xls.

9. Hernando de Soto, *The Mystery of Capital: Why Capitalism Triumphs in the West and Fails Everywhere Else* (New York: Basic Books, 2000).

10. Michael O'Sullivan, "Global Trends: Analyzing the Wealth of the World's Adult Population," Credit Suisse, October 19, 2011, https://infocus.credit-suisse.com/app/article/index.cfm?fuseaction=OpenArticle&aoid=323370&video=true&coid=118&void=324171&lang=EN.

11. "Labour productivity levels in the total economy," OECD, accessed January 9, 2013, http://stats.oecd.org/Index.aspx?DatasetCode=LEVEL.

12. O'Sullivan, "Global Trends."

13. "Comeback kid: America's economy is once again reinventing itself," *The Economist*, July 14, 2012, http://www.economist.com/node/21558576

14. Lori Robertson, "Health Care Bill Bankruptcies," Annenberg Public Policy Center, December 18, 2008, http://www.factcheck.org/2008/12/health-care-bill-bankruptcies/; and Filip Spagnoli, "Statistics on Prison Population Rates," *P.a.p.-Blog,* accessed January 9, 2013, filipspagnoli.wordpress.com/stats-on-human-rights/statistics-on-freedom/statistics-on-prisoner-population-rates.

15. "World's 50 Safest Banks 2011," *Global Finance,* August 18, 2011, http://www.gfmag.com/tools/best-banks/11341-worlds-50-safest-banks-2011.html.

16. "World's 50 Biggest Banks 2011," *Global Finance,* September 7, 2011, http://www.gfmag.com/tools/best-banks/11382-worlds-50-biggest-banks-2011.html.

17. Hobart King, "Who Owns the Arctic Ocean?," Geology.com, http://geology.com/articles/who-owns-the-arctic.shtml.

18. C.J. Schenk, K.J. Bird, P.J. Brown et al., "Assessment of Undiscovered Oil and Gas Resources of the West Greenland–East Canada Province, 2008," U.S. Geological Survey Fact Sheet 2008–3014, May 2008, http://pubs.usgs.gov/fs/2008/3014/pdf/FS08-3014_508.pdf.

19. "Future of the Arctic: A New Dawn for Exploration," Wood Mackenzie, http://www.woodmacresearch.com/cgi-bin/wmprod/portal/energy/productMicrosite.jsp?prodID=503.

20. "Canadians and the Great Escape," Canada at War, http://www.canadaatwar.ca/content-91/world-war-ii/canadians-and-the-great-escape.

21. "Cushing Defends Right of Dissent," *The New York Times,* December 11, 1966.

22. "World military spending reached $1.6 trillion in 2010, biggest increase in South America, fall in Europe according to new SIPRI data," Stockholm International Peace Research Institute, April 11, 2011, http://www.sipri.org/media/pressreleases/2011/milex.

23. "Active Duty Military Strength Report for March 30, 2012," U.S. Department of Defense, http://siadapp.dmdc.osd.mil/personnel/MILITARY/ms1.pdf.

24. Lawrence Kapp, "Reserve Component Personnel Issues: Questions and Answers," Congressional Research Service, http://www.fas.org/sgp/crs/natsec/RL30802.pdf.

25. "American Veterans by the Numbers," Infoplease.com, http://www.infoplease.com/spot/veteranscensus1.html.

26. "The Budget and Economic Outlook: Fiscal Years 2012 to 2022," Congressional Budget Office, January 31, 2012, http://www.cbo.gov/sites/default/files/cbofiles/attachments/01-31-2012_Outlook.pdf. Total outlays in FY2011 were $3.598 trillion, of which defense spending accounted for $700 billion, or 19.5 percent.

27. International Monetary Fund, "Report for Selected Countries and Subjects," World Economic Outlook Database, April 2012, http://www.imf.org/external/pubs/ft/weo/2012/01/weodata/weorept.aspx?sy=2010&ey=2017&scsm=1&ssd=1&sort=country&ds=.&br=1&pr1.x=61&pr1.y=8&c=111&s=GGXWDG_NGDP&grp=0&a=.

28. David Alexander, "House approves $649 bln for defense in 2012," Reuters, July 8, 2011, http://www.reuters.com/article/2011/07/08/usa-budget-defense-idUS-N1E7670UA20110708.

29. "OECD Health Data 2012—Frequently Requested Data," OECD, October 2012, http://www.oecd.org/els/healthpoliciesanddata/OECDHealthData2012FrequentlyRequestedData_Updated_October.xls.

30. Diana Farrell, Eric Jensen, Bob Kocher et al., "Accounting for the cost of US health care: A new look at why Americans spend more," McKinsey Global Institute, December 2008, http://www.mckinsey.com/Insights/MGI/Research/Americas/Accounting_for_the_cost_of_US_health_care.

31. Theresa Tamkins, "Medical bills prompt more than 60 percent of U.S. bankruptcies," CNN Health, June 5, 2009, http://articles.cnn.com/2009-06-05/health/bankruptcy.medical.bills_1_medical-bills-bankrupcties-health-insurance?_s=PM:HEALTH.

32. "Taking apart the federal budget," The Washington Post, http://www.washingtonpost.com/wp-srv/special/politics/budget-2010.

33. "Labour productivity levels in the total economy," OECD, accessed January 9, 2013, http://stats.oecd.org/Index.aspx?DatasetCode=LEVEL.

34. Canada, Royal Commission on the Economic Union and Development Prospects for Canada, *Report of the Royal Commission on the Economic Union and Development Prospects for Canada* (Ottawa: Minister of Supply and Services Canada, 1985) 1: 208, 379, 382.

35. Thomas L. Friedman, *The Lexus and the Olive Tree* (New York: Farrar, Straus and Giroux, 1999).

36. "GDP per capita (US$)," The World Bank, http://data.worldbank.org/indicator/NY.GDP.PCAP.CD.

37. Diane Francis, "Canada's case of 'Dutch Disease,'" *Financial Post,* April 16, 2011, http://opinion.financialpost.com/2011/04/16/canadas-case-of-dutch-disease.

38. John Powell, *Encyclopedia of North American Immigration* (New York: Facts on File, 2005): 47–48.

39. "Table 2: Persons Obtaining Legal Permanent Resident Status by Region and Selected Country of Last Residence: Fiscal Years 1820 to 2011," *2011 Yearbook of Immigration Statistics,* U.S. Department of Homeland Security, Office of Immigration Statistics, http://www.dhs.gov/sites/default/files/publications/immigration-statistics/yearbook/2011/ois_yb_2011.pdf.

40. "Create a list," Nobel Prize official website, http://www.nobelprize.org/nobel_prizes/lists/all/create.html?active=1&cat_all=all&year1=Type+year&year2=Type+year&laureate=Type+a+name+or+names+of+a+Laureate&born_in[]=7&born_in[]=52&born1_year=0&born1_month=0&born1_day=0&born2_year=0&born2_month=0&born2_day=0&citation=Type+a+word+or+words+from+the+prize+motivation+text&sorting=default.

CHAPTER FOUR: THE BENEFITS OF A MERGER

1. Michael Greenstone and Adam Looney, "Understanding the 'Jobs Gap' and What It Says About America's Evolving Workforce," Brookings Institution, March 9, 2012, http://www.brookings.edu/blogs/jobs/posts/2012/03/09-jobs-greenstone-looney.

2. "Foreign control in the Canadian economy, 2010," Statistics Canada, *The Daily,* June 22, 2012, http://www.statcan.gc.ca/daily-quotidien/120622/dq120622b-eng.htm.

3. "Foreign ownership of U.S. companies jumps," Reuters, August 27, 2008, http://www.reuters.com/article/2008/08/27/us-companies-ownership-usa-idUSN2744743020080827.

4. Ian F. Fergusson, "United States–Canada Trade and Economic Relationship: Prospects and Challenges," Congressional Research Report, fpc.state.gov/documents/organization/174202.pdf.

5. "Canada's State of Trade: Trade and Investment Update 2011," Foreign Affairs and International Trade Canada, last modified March 12, 2012, http://www.international.gc.ca/economist-economiste/performance/state-point/state_2011_point/2011_6.aspx?lang=eng&view=d.

6. David Payne and Fenwick Yu, "Foreign Direct Investment in the United States," U.S. Department of Commerce, Economics and Statistics Administration, http://www.esa.doc.gov/sites/default/files/reports/documents/fdiesaissuebriefno2061411final.pdf.

7. "International Sales Continue to Climb in U.S. Market, Realtors Report," National Association of Realtors, June 11, 2012, http://www.realtor.org/news-releases/2012/06/international-sales-continue-to-climb-in-us-market-realtors-report.

8. "U.S. Relations with Canada," U.S. Department of State, http://www.state.gov/r/pa/ei/bgn/2089.htm.

9. Michael Arrington, "Strength in Numbers: Canadian Entrepreneurs Flock to the C100," TechCrunch.com, March 8, 2010, http://techcrunch.com/2010/03/08/strength-in-numbers-canadians-entrepreneurs-flock-to-the-c100; Robert L. Phillips Jr., Stephen Petterson, George E. Fryer Jr. and Walter Rosser, "The Canadian contribution to the US physician workforce," *Canadian Medical Association Journal* 176, no. 8 (April 10, 2007), http://www.cmaj.ca/content/176/8/1083.full; Katy Eager and Jennifer Blythe, "Canadian Nurse Migration to the United States of America," Nursing Effectiveness, Utilization and Outcomes Research Unit, McMaster University and University of Toronto, December 2003, http://www.nhsru.com/wp-content/uploads/2010/11/Nursing-Migration-to-the-U.S.-edited-Apr-05041.pdf; and author interview with Windsor Mayor Eddy Francis, 2010.

10. "The Canada–U.S. border: by the numbers," *CBC News*, December 7, 2011, http://www.cbc.ca/news/canada/story/2011/12/07/f-canada-us-border-by-the-numbers.html.

11. Steve Blank, "The Secret History of Silicon Valley Part VI: Every World War II Movie

Was Wrong," *SteveBlank.com* (blog), April 27, 2009, http://steveblank.com/2009/04/27/the-secret-history-of-silicon-valley-part-vi-the-secret-life-of-fred-terman-and-stanford.

12. Omar Tawakol, "Why Silicon Valley Is Bucking the National Unemployment Trend," *Forbes,* November 8, 2011, http://www.forbes.com/sites/realspin/2011/11/08/why-silicon-valley-is-bucking-the-national-unemployment-trend.

13. "Welcome," Engineers Canada, http://www.engineerscanada.ca/e/index.cfm.

14. "What Is Industrial Engineering?," Ohio State University Integrated Systems Engineering Department, accessed January 9, 2013, http://www.ise.osu.edu/overview_whatisind.cfm.

15. *Ibid.*

16. *2012 Global Re&D Funding Forecast,* Battelle Memorial Institute, http://www.battelle.org/docs/default-document-library/2012_global_forecast.pdf.

17. *2013 Global Re&D Funding Forecast,* Battelle Memorial Institute, http://www.battelle.org/docs/default-document-library/2013-R-and-D-Funding-Forecast.pdf.

18. "Electricity Explained: Electricity in the United States," U.S. Energy Information Administration, last updated May 2, 2012, http://www.eia.gov/energyexplained/index.cfm?page=electricity_in_the_united_states; and "Canada's Electricity Industry," Canadian Electricity Association, http://www.electricity.ca/media/Electricity101/Electricity 101.pdf.

19. Canadian Hydropower Association, "Hydropower in Canada: Canada's Number One Electricity Source (Presentation to the Standing Committee on Energy, the Environment and Natural Resources, Senate of Canada)," November 16, 2010, http://www.canadianenergyfuture.ca/wp-content/uploads/2010/11/Hydro-EN1.pdf.

20. Thomas Kierans, "Thomas Kierans on his GRAND Canal project," *The Globe and Mail* video, October 22, 2010, http://www.theglobeandmail.com/report-on-business/25/the-nominees/thomas-kierans-on-his-grand-canal-project/article1768581.

21. John D. Jorgenson, "Iron Ore," U.S. Geological Survey, Mineral Commodity Summaries, January 2011, http://minerals.usgs.gov/minerals/pubs/commodity/iron_ore/mcs-2011-feore.pdf.

22. "Minerals and Metals," Natural Resources Canada, last modified July 27, 2007, http://www.nrcan.gc.ca/statistics-facts/minerals/902.

23. "Defining the World's New Zinc Supply," Selwyn Resources, http://www.selwynresources.com/en/index.cfm.

24. "Facts and Statistics," Alberta Energy, http://www.energy.alberta.ca/oilsands/791.asp.

CHAPTER FIVE: HOW A MERGER DEAL MIGHT BE STRUCTURED

1. Nicholas Kulish, "Germany Looks to Its Own Costly Reunification in Resisting Stimulus for Greece," *The New York Times,* May 25, 2012, http://www.nytimes.com/2012/05/26/world/europe/german-reunification-pains-inform-stance-on-greece.html.

2. "Germany—The Economy," Mongabay, http://www.mongabay.com/reference/country_studies/germany/ECONOMY.html.

3. "GDP (current US$)," The World Bank, http://data.worldbank.org/indicator/NY.GDP.MKTP.CD?order=wbapi_data_value_2011+wbapi_data_value+wbapi_data_value-last&sort=desc.

4. "Country Comparison: Exports," *World Factbook,* https://www.cia.gov/library/publications/the-world-factbook/rankorder/rankorderguide.html.

5. Walter Russell Mead, "How Bush Could Get a Head on Mt. Rushmore," *Los Angeles Times,* http://articles.latimes.com/1992-07-19/opinion/op-4526_1_mount-rushmore.

6. James Pethokoukis, "North Korea's horrific economy and the cost of reunification," *AEIdeas* (American Enterprise Institute public policy blog), December 19, 2011, http://www.aei-ideas.org/2011/12/north-koreas-horrific-economy-and-the-cost-of-reunification.

7. "North Korea 'sunk South Korean warship,' killing 46 sailors," *News.com.au,* April 22, 2010, http://www.news.com.au/world-old/north-korea-sunk-south-korean-warship-killing-46-sailors/story-e6frfkyi-1225856989612.

8. Peter Foster, "North Korea warns South over 'declaration of war,'" *Telegraph* (UK), January 24, 2010, http://www.telegraph.co.uk/news/worldnews/asia/northkorea/7067362/North-Korea-warns-South-over-declaration-of-war.html.

9. "Details of proposed Korean unification tax," *Korean Unification Studies* (blog), August 19, 2010, http://koreanunification.net/2010/08/19/details-of-proposed-korean-act-those-that-can-least-afford-it-unification-tax.

10. "National Accounts Main Aggregates Database," United Nations Statistics Division, http://unstats.un.org/unsd/snaama/resCountry.asp.

11. "Germany—Government Expenditures and the National Debt, Government Subsidies," Mongabay, data as of August 1995, http://www.mongabay.com/history/germany/germany-government_expenditures_and_the_national_debt_government_subsidies.html.

12. "National Accounts Main Aggregates Database," United Nations Statistics Division, http://unstats.un.org/unsd/snaama/resCountry.asp.

13. "Germany," *World Factbook,* Central Intelligence Agency, https://www.cia.gov/library/publications/the-world-factbook/geos/gm.html.

14. "Ten largest stock exchanges in the world by market capitalization in 2011," World Stock Exchanges, http://www.world-stock-exchanges.net/top10.html; "Global Leaders in Mining," TMX Group (Toronto Stock Exchange), http://www.tmx.com/en/listings/sector_profiles/mining.html; and "MineAfrica Directory of TMX Group Listed Mining Companies Active in Africa," MineAfrica, http://mineafrica-directoryoftmx.eventbrite.com.

15. "General Government Revenue (National Currency) Data for All Countries," Economy Watch, http://www.economywatch.com/economic-statistics/economic-indicators/General_Government_Revenue_National_Currency.

16. "Seven Ways to Compute the Relative Value of a U.S. Dollar Amount—1774 to Present," Measuring Worth, http://www.measuringworth.com/uscompare.

17. "Northwest Territories," ExxonMobil, http://www.exxonmobil.com/Corporate/energy_production_arctic_nwterritory.aspx; and Dave Cooper, "Northwest Territories government banging the oil drum in Houston," *Calgary Herald,* December 5, 2012, http://www2.canada.com/calgaryherald/iphone/news/latest/story.html?id=7657028.

18. Reuters, "Russia beats Saudi to emerge as biggest oil producer in 2012," *Financial Post,* http://business.financialpost.com/2013/01/02/russia-beats-saudi-to-emerge-as-worlds-biggest-oil-producer-in-2012.

19. "Alaska's Oil and Gas Industry," Resource Development Council for Alaska, http://www.akrdc.org/issues/oilgas/overview.html.

20. John W. Schoen, "Would drilling more Alaskan oil cut prices?," MSNBC Answer Desk, http://www.msnbc.msn.com/id/12993250/ns/business-answer_desk/t/would-drilling-more-alaskan-oil-cut-prices.

21. "Fund Market Value," Alaska Permanent Fund Corporation, http://www.apfc.org/home/Content/home/index.cfm.

22. "Annual Dividend Payouts," Alaska Permanent Fund Corporation, http://www.apfc.org/home/Content/dividend/dividendamounts.cfm.

23. "2012 Permanent Fund Dividend is $878," Office of Gov. Sean Parnell, http://gov.alaska.gov/parnell/press-room/full-press-release.html?pr=6257.

24. "Market value of the Government Pension Fund," Norway Ministry of Finance, http://www.regjeringen.no/en/dep/fin/Selected-topics/the-government-pension-fund/market-value-of-the-government-pension-f.html?id=699635. US$1=5.6072 Norwegian krone.

25. "Ownership stakes," Norway Ministry of Finance, http://www.regjeringen.no/en/dep/fin/Selected-topics/the-government-pension-fund.html?id=1441.

26. "Heritage Fund—Historical Timeline," Alberta Treasury Board and Finance, http://www.finance.alberta.ca/business/ahstf/history.html.

27. "What are the income tax rates in Canada for 2013?," Canada Revenue Agency, http://www.cra-arc.gc.ca/tx/ndvdls/fq/txrts-eng.html.

28. "United States," *World Factbook,* Central Intelligence Agency, https://www.cia.gov/library/publications/the-world-factbook/geos/us.html; and "Canada," *World Factbook,* Central Intelligence Agency, https://www.cia.gov/library/publications/the-world-factbook/geos/ca.html.

29. Valentina Pasquali and Tina Arida, "Total Debt in Selected Countries Around the World," *Global Finance,* http://www.gfmag.com/tools/global-database/economic-data/11855-total-debt-to-gdp.html. U.S. debt = 80 percent of GDP, or $12.06 trillion. Canada's debt = 75 percent of GDP, or $1.046 trillion. Blended would bring combined rate to 77.3 percent.

30. *Ibid.*

31. "How much gasoline does the United States consume?," U.S. Energy Information Administration, http://www.eia.gov/tools/faqs/faq.cfm?id=23&t=10.

32. Pasquali and Arida, "Total Debt." United States government debts in 2011 = 80 percent of GDP. Canadian government debts in 2011 = 69% of GDP. Blended 79 percent of GDP is calculated by dividing their combined debts by their combined GDP.

33. "Greece," *World Factbook;* "Germany," *World Factbook*; and "Japan," *World Factbook,* Central Intelligence Agency, https://www.cia.gov/library/publications/the-world-factbook/.

34. "Population estimates by sex and age group as of July 1, 2011, Canada," Statistics Canada, *The Daily,* September 28, 2011, http://www.statcan.gc.ca/daily-quotidien/110928/t110928a4-eng.htm.

35. Mining Association of Canada, *F&F 2011: Facts & Figures of the Canadian Mining Industry,* http://www.mining.ca/www/media_lib/MAC_Documents/F&F2011-English.pdf: 49.

36. "Alaska's Mining Industry," Resource Development Council for Alaska, http://www.akrdc.org/issues/mining/overview.html.

37. "Skilled Labour Crisis," Greater Sudbury Chamber of Commerce, http://sudburychamber.ca/policy/skilled-labour-crisis.

38. "Mining in Colombia: Digging Deeper," *The Economist,* August 4, 2012, http://www.economist.com/node/21559963.

CHAPTER SIX: MERGER POLITICS

1. Fiona Collie, "Uncertainty leaves Canadians pessimistic on economy: survey," *Investment Executive,* http://www.investmentexecutive.com/-/uncertainty-leaves-canadians-pessimistic-on-economy-survey.

2. "Only Half of Americans Believe the American Dream Exists," Marketing Charts, http://www.marketingcharts.com/wp/topics/demographics/only-half-of-americans-believe-the-american-dream-exists-22254.

3. "Sharp Drop in American Enthusiasm for Free Market, Poll Shows," World Public Opinion.org, http://www.worldpublicopinion.org/pipa/articles/btglobalization-tradera/684.php.

4. Michiko Kakutani, "Surveying a Global Power Shift: 'Strategic Vision,' by Zbigniew Brzezinski," *The New York Times,* January 29, 2012, http://www.nytimes.com/2012/01/30/books/strategic-vision-by-zbigniew-brzezinski.html.

5. Ian Bremmer, "Winners and losers in a G-Zero World," *The Economist,* http://www.economist.com/blogs/prospero/2012/06/ian-bremmer-every-nation-itself.

6. Jennifer Rubin, "Robert Kagan: The World America Made" (book review), *The Washington Post,* February 14, 2012, http://www.washingtonpost.com/blogs/right-turn/post/robert-kagan-the-world-america-made/2012/02/13/gIQARYQ7BR_blog.html

7. Canada, Royal Commission on the Economic Union and Development Prospects for Canada, *Report of the Royal Commission on the Economic Union and Development Prospects for Canada,* http://epe.lac-bac.gc.ca/100/200/301/pco-bcp/commissions-ef/mcdonald1985-eng/mcdonald1985-report1-eng/mcdonald1985-report1-part2-eng.pdf: 375.

8. Will Ferguson, *Why I Hate Canadians* (Vancouver: Douglas & McIntyre, 1997).

9. Susan Hardwick and Jack Jedwab, *Boundaries of Identity: Geographic Knowledge, Identities and Migration in Canada and the United States,* International Association for the Study of Canada, http://www.acs-aec.ca/pdf/polls/12488060185351.ppt.

10. The Canada–U.S. Institute, University of Western Ontario, *Moving Closer or Drifting Apart? Assessing the State of the U.S.–Canada Relationship,* www.wilsoncenter.org/events/docs/Moving Closer or Drifting Apart, Anderson and Stephenson April 9.pdf.

11. Public Policy Forum, *Policy Choices: Improving Our Relations with the United States: Conference Outcomes Report,* June 2006, www.ppforum.ca/sites/default/files/canada_us_relations.pdf.

12. Pew Research Global Attitudes Project, "Confidence in Obama Lifts U.S. Image Around the World," July 23, 2009, http://www.pewglobal.org/2009/07/23/confidence-in-obama-lifts-us-image-around-the-world.

13. Angus Reid Public Opinion, "Obama Clearly Preferred Over Romney in Canada

and Britain," October 30, 2012, http://www.angus-reid.com/polls/47461/obama-clearly-preferred-over-romney-in-canada-and-britain.

14. Patrick Cain, "Poll: Six in 10 Canadians more concerned about a terrorist attack now than before 9/11," *Global News*, September 6, 2011, http://www.globalnational.com/poll+six+in+10+canadians+more+concerned+about+a+terrorist+attack+on+canada+now+than+before+911/6442476365/story.html.

15. "Canada-US Relations," Leger Marketing, http://www.annexation.ca/reports/2004%20Leger%20Marketing%20-%20Canada%20US%20Relations.pdf.

16. Karl McNeil Earle, "Cousins of a Kind: The Newfoundland and Labrador Relationship with the United States," *American Review of Canadian Studies* 28, no. 4 (1998): 387–411.

17. "Historical Election Results," U.S. National Archives and Records Administration, http://www.archives.gov/federal-register/electoral-college/votes/index.html.

18. "Same Sex Marriage Laws," National Conference of State Legislatures, last modified December 10, 2012, http://www.ncsl.org/issues-research/human-services/same-sex-marriage-laws.aspx.

19. Ebong Udoma, Reuters, "Connecticut abolishes death penalty," *CNews*, April 25, 2012, http://cnews.canoe.ca/CNEWS/World/2012/04/25/19678686.html.

20. Jack Healy, "Voters Ease Marijuana Laws in 2 States, but Legal Questions Remain," *The New York Times*, November 7, 2012, http://www.nytimes.com/2012/11/08/us/politics/marijuana-laws-eased-in-colorado-and-washington.html.

21. Jaime Joyce, "The Evolving State of Physician-Assisted Suicide," *The Atlantic*, July 16, 2012, http://www.theatlantic.com/health/archive/2012/07/the-evolving-state-of-physician-assisted-suicide/259862.

22. Jack Jedwab, "Canada and the United States: The Distance Between Us," Association for Canadian Studies, March 14, 2011, http://www.acs-aec.ca/en/social-research/canada-us-international/.

23. "Views on Canadian Oil and Gas," Ipsos, May 3, 2012, http://www.ipsos-na.com/news-polls/pressrelease.aspx?id=5614.

24. Elizabeth Mendes, "Americans Favor Keystone XL Pipeline," Gallup, March 22, 2012, http://www.gallup.com/poll/153383/americans-favor-keystone-pipeline.aspx.

25. "Division Over Gun Control," Pew Research Center, January 10, 2011, http://www.pewresearch.org/daily-number/division-over-gun-control.

26. Mark Kennedy, "Two-thirds of Canadians back long-gun registry," *National Post,* October 5, 2010, http://news.nationalpost.com/2010/10/05/two-thirds-of-canadians-back-long-gun-registry-poll.

27. "Fact Sheet: Public Opinion on Economic Inequality," Public Religion Research Institute, February 29, 2012, http://publicreligion.org/research/2012/02/public-opinion-on-economic-inequality.

28. "Pew Poll Notes Rise in Independent Voters," *All Things Considered,* May 21, 2009, http://www.npr.org/templates/story/story.php?storyId=104406480.

29. "It'll Cost You: Scottish independence would come at a high price," *The Economist,* April 14, 2012, http://www.economist.com/node/21552564.

30. "Full UMR research poll results on Aust–NZ union," *TVNZ One News,* March 14, 2010, http://tvnz.co.nz/national-news/full-umr-research-poll-results-aust-nz-union-3414686.

31. "Australia and NZ merger 'inevitable,'" *The New Zealand Herald,* March 14, 2010, http://www.nzherald.co.nz/nz/news/article.cfm?c_id=1&objectid=10631994.

32. "Australia and New Zealand merger 'not going to happen' says Keys," New Zealand Visa Bureau, March 15, 2010, http://www.visabureau.com/newzealand/news/15-03-2010/australia-and-new-zealand-merger-not-going-to-happen-says-keys.aspx.

CHAPTER SEVEN: IF THERE IS NO MERGER SOON

1. "Foreign control in the Canadian economy, 2010," Statistics Canada, *The Daily,* June 22, 2012, http://www.statcan.gc.ca/daily-quotidien/120622/dq120622b-eng.htm.

2. "Leading Retailers Take a Big Bite Out of the Canadian Retail Pie," Ryerson University press release, June 28, 2012, http://www.newswise.com/articles/leading-retailers-take-a-big-bite-of-out-the-canadian-retail-pie.

3. "International Trade: Canadian Economy (NAICS 11–91)," Industry Canada, last modified November 24, 2011, http://www.ic.gc.ca/eic/site/cis-sic.nsf/eng/h_00029.html.

4. Author interview with Luc Bertrand, head of the Maple Group consortium, controlling shareholder of TMX Group, 2012.

5. "Foreign control in the Canadian economy, 2010," Statistics Canada, The Daily, June 22, 2012, http://www.statcan.gc.ca/daily-quotidien/120622/dq120622b-eng.htm.

6. "Canada and Florida: An Economic Impact Study," Canadian Trade Commissioner Service, March 2011, http://www.tradecommissioner.gc.ca/eng/document.jsp?did=1247 94&cid=0092&oid=359.

7. "Gross domestic product, expenditure-based, by province and territory," Statistics Canada, last modified November 19, 2012, http://www.statcan.gc.ca/tables-tableaux/ sum-som/l01/cst01/econ15-eng.htm.

8. Margaret Michalowski and Kelly Tran, "Canadians Abroad," Statistics Canada, last modified November 21, 2008, http://www.statcan.gc.ca/pub/11-008-x/2008001/ article/10517-eng.htm.

9. Diane Francis, "Is Canada headed for demographic disaster?," Financial Post, September 21, 2012, http://opinion.financialpost.com/2012/09/21/is-canada-headed-for-demographic-disaster.

10. Francis Fukuyama, "The right must learn to love the state again," Financial Times, July 20, 2012, http://www.ft.com/intl/cms/s/0/ace4f55a-d0e2-11e1-8957-00144feabdc0.html.

11. Ipsos, "Half (49%) of Canadians Outside Quebec Agree They Don't Care If Quebec Separates from Canada," June 29, 2012, http://www.ipsos-na.com/news-polls/ pressrelease.aspx?id=5683.

12. Joe Friesen, "Why Canada needs a flood of immigrants," The Globe and Mail, May 4, 2012, http://www.theglobeandmail.com/news/national/time-to-lead/why-canada-needs-a-flood-of-immigrants/article4105032.

13. Edward Glaeser, "What the U.S. Can Learn From Australia's Coal Mines," Bloomberg, July 11, 2012, http://www.bloomberg.com/news/2012-07-11/what-the-u-s-can-learn-from-australia-s-coal-mines.html.

14. Mortimer B. Zuckerman, "We Must Reignite America's Can-Do Spirit," *U.S. News & World Report*, January 6, 2012, http://www.usnews.com/opinion/mzuckerman/articles/2012/01/06/mort-zuckerman-we-must-reignite-americas-can-do-spirit.

15. Arianna Huffington, "The Inspirationals: Jeff Skoll, Doubling Down on the Things That Work," *The Huffington Post*, May 25, 2012, http://www.huffingtonpost.com/arianna-huffington/jeff-skoll-order-of-canada_b_1544322.html.

16. O'Sullivan, "Global Trends."

17. "Muskrat Falls Hydroelectric Power Project," *The International Resource Journal*, http://www.internationalresourcejournal.com/renewable_energy/re_feb_11/massive_hydroelectric_project_to_develop_muskrat_falls.html.

18. Canadian Press, "N.B. Premier Shawn Graham calls off $3.2-billion NB Power sale to Hydro-Quebec," *The Telegram* (St. John's, N.L.), March 24, 2010, http://www.thetelegram.com/Arts—-Life/Education/2010-03-24/article-1446837/N.B.-Premier-Shawn-Graham-calls-off-$3.2-billion-NB-Power-sale-to-Hydro-Quebec/1.

19. Rhéal Séguin, "Quebec warns it will fight federal funding of Newfoundland energy project," *The Globe and Mail*, November 30, 2012, http://www.theglobeandmail.com/news/politics/quebec-warns-it-will-fight-federal-funding-of-newfoundland-energy-project/article5842575.

20. Steffen Bach, Hansjörg Blöchlinger and Dominik Wallau, "The Spending Power of Sub-Central Governments: A Pilot Study," OECD Network on Fiscal Relations Across Levels of Government," 2009, www.oecd.org/dataoecd/28/6/42783063.pdf.

21. "Aboriginal Peoples—Release No. 5: January 5, 2008," Statistics Canada, last modified April 19, 2012, http://www12.statcan.ca/census-recensement/2006/rt-td/ap-pa-eng.cfm.

22. Gregory Reynolds, "Canada's Federal Government Making a Mess of Aboriginal Land Claims and Mining Issues," *Republic of Mining*, June 30, 2008, http://www.republicofmining.com/2008/06/30/canadas-federal-government-making-a-mess-of-aboriginal-land-claims-and-mining-issues-gregory-reynolds.

23. "Australia's Foreign Investment Policy," Foreign Investment Review Board (Australia), www.firb.gov.au/content/_downloads/AFIP_Aug2012.pdf.

24. David Curtis Wright, "The Panda Bear Readies to Meet the Polar Bear: China Debates and Formulates Foreign Policy Towards Arctic Affairs and Canada's Arctic Sovereignty" (policy paper, 2011), http://www.cdfai.org/PDF/The%20Panda%20Bear%20 Readies%20to%20Meet%20the%20Polar%20Bear.pdf.

25. Jon Stewart, *Unleavened* (HBO television special), September 1996, http://www.you-tube.com/watch?v=TjxYPMm4Ru4.

26. Stephen Clarkson, "Stephen Clarkson: The slow path to a North American union," *National Post,* June 9, 2012, http://fullcomment.nationalpost.com/2012/06/09/stephen-clarkson-the-slow-path-to-a-north-american-union.

27. J.L. Granatstein, "J.L. Granatstein: 50 years of Americans trying to conquer what they coveted," *National Post,* June 9, 2012, http://fullcomment.nationalpost.com/2012/06/09/j-l-granatstein-50-years-of-americans-trying-to-conquer-what-they-coveted.

28. "Rick Mercer," CBC Program Guide, http://www.cbc.ca/programguide/personality/rick_mercer.

Index

D